# Public-Private Partnerships

A Practical Analysis

Consulting Editor **Nicholas Avery**

**Consulting editor**
Nicholas Avery, Ashurst

**Publisher**
Sian O'Neill

**Editor**
Carolyn Boyle

**Marketing manager**
Alan Mowat

**Production & design**
Russell Anderson, John Meikle

**Publishing directors**
Guy Davis, Tony Harriss, Mark Lamb

*Public-Private Partnerships: A Practical Analysis*
**is published by**
Globe Law & Business
Globe Business Publishing Ltd
New Hibernia House
Winchester Walk
London Bridge
London SE1 9AG
United Kingdom
Tel +44 20 7234 0606
Fax +44 20 7234 0808
Web www.gbplawbooks.com

Printed by Antony Rowe Ltd

ISBN 1-905783-00-0 / 978-1-905783-00-7

*Public-Private Partnerships: A Practical Analysis*
© 2006 Globe Business Publishing Ltd

All rights reserved. No part of this publication may be reproduced or transmitted in any form by any means without the prior written permission of Globe Business Publishing Ltd, or as expressly permitted by law.

**DISCLAIMER**
This publication is intended as a general guide only. The information and opinions which it contains are not intended to be a comprehensive study, nor to provide legal advice, and should not be treated as a substitute for legal advice concerning particular situations. Legal advice should always be sought before taking any action based on the information provided. The publishers bear no responsibility for any errors or omissions contained herein.

# Table of contents

**Introduction** — 5
Nicholas Avery
Ashurst

**Roads** — 11
Joss Dare
Ashurst

**Railways** — 45
Tom Winsor
White & Case LLP

**Health** — 59
Paul Smith
CMS Cameron McKenna LLP

**Prisons** — 87
Cameron Smith
Ashurst

**Education** — 117
Frank Suttie
Giles Taylor
Beachcroft LLP

**Defence** — 143
Dan Hood
David Nelligan
Simmons & Simmons

**EU procurement** — 159
Matthew Hall
Ashurst

**Partnerships UK** — 181
Edward Farquharson
Partnerships UK

**Financing public-private** — 187
**partnerships: the**
**changing market**
Chris Brown
Norton Rose

**About the authors** — 197

# Introduction

**Nicholas Avery**
Ashurst

The extensive and increasing involvement of the private sector in the provision of infrastructure and services which were previously the sole domain of public authorities is seemingly irreversible. It is also very often highly controversial.

There are those who feel that there is no place for the private sector and its all-pervading profit imperative in the provision of health, educational, penal or other social services. Feelings can run very high and, generally speaking, there are no easy votes to be won by a government that argues the case for more private sector involvement. The electorate seems to want new roads, better hospitals, more modern schools facilities and so on, but few would credit improvement in these matters to the public-private partnership (PPP) model. Nonetheless, governments of all political colours, in the capitalist world at least, have grasped the opportunity that private sector participation offers to modernise and improve on their ageing infrastructure. For a time in the United Kingdom, it seemed that before any such investment decision could be taken it was necessary to first answer the question, "Why not use a private finance solution?"

Changing governments have led to a change in emphasis or, perhaps, in methodology, but have barely held back the tide. Private finance is big business and it has changed the landscape of public procurement. It may prove too much to say that PPP is here to stay, but its legacy will be with us for a long time – not only in the changes that have been made in approaches to procurement and contracting, but also in the fact that even the earliest deals have at least a decade left to run. If we never closed another private finance deal, it would be well into the third decade of this century before the deals that have been completed cease to be relevant to government policy and the public purse.

The UK construction industry, for example, has reshaped itself around PPP, with many construction businesses redefining themselves as facilities managers. These new businesses provide potential for longer-term revenues, which in turn increases the certainty of stable dividends and improvements in shareholder value.

The banking and finance markets have moved to accommodate the needs of these sorts of transaction. At its most basic, we have seen an extraordinary change in the length of time for which financial institutions are willing to lend. Loan maturities of 10 or 12 years were unusual in the 1980s; now we see repayment periods of 30 or 35 years (and beyond). Because the way in which these infrastructure transactions are structured delivers the comfort of a high degree of certainty of stable cash flow in the project, credit committees can accept long-term lending. At the same time, and almost by happenstance, pension funds have an almost unquenchable thirst for long-term fixed-income investments. This area of activity delivers those investments and, in part, helps to resolve some of the issues that arise as society becomes on average older, requires more infrastructure and more services, and has a declining population in work.

On a micro level, very many individuals now owe their livelihoods to PPP. Vast armies of lawyers, accountants, insurance specialist and technical advisers are engaged in this sector. It would be a brave government that brought an end to all of this.

This book does not aim to be an apologist for PPP. Indeed, the private opinions of the contributors to each chapter are barely relevant. It rather aims to provide a greater understanding of how and why these transactions are structured the way they are, and to draw on the insight of individuals who, on a daily basis, share the responsibility for making them happen.

Each contributor addresses a sector or facet of the PPP industry with which he is intimately involved. Contributors have not been asked to follow a set chapter structure; this is not intended to be an exercise in comparative legal or sectoral practice. Instead, each contributor has looked to what he regards as relevant and instructive to the reader of the issues and concerns in the area on which he focuses: specifically, to address what, in his personal opinion, is needed to be understood to appreciate how transactions are structured and are developing. Of course, for the reader to make the most of this, it is appreciated that a starting point is needed: a basic model for a privately financed project against which to test what is written. This is what follows below.

It is axiomatic that in public-private transactions there must be a public participant. The 'authority' side comes in many guises. Most straightforwardly, we are talking about government entities at the national or federal level. The powers of these parties are clear to understand and the strength of the promises they make equally so; one takes political risk, pure and simple, when contracting with these parties.

But many projects are led at a local or regional government level. The powers here may be more constrained, and there is a need to understand how these bodies are financed and to whom they are accountable. Many of the socially important projects happen at local government level. For example, in the United Kingdom, the provision of schooling in the state sector falls to local authorities.

Then there are the bodies which are quasi-public authorities. Again, to take an example from the United Kingdom, much of the state-provided health service is delivered through health trusts – entities which are creatures of statute, technically independent from central government although wholly reliant on central government for funding and financial supervision. Parties wishing to engage in transactions with these sorts of entity need to pay close attention to the limits of their powers, their freedom to contract and the likely outcome of central government intervention if and when they fail financially. Many of these public service entities will have been established at a time when private sector participation in their area of influence would never have been contemplated. As will be seen in the chapters that follow, in order to provide robust, financeable structures in many cases it has been necessary for there to be primary legislation.

As can be seen, the authority side contains an infinite variety. On a legal and structural level, this may be simply a challenge for the lawyers involved. On a practical level, this breadth creates real issues in developing rapidly the necessary experience, skills and transaction knowledge on the authority side. Without this depth of experience, progress can be slow. As described in the pages that follow, effective steps can be taken which produce small returns at first, but later snowball to have much greater positive effect.

The authority is often under a statutory or other legal duty to provide public services. This will place further constraints on the manner in which transactions are structured, and the circumstances in which the authority must be able to intervene and to unpick the strict contractual position so as to satisfy its public service duty. Further, because these transactions involve the entering into of large-scale contracts by the public sector, the role of supranational bodies such as the European Union cannot be ignored. Relevant developments in EU law are described later in this book.

Most usually, the private sector participation is funnelled through a company or entity specifically established for the purposes of undertaking the transaction in question. Most often, the special purpose vehicle (SPV) will have at least two shareholders and those shareholders will have an interest in themselves carrying out some of the activities relating to the project. They will do this as subcontractors of the SPV. As the sector has developed, we see more and more shareholders whose interests are limited purely to the investment returns available from the project. Most recently, a plethora of new market entrants have been seen acquiring the equity positions of the contractor shareholders. The original justification given by construction companies for taking a small equity investment in a project that it was necessary to use a sprat to catch a mackerel have been replaced by the economic reality that these transactions provide long-term, stable cash flows to their participants at all levels. The financial innovations that have resulted from such a position are examined further later in this book.

The SPV enters into a contract with the authority. In most cases, this requires the creation of a new asset or the enhancement of an existing asset. By and large, the obligation on the SPV is to deliver something which is 'output based'. By this we mean that, rather than providing the SPV with a blueprint and a full set of architects' drawings, the challenge set is to deliver, say, 15 trams a day down a given street at not greater than five-minute intervals capable of carrying a total of 2,000 passengers. It is for the private sector, through innovation and design, to meet the output specification.

In some cases, the SPV is exposed to demand risk; that is to say, the fortunes of the SPV rise and fall with the number of passengers actually riding its tramway. An alternative model sees the SPV receiving payment for simply making the infrastructure available. In our tram example, on an availability basis it would not matter that there were no fare-paying passengers, provided that trams ran up and down the designated street sufficiently often to meet the output specification. Taking demand (or traffic) risk clearly is more appropriate to some projects than to others. There also may be political sensitivities; generally, in healthcare PPP an availability model prevails because of concerns over the involvement of the private sector in clinical matters.

SPVs tend not to have massive workforces of their own, but to rely on a series of subcontractors to which they pass the obligations they assume from the authority.

The construction of the new infrastructure asset will be entrusted to a specialist construction company or a joint venture formed by a number of specialist construction companies. Often, as mentioned above, there is a direct link between the chosen construction company and one or more shareholders of the SPV.

In setting its output specification, the authority will have imposed time limits by which it requires the output to be delivered. It is crucial, therefore, that the construction contractor delivers the infrastructure within that timeframe. Further, in order to ensure the long-term stable cash flows which permit for the financing of these transactions, it is equally crucial that construction costs do not overrun.

The imperative to deliver both to time and to budget cannot be overestimated when considering the fundamental structure of these transactions. When first promoted in the United Kingdom, PPP was argued to be a great way by which infrastructure could be provided by the state without increasing its public sector borrowing requirement. In recent times, it is the fact that the vast majority of these sorts of project are delivered to time and on budget which is now used as one of the primary justifications for this approach to infrastructure procurement.

Of course, in some projects there will be delay and it is therefore necessary in all projects to anticipate the possibility of late delivery. There will be a careful allocation of the construction risks, most usually along the lines of the often heard, well-used mantra that the party most able to manage a risk should be the party who takes that risk. In the end, time is money, and if the project is to deliver certainty to its financiers that the debt will be serviced without default, then somebody will need to replace the lost revenue (be it demand or availability based) arising due to a delay in completion of the infrastructure. Assuming the delay arises by reason of one of the risks allocated to the construction contractor, it falls to that party through the payment of liquidated damages to keep the project whole. In essence, this means providing cash payments sufficient to cover debt service and other unavoidable costs of the SPV during the delay period. Inevitably, by accepting these additional risks the construction contractor will need to increase its price for delivering the infrastructure (another criticism of the PPP model). It is undeniable that a contractor will bid a higher price for taking more risk (and for accepting a fixed price at all), but it is the final turn-out cost that really matters. The public sector seems very willing to accept a higher price in return for greater certainty that this will be the final price for the infrastructure it desires.

Most projects are divided into a (relatively) short construction period followed by a much longer period of operations. It is during the period of operations that the SPV earns the revenue which allows it to repay the capital costs expended during the construction period. Because these capital costs are debt financed, there is inevitably a build-up of interest during the construction period and it is only once revenues are flowing that the project can afford to pay interest and begin to reduce its principal outstanding. To be able to model reliably the cash flows arising during two or three decades of service provision, prospective financiers need as much certainty as possible during that period. Accordingly, a range of contracts will be entered into with service providers. This may be for maintenance of the fabric of the infrastructure, for provision of cleaning, laundry or landscaping services or, more recently, for the provision of trained personnel to undertake specific tasks. However, 20-year fixed price contracts for these matters are not practical and are not seen to deliver value to the authority. Contracts divided into short periods with processes for re-tendering or testing against the prevailing market on a periodic basis are the norm. Of course, failings by these service providers in the service period are just as likely to interrupt the stability of the overall cash flow. However, the reality is that these parties are unable to provide the level of financial backing for their obligations that can be demanded from construction contractors. There is likely to be some provision for liquidated damages on default, but establishing a framework for ensuring stable cash flows during the services period requires more active monitoring and intervention by the various parties during that period and a much more subtle and complex web of interrelating contractual obligations. This is not the glamorous end of the transaction during its negotiation, but in many ways the structure adopted here provides the engine room by which the transaction becomes financeable over the long term.

The 'glamour boys' of the transaction are, of course, the debt financiers. It is they who will be providing the bulk of the funds and (they will say) who are taking the majority of the risk. In the early years of PPP, the financiers were in an extremely powerful negotiating position, but as competition between financiers has increased and the public sector, in particular, has reached a critical mass of experience, the emphasis has begun to change. Debt financiers still have their fundamental demands, but these are now much better understood and thus dealt with more easily. Standardisation of contractual terms has gone a long way towards reining in the worst excesses of some financiers and the role of standardisation is touched upon by a number of the contributors to this book.

The classic schematic for a PPP transaction looks like this:

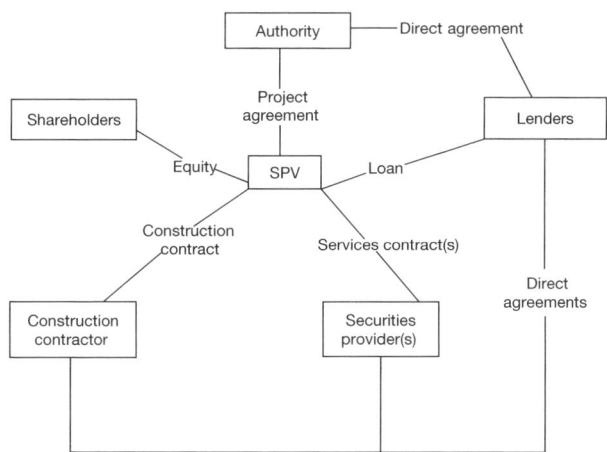

The final pieces of the jigsaw not so far referred to are the direct agreements between the lenders and the various other project participants. Because the lenders are reliant on future cash flow to make full recovery in default scenarios, they have a vested interest in keeping the intricate contractual web together. It is very unlikely that the lenders will benefit from simply enforcing their security and selling the project to the highest bidder: the physical assets will be nowhere near sufficiently valuable and the future revenues are assured only by a watertight set of contracts. Through this direct agreement (the theory goes), lenders will be able to keep the project together long enough to find a solution to whatever has put the SPV into default. This is largely untested – despite the huge numbers of PPP transactions now closed, there have been very few defaults. Where problems have arisen, it has been mostly because either demand risk has been taken (and the forecasted demand has failed to materialise) or a construction contractor group has failed generally and is unable to complete the works on a range of unassociated projects.

With this general description of PPP transactions and their structures in mind, readers can explore the differences and developments highlighted by the contributors in their various chapters. As stated above, each of the contributors is a fully engaged participating member of the PPP industry. Their experience is current and highly relevant, and I am grateful to all of them for taking the time out of their professional lives to make this book possible.

# Roads

Joss Dare
Ashurst

1. **Introduction**
Roads are at the heart of how we live today. They are part and parcel of our individual lives, and are fundamental to facilitating and encouraging economic growth across regions, countries and continents. Along with the rail network, they are the primary means of most economies – first world and developing alike – of transporting goods from the point of production to the marketplace; they are the arteries through which imports and exports flow; they are one of the primary means by which citizens access markets and commute to and from work. Governments the world over are keenly aware that an underdeveloped road network is likely to be associated with suboptimal economic performance and quality of life. Accordingly, it is no surprise that those governments are constantly looking for ways to develop their road networks and other transport links in the manner that best suits their economic, political and social needs.

In some jurisdictions, this will mean predominantly building brand new roads; in other perhaps more developed areas, it will mean a focus on refurbishing and/or widening old ones – either singly or in groups across a region. It may be that a new trading partner now exists requiring a new strategic route for goods; perhaps the internal economic dynamics of the country have changed, creating a need for a new internal route. Sometimes new roads are built to relieve congestion on existing routes (eg, the Birmingham Northern Relief Road in the United Kingdom); sometimes a river crossing is created to change the traffic patterns in a city or region (eg, as was partly the case for the Waterford Bypass in Ireland), or even to attempt to regenerate the local economy by connecting two previously isolated economic regions (as with the mooted Thames Gateway Bridge in East London).

The nature of road projects varies considerably from project to project and is driven by the local, national or even international factors that make that project a necessity in the first place. Whatever form these projects take, rare indeed is the government with the resources required simultaneously to build every major infrastructure project it wishes. Generally speaking, government income is ultimately derived only from taxation and borrowing, and either of these mechanisms, used excessively, is likely to lead to trouble eventually – especially perhaps for a democratic administration with an eye for future re-election. It was from this financial imperative – allied to a desire to harness the efficiencies and innovation of the private sector – that the concept of utilising private sector funds to realise this infrastructure was born. Design-build-finance-operate (DBFO) and public-private partnership (PPP) structures have now been extensively used in Europe, the Americas, Australasia and South Africa, and are consistently perceived to demonstrate advantages over 'traditional' design and build project structures in terms of value for money, speed and quality of construction and operations.

This chapter focuses on project finance in the roads sector and the various ways that private finance is used to develop these projects. It takes in a review of the main payment structures (perhaps the most fundamental taxonomical category for road deals); an analysis of the key risks in roads deals and how they may be dealt with; a consideration of some factors that the private sector will consider when choosing whether to bid for a road project in a particular jurisdiction; a brief overview of the impact of the project being procured within the confines of the European Union (including a brief review of the relevant EU procurement rules); and recent trends and the possible future direction for roads deals worldwide.

This chapter uses the term 'road' or 'project road' generically to apply to all relevant infrastructure: for example, national roads, motorways, bridges and tunnels – unless there is a need in a particular instance to differentiate between these types of infrastructure.

Similarly, the term 'authority' is used to refer to the public sector organisation procuring the project road and 'concessionaire' to the private sector party building and operating it. In practice, of course, many different terms are used for these entities, from project to project.

## 2. Traffic risk/revenue risk

The terms 'traffic risk' (sometimes also referred to as 'demand risk') and 'revenue risk' tend to be used quite liberally in discussing and analysing road transactions, and it is helpful to understand the distinction between the two terms as different project structures (which are analysed at section 3) can be aimed at transferring to the private sector one or the other risk, both risks or neither.

In this chapter:
- 'traffic risk' is simply the risk of how many vehicles (of various types) will travel up and down the road over the life of the concession; and
- 'revenue risk' is a factor of both traffic volumes/toll rates and collection/enforcement risk (see section 4.1(b) for more detail).

Pure 'availability'-based payment structures generally transfer neither of these risks (see section 3). 'Shadow toll' structures are generally seen as transferring traffic risk, but not revenue risk (since there is no actual toll to collect or enforce). Real-tolled structures are usually considered capable of transferring both traffic risk and revenue risk.

## 3. Payment mechanism options

In PPP projects in other sectors of the industry, the project company is very often paid a unitary charge by the authority in return for the availability of the project asset and/or the provision of desired service(s). However, this is not necessarily the case for road projects. Accordingly, among the first questions one might consider when analysing a road deal is how the concessionaire will be paid.

When considering what the answer to this question should be for a particular project, a whole range of factors fall to be considered; some of these are examined below. At the heart of the decision, however, lies the prediction of how many drivers are expected to use the project road. These traffic forecasts will form a key tool to help the authority in structuring the payment mechanism for the deal (since it is only if expected traffic volumes are sufficiently high that real tolling can be considered as a realistic option), and enable bidders/financiers to analyse the attractiveness of the deal and, for real-tolled projects, the size of any grant funding or other instruments that they require to support the project revenues.

## 3.1   Real tolls

Perhaps the most fundamental differentiating factor between road projects is the question of whether the project will involve the payment of 'real tolls' – that is, individual users of the road paying to use that asset. Without real tolling, the cost of the road is invisible to the consumer at the point of use and the perceived resistance/willingness of the target users of the road to pay real tolls will be a key issue in forecasting the expected traffic flows for the road. But real tolling holds a number of attractions for authorities as set out below.

While many of the facets of real tolling quickly become extremely technical in nature on closer inspection (and as such are beyond the remit of this chapter), some of the main points to arise in dealing with real tolls are overviewed in section 4.1. This section confines itself to a consideration of the pros and cons of real tolling when compared to other options.

*(a)   Advantages/disadvantages*

*(i)   Cost*

Chief among the benefits for awarding authorities in seeking a real-tolled payment structure is the, undeniably attractive, prospect of procuring an important piece of infrastructure at a net zero cost to the public purse. In a perfect world, the demand from users would be such that the projected traffic flows at the projected toll rates would be sufficient in their own right to service the required debt and produce an appropriate return on equity for the project 'sponsors'. In reality, however, the very high capital construction costs of significant road projects means that projected traffic volumes are often considered an insufficient revenue stream to achieve this without some form of governmental/intra-governmental subsidy – and/or an exceptionally long concession period.

While the goal of a 'free' road for the authority may – from the public sector perspective – be realised all too rarely, there are undoubted cost benefits to governments in instituting nationwide toll road programmes. From 1973 to 1995, for example, France is thought to have reduced central government contributions to its national road system from around 55% to nearer 20%, with a proportional increase in toll revenue. During a similar period Spain, by some accounts, reached a position whereby it funded nearly half of its national roads system budget from toll revenue. This revenue-generation aspect of real-toll projects is in sharp contrast to pure shadow-tolled projects, where the user does not pay to utilise the project road. The cost benefits of real tolling over shadow tolling are well illustrated by Portugal's recent plans to convert many of the shadow-tolled 'scut' concessions into real-tolled projects – the primary driver for which was the need to reduce the burden on the state budget of higher than expected traffic flows (see section 3.3 for further details on shadow tolling).

From a government perspective, then, real tolling has the very real attraction of reducing the level of road costs that must be borne from the public purse. Conversely, because they generally involve the transfer of revenue risk, real-tolled projects are often seen as inherently more risky for concessionaires than shadow and (even more so) availability-based mechanisms (although the degree of perceived risk in real-tolled deals will inevitably vary from project to project, depending on the strength of the individual traffic case). This perception is expressed in the general reluctance of the generally risk-averse capital markets to fund real-tolled projects to date. It would, however, be naïve for awarding authorities to attempt a real-toll solution for every project. Numerous factors must be weighed when deciding whether to adopt real tolling (see section 3.2).

*(ii) Consumer resistance*

The concept of user-paid tolling has been well established and accepted in continental Europe and elsewhere for many years, whereas in the United Kingdom there is widely perceived resistance to the idea among the general public. This perception seems to have a true historical footing: real tolling began in the United Kingdom as early as the eighteenth century with the establishment of the 'turnpike trusts' to manage the English road network originally established by the invading Roman army. At one point there were over 1,000 such trusts operating 35,000 kilometres of road, a fifth of all highways in the country. However, the charges were high and the tollgates were regularly destroyed (indeed, as one well-known financier in today's DBFO roads market is fond of pointing out, at one stage in 1734 not a single turnpike tollgate was left standing between Bristol and Gloucester). It is probably fair to say, then, that the United Kingdom has something of a chequered history with real tolls. Recent UK experience has been rather different, however: both the M6 toll and the Central London Congestion Charge received considerable negative media coverage when introduced, but both schemes have shown that the English public will, in fact, pay for access to certain roads/road systems.

In reality, the willingness of the local population to pay tolls at the point of delivery varies from area to area, from jurisdiction to jurisdiction and from project to project, and it will change over time as attitudes develop. The analysis of the expected levels of consumer resistance can be complex and may take in such factors as:
- the historical attitude of the region to real tolling (if any);
- prevailing media attitudes and their likely effect on public perception of the project;
- whether the tolled road confers a sufficient advantage on the user (eg, time savings, increased comfort/safety and so on) over existing alternatives – if the road is seen as a sufficiently attractive proposition (perhaps because of very

bad congestion on alternative routes, as was the case for the M6 toll), this may help overcome any reluctance to pay tolls;
- whether the road is an inter-urban route or a 'crossing' project (ie, a bridge or a tunnel across, for example, a river, estuary or harbour, or through a mountain pass) or an intra-urban road charging scheme;
- the quality, price and availability of competing roads – or indeed other transport modes (see section 4.2);
- the prevailing taxation regime – in high tax jurisdictions, there can be a reluctance to 'pay twice' for transport infrastructure, once through general taxation and once for user-paid tolls. This argument is sometimes advanced (perhaps rather simplistically) to explain the relatively low numbers of toll roads in countries such as Finland and Denmark;
- the toll rate compared to the ability of the target user groups to pay; and
- the proposed tolling technology (see section 4.1).

If consumer resistance is considered high in the area/jurisdiction where a project is proposed, this is will have a negative impact on projected traffic volumes, and therefore on the view of bidders and their funders as to the attractiveness of the project and it will increase the perceived need for grant support or traffic guarantee mechanisms in the concession agreement.

Consumer resistance is therefore generally a negative factor for projects seeking a real-tolled solution (although see section 3.1(a)(iii) re the use of consumer resistance in congestion charging schemes). It is also worth noting that where the intention of the scheme is to promote the use of the road (rather than to reduce it, as may be the case for congestion regulation schemes), consumer resistance is a risk not just for the private sector. As noted above, governments often promote road projects to help achieve a wider economic, sociological or political objective. These goals are unlikely to be well achieved if no one uses the road in question.

(iii)   *Traffic control/regulation*
As noted above, the existence of consumer resistance to the concept of paying tolls for the use of the road is therefore usually a disadvantage. Occasionally, however, it is part and parcel of the project itself. That is, it is possible deliberately to dis-incentivise the use of a road by charging for its use. In this way, the transport burden of a nation or region can be eased (by easing traffic onto other transport modes, encouraging it to move to different times of travel or eliminating it altogether) and the environmental impact of the project road can be eased accordingly.

For example, the Central London Congestion Charge recently introduced by Transport for London sought actively to reduce traffic in the central London area so as to speed up journey times, raise revenue and improve pollution levels. Such schemes can be regarded either as taking advantage of an inherent willingness of the consumer to pay for a desirable service or, conversely, as tacitly recognising that paying for something is inherently undesirable. For similar reasons, the Eurovignette Directive (see section 6.2) allows for increases in toll rates of up to 25% in particularly environmentally sensitive areas (eg, mountain ranges).

*(iv)   An equitable alternative to general taxation?*

If the government pays for a project through its own budget, the cost of the project road is borne by all taxpayers – notwithstanding that many will never use the road or benefit from it. To the extent that a project is real tolled, it is paid for by those who actually use it. This is arguably a more equitable position (although a strategic route could also be argued to benefit the nation as a whole and therefore be deserving of central government funding).

## 3.2   Shadow tolls

### (a)   *History and current usage*

Most commentators agree that the concept of the shadow toll was created in the United Kingdom around 1994 in the early stages of the ongoing wave of Private Finance Initiative (PFI) projects. During the remainder of the 1990s a number of DBFO roads were brought to market in the United Kingdom using this mechanism, although the deal flow has dried up somewhat during the current decade. Since then, various countries have adopted shadow tolling to a greater or lesser degree – including Portugal, Belgium, Finland, Spain, the Netherlands and, most recently, Israel, with the $402 million '431 Highway' (the southern section of the Tel Aviv ring road) reaching financial close in July 2006. Its greatest usage, however, probably remains in the United Kingdom.

### (b)   *What is a shadow toll?*

Shadow-tolled projects are generally characterised by transferring traffic risk (how many people drive up and down the road) but not revenue risk (what they are prepared to pay for that privilege). This is because in a shadow-tolled project, no actual tolls are collected from the public; accordingly, the road is free from the perspective of the driver. Instead of deriving its revenue directly from the public, the concessionaire operating the road is paid by the authority by reference to the utilisation of the road by the public: in simple terms, the more the road is used, the more the concessionaire is paid.

In practice, of course, these mechanisms are somewhat more complicated than this. They usually adopt a 'banding' mechanism (which is bid by tenderers as part of the procurement process), which applies different shadow toll payments to various levels of traffic. There are commonly about four such bands – the lowest of which is usually set at a conservative 'base case' level designed to service senior debt but not provide a return on equity (which is provided by higher bands of traffic levels). The top band is always usually given a 'toll rate' of zero – thus capping the amount payable to the concessionaire.

It is vital, therefore, that shadow-tolled projects have very reliable traffic counting systems to ensure that the correct payments are made.

It is common for shadow-toll structures to be augmented by performance-related matters (see section 3.4).

### (c)   *Why use a shadow toll?*

When they were introduced in the United Kingdom, the main reasons generally given for the use of shadow tolls were twofold:

- to access the benefits of a DBFO/PPP-type structure (eg, in terms of value for money, encouraging the consideration of whole-life costing in the design, construction and operation of the road, and incentivising construction completion to timetable and to budget) in an environment perceived to be hostile to real tolls; and
- to prepare the way for real-tolled roads in due course by cultivating an industry used to bearing traffic risk.

Other reasons sometimes advanced in favour of the use of shadow toll mechanisms include the following:
- A lower level of consumer resistance is associated with shadow-tolled roads – traffic levels are not impaired by the visibility of real tolls (or toll increases).
- Multiple sources of revenue can be drawn upon by the government to contribute to the shadow toll fund.
- The minimisation of traffic risk transfer should reduce the complexity of the project and therefore reduce the level of due diligence required by the private sector, enabling a more streamlined procurement process. The absence of revenue risk can also enable keener pricing of senior debt by financiers.
- Some projects are simply not capable of being real tolled; in such circumstances, a shadow-toll mechanism enables the transfer of traffic risk to the private sector.

The arguments against shadow tolls are as follows:
- The above factors in favour of shadow tolling may have merit when the alternative is a traditional design and build project structure, but some road practitioners argue that availability-based mechanisms (in respect of which see section 3.4) can achieve a similar effect without the arguably needless artifice of a shadow toll. In addition, the benefit of transferring traffic risk to the private sector without transferring revenue risk is not particularly obvious. Some claim that, if ever there was a benefit in seeking to prepare the industry for real tolls, this has dissipated in a world where a considerable number of major international contractors now operate numerous toll concessions in many countries worldwide.
- Crucially, shadow tolling does not act as a revenue generation device in the way that real tolls do. Accordingly, the total cost of the project (including the private sector return and funding costs) falls to the public purse, albeit over a long-term concession period.
- If traffic volumes are significantly in excess of those forecast, the government may find itself paying more 'toll' than it budgeted for. If this happens across a nationwide roads programme, the responsible roads authority may even find that its operational budget is coming under pressure. As noted above, this is indeed what happened to the 'scut' shadow-toll programme in Portugal, prompting consideration of an attempt to convert operational shadow-tolled projects into real-toll projects mid-concession – perhaps never likely to be an easy exercise in practice.

## 3.3 Availability/performance-based payment mechanisms

*(a) Availability*

As the name implies, under these mechanisms the concessionaire is essentially paid for making the road available for public use, rather than by reference to traffic volumes. Save in respect of the level of wear and tear inflicted on the road, the concessionaire is therefore not particularly concerned as to whether anyone actually uses the project road. Accordingly, pure availability-based payment mechanisms are generally considered to transfer neither traffic nor revenue risk to the private sector (a fact that tends to make them popular with financiers of the concession).

For projects adopting a 'pure' availability-based payment mechanism, the concessionaire will typically bid a level of availability payment as part of the tender competition. It then suffers reductions in payment for lane closures on the project road. If an availability mechanism is mixed with a real-tolled project (as is the case for the current round of Irish real-tolled roads), it might be that no separate availability payment is bid and that, instead, the concessionaire is required to make 'non-availability' payments to the authority out of earned toll revenue. In either case, the amount of the deduction/non-availability payment will usually be determined by reference to a number of factors, including:

- the length of the project road that is unavailable;
- the number of lanes affected;
- how long the unavailability lasts; and
- the time of day at which the unavailability occurs.

Relief is usually given for closures made in certain circumstances (eg, during an emergency or during the night for routine maintenance). Similarly, the mechanism can be structured so that loss of availability of particular sections of the project road or unavailability at particular times of day can give rise to greater financial loss for the concessionaire – thus incentivising the availability of key sections of the project road at key times.

Availability-based mechanisms have several advantages. In particular, the absence of any transfer of traffic/revenue risk simplifies matters somewhat in that it:

- obviates the need for extensive traffic due diligence by sponsors and financiers;
- reduces the level of risk borne by the concessionaire, resulting in cheaper finance (including, potentially, facilitating access to the bond market);
- removes the emphasis on the monitoring of traffic flows during the operational period that is so key to shadow-tolled mechanisms; and
- removes any consumer resistance concerns that would arise from real tolls and any attendant political difficulties for the government arising out of their potential unpopularity.

However, the absence of real tolls means that, like shadow-tolled deals, the cost of availability-based projects must ultimately be borne entirely by the public sector budget (albeit spread over a number of years). Clearly, this is of direct concern to procuring authorities which must balance their books, but there may also be an indirect effect in making EU assistance for the project more difficult to access – given that the European Commission seems currently to favour user-paid payment options (see section 6 regarding the introduction of the Eurovignette and Interoperability Directives and the commission's strategy for funding the completion of the Trans-European Network – Transport (TEN-T)).

*(b)*   *Performance*

It is not unusual for any of the various payment mechanism options mentioned to be supplemented by various performance-based criteria that can result in reduced payments if they are not met.

Potential criteria include the following:
- Safety improvements must be created;
- Ride-quality thresholds must be met;
- Rut-depth values must not be exceeded;
- Skid-resistance tests must be met;
- Loss of road surfacing must not exceed agreed thresholds; and
- Services must be delivered (eg, grass cutting, sign cleaning).

These criteria may also be extended to include such matters as reductions in 'end-to-end' journey times, although this may be resisted by the private sector on the basis that this is so heavily affected by factors beyond its control (eg, the way people drive).

Monitoring of achievement of these criteria (and indeed availability of lanes) is usually carried out in the first instance by the concessionaire. If this is seen as too contentious an issue to be monitored purely by the private sector, it is possible to capture evidence by closed circuit television (but this is perhaps an unattractive option given the time/cost involved in sifting through hours of uneventful video tape).

3.4   **Grant funding**

As noted above, real-tolled projects involve the passing of revenue risk to the private sector (ie, in its purest form, the concessionaire is paid only what it extracts from users of the project road). However, road projects are usually associated with a very high capital cost. In some such projects, therefore, forecast traffic volumes will often not be enough to create a sufficient revenue stream to satisfy both project sponsors and their financiers. In such circumstances, the authority may choose to support the project with construction grants (to reduce the level of senior debt required to complete the road) and/or operation grants to assist with ongoing operational costs. As noted in section 3.6, this sort of grant funding will very often be 'mixed' in with other facets of the payment mechanism (eg, real tolls and provision for non-availability payments). Authorities in some jurisdictions (including the United Kingdom) will take care in balancing the payment mechanism with the transfer of sufficient demand risk so as to ensure that grant payments do not result in an unfavourable balance sheet treatment (which, in many cases, will threaten the viability of the project).

## 3.5 Hybrids and other options

There is a great deal of scope to mix any and all of these payment options according to the need of the project, as well as other possibilities, as the following examples illustrate:

- The project road could include a 'multi-occupancy' lane (ie, one which attracts a lower payment for, or is simply reserved for use by, vehicles containing a minimum number of people).
- An availability-based mechanism could be adopted that includes scope for increased payments for higher traffic volumes to compensate for increased maintenance.
- The project could utilise variable toll rates – not only for differing types of vehicle, as is commonplace, but potentially also discounts for local vehicles (taking care not to breach EU/local anti-discrimination rules) or those travelling at non-peak hours.
- In real-tolled projects, the authority may wish to include a mechanism (sometimes called 'gain-sharing' or 'revenue sharing') to share with the concessionaire the benefits of higher than expected traffic volumes. Sometimes these mechanisms seek to share pure revenue (ie, regardless of the concessionaire's debt service/operational or other costs); other mechanisms share only the concessionaire's profit above a pre-agreed level, for example, by reference to a threshold internal rate of return level.
- Even in a real-tolled project the authority could retain revenue risk by having toll revenue paid over to it by the concessionaire – with the concessionaire being remunerated by other means (eg, shadow tolls or availability payments – or both). This mechanic gives the authority the benefit of raising revenue to pay for the project directly from users (thus easing the burden on taxation/public borrowing referred to earlier) without transferring this risk to the private sector (which may be difficult if traffic forecasts are not sufficiently robust).

## 3.6 Conclusion

It is sometimes difficult to resist the notion that the choice of payment mechanisms responds to some extent to the vagaries of fashion. In the 1990s shadow tolling seemed to be gaining in popularity; in the middle of the current decade, availability-based mechanisms appeared increasingly in various jurisdictions. Currently, it is real tolling that seems to be the most popular option. If there is such a trend, then the key drivers towards real tolling are likely to be:

- a belief in a robust traffic case by the public sector;
- the attraction of not having to fund desirable but expensive infrastructure entirely out of general taxation or government debt; and
- concern over the cost to the public purse of availability-based mechanisms and shadow-tolled projects (especially, in the latter case, if traffic volumes exceed expectations).

## 4. Key risk areas

### 4.1 Issues for real-tolled projects
If the road is to be real tolled, a whole range of factors will fall to be considered. Some of the key issues are examined briefly below.

*(a)* *Toll collection technology*

*(i)* *What is the most suitable toll collection system?*
There is a range of options available as to how real tolls can be collected and processed. Specialist consultants will consider the best option for each different project, having considered a wide variety of factors and the objectives of the scheme in question. Such factors will include the following:
- Cost – how much will one system cost to build and operate compared to the alternatives?
- System performance – what are the expected traffic volumes for the project road? Is it essential that the toll collection system can handle very high throughputs of vehicles?
- Land take – how much land does the toll collection system require? What land is available for the project road?
- Flexibility – is there a need for differential tolling (eg, different rates for different vehicles and/or different times of travel)?
- Interoperability – how well will the system interact with other user-paid charging systems? (Note the Interoperability Directive in this respect – see section 6.3.)
- Environmental impact – what is the environmental sensitivity of the area in which the project road is to be situated?
- Ease of use – how easy will the system be to use; how will this differ if payments are to be made other than with cash?

*(ii)* *What are the options?*
At the risk of oversimplifying matters, it can be considered that there are a number of variants to two main themes for toll collection systems:
- 'Traditional' toll plazas: Traditional plazas are those with a physical barrier that is raised as each car pays its toll. These can be augmented by adding one or more electronic toll collection lanes, which tend to operate using either utilising either tags or smart cards.
- 'Free-flow' systems: A free-flow system has no toll plaza and no physical barrier. Users drive over the project road as they would any other road and pay for it separately.

When the ability to deal with all aspects of the transaction on site is removed in this way, a degree of complication arises. The toll payment transaction in these circumstances can be divided into the following individual process steps (although there is probably a number of different ways of looking at this):

- Collection – this may include the operation of a 'back office' to register users (noting any applicable exemptions/discounts), deal with customer enquiries, accept payment and generally handle user accounts. This could be by phone, by post or over the Internet.
- Monitoring – the system must be aware of each user driving over the project road. This can be achieved by various means (including a combination of these methodologies):
    - Automatic number plate recognition (ANPR) – this is the system currently used in London's congestion charging scheme. It uses special cameras to note the number plate of each car using the road. This information is then fed into the collection system (and, if necessary, the enforcement system) – in respect of which, see below.
    - Tag and beacon – this is a system whereby each user keeps an on-board unit in the vehicle. This identifies itself to the monitoring system, often mounted on the gantries by the roadside, as the vehicles pass along the project road.
    - Satellite tracking – this is a system using a global positioning satellite (GPS) system to monitor use of the project road by users.
- Identification – the system must be capable of distinguishing users who have paid from those who have not. This will be an exercise in taking the information from the monitoring system and comparing it against the data held by the collection system.
- Enforcement – if a user fails to pay, action is taken to identify that user (eg, by reference to the jurisdiction's central number plate registry) and recover the unpaid toll, possibly together with costs and/or a fine. Note that the party to which enforcement responsibility is given under the concession agreement will wish to be satisfied as to the statutory regime governing recovery of the lost toll and so on, and what processes/powers are conferred on it. If enforcement is to be retained by the authority, the concessionaire will wish to be comforted that violators will be properly pursued or be kept whole from the financial consequences of any failure to enforce.

This process could be expressed as in the following flow diagram:

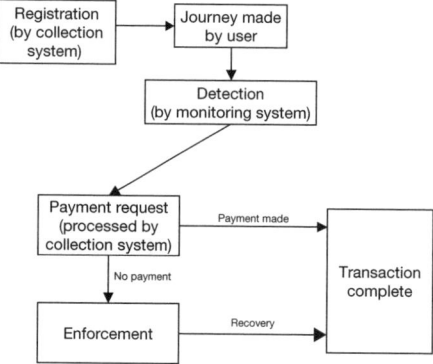

All of these various processes could be carried out by the concessionaire, or some/all could be retained by the authority or let to a third party. Each project will have its own optimum solution.

(iii) *Pros and cons*

**Traditional plazas:** These systems have the following characteristics/points of interest:
- They are based on reliable, tried and tested technology.
- The throughput of vehicles they are capable of delivering is relatively low (since each car must stop and pay its toll before the barrier is lifted to allow it to pass). This can lead to congestion, which can lead to consumer resistance and, ultimately, to lowered traffic volumes.
- Vehicle throughput can be increased by adding a dedicated electronic toll collection lane or by creating more toll booths – but this increases the required land take for the project (and land take is already higher than for free-flow systems).
- Toll plazas will need to be positioned with care at strategic points on the project road (assuming it is not practicable to position them at every entrance and exit) in order to ensure the majority of traffic is captured.
- Toll booths are good at accepting cash payments. They are less well suited to more modern, paperless payment methods.
- The environmental impact of toll plazas is relatively high compared to free-flow systems, as there is simply more infrastructure to be built. This is exacerbated if more lanes/booths are added – either to accommodate an electronic toll collection lane or otherwise to increase traffic throughput.
- Toll plazas (especially those with automatic machines rather than manual booths) are not well suited to differential tolling and are less amenable to the benefits of interoperability with other tolling/user charging schemes sought by the European Commission.

**Free-flow systems:** The advantages of free-flow system include the following:
- They are usually cheaper to install and run than traditional plaza-based systems.
- As the name implies, they are much less disruptive to traffic flows than traditional systems (which require drivers to slow down, often queue and pay before the barrier is lifted before the journey continues).
- They are often championed as being easy to use and as creating a good driving experience – both of which may help reduce consumer resistance to real tolling.
- They generally require less 'land take' than their traditional counterparts. This reduces the amount of land the authority must acquire (and extensive compulsory purchase processes are not without their difficulties) and reduces the environmental impact of the scheme.
- They are well suited to offering differential tolling options and interoperability benefits.

The disadvantages include the following:
- Tag and beacon technology is not well suited to occasional users (but ANPR can be used in conjunction with a tag and beacon to help deal with this).
- GPS technology is sometimes regarded as not yet sufficiently reliable for small scale intra-urban schemes. In addition, onboard unit costs for GPS-based systems are high. Apart from the lorry road user charging system recently established in Germany, satellite technology has yet to be adopted in road projects to any significant degree (indeed, the UK equivalent of that scheme was eventually dropped by the current government).
- ANPR systems are not 100% reliable. Cameras do fail to read or 'mis-read' plates occasionally. However, ANPR used as a support to tag and beacon technology has been used several times worldwide to good effect (eg, Melbourne City Link).
- Free-flow systems are more prone to toll evasion (since there is no physical barrier to prevent it). This places a heavy emphasis on the enforcement methodology and the legislative framework that supports it.

*(b)* *Collection/enforcement risk*

Most real toll projects will oblige the concessionaire to collect the tolls – either for itself or on behalf of the authority. If the concessionaire sets the levels of real tolls, collects those tolls and enforces against toll evaders, it can be said to be bearing true revenue risk. In these circumstances it might be regarded as more of a 'real' business than most PPP project companies since it deals with its customers directly and controls the way in which it interacts with them. The transfer of each component of revenue risk can also give rise to concerns for the concessionaire and its funders, such as the following:
- What are the limits on increases/decreases to the toll levels (both as to amount and frequency)?
- Are there any other limiting factors on such changes (eg, authority consent, the terms of any implementing legislation such as a toll order)?
- What is the expected performance of the toll collection system in terms of throughput, reliability effect on consumer resistance and likely violation rates?
- What ability/freedom does the concessionaire have to recover the evaded toll?
- Can it recover its costs of recovery?
- Is there scope for the imposition of a fine to discourage other offenders?

*(c)* *EU legislation*

Certain EU legislation applies only to real-tolled projects. These are examined in more detail in section 6.

## 4.2 Traffic issues

Shadow and real-tolled projects involve the transfer of traffic risk. As a result, a comprehensive series of studies will be carried out at various stages of the procurement process by specialist technical consultants on behalf of the authority, the concessionaire and the financiers. These studies will look to determine the likely volume of usage of the road over the concession period for various categories of vehicle based on a number of assumptions (eg, as to population levels, gross domestic product growth in the relevant areas, car ownership in target user groups), as well as considering the likely 'elasticity of demand' (ie, the degree to which appetite for a product varies in reaction to pricing changes) at various toll levels. This will establish a 'base case' traffic forecast as well as examining best and worst-case scenarios.

The use of shadow tolling gives a different complexion to traffic forecasting than that which prevails for real-tolled projects, as many of the factors that might create consumer resistance to a real tolled project (and therefore act to reduce utilisation of the road) are no longer a factor.

The details of traffic forecasting are of a technical nature and as such are beyond the ambit of this chapter. The transfer of traffic risk itself will, however, give rise to certain legal/commercial considerations, as outlined below.

(a) *Not enough traffic*

There a number of key risks for the concessionaire to manage – not least the challenge of reaching construction completion on time and on budget. Real-tolled (and indeed shadow-tolled) projects have the added problem that the traffic forecasts used to set up the project's financial dynamics are not always as accurate in practice as might be hoped. This is sometimes less of an issue for shadow-tolled projects, as historically they have tended to be used in projects for the refurbishment/upgrade of existing routes (which therefore already have an established – and therefore hopefully more reliable – traffic case).

If the forecasts have proven dramatically optimistic, the concessionaire's practical options to remedy the situation are probably quite limited. One option might be to lower the tolls in a bid to increase the traffic volume – assuming it has the power to do so. The extent to which this would be effective will depend on a number of factors, including the elasticity of demand for that project, and indeed whether the strategic need for the project itself was misconceived in the first place (if nobody wants to travel between the places linked by the project road, reducing the cost of doing so will not help very much). For this reason, the concessionaire and its funders will always prefer to have control over the toll rates for the project road, although this may not always be forthcoming from the authority – either as a matter of policy or as a result of the applicable statutory/regulatory framework.

There are, however, potential advantages for the concessionaire in taking traffic risk. For example, if a concessionaire has miscalculated its whole life costings in an availability-based deal, it may find itself in financial trouble during the operational period. Having real tolls as a revenue stream on a project at least allows the possibility that better than expected traffic can help solve such a problem.

(b) *Traffic guarantee*

If forecasted traffic volumes are a cause for concern in the context of the capital cost of the road (and the resultant size of the senior debt requirement), the authority may consider offering some form of 'traffic guarantee'. This is a mechanism whereby traffic levels are measured over the life of the concession (or, alternatively, only during a particularly risky period of the concession – for example, during the 'ramp-up' or the first few years of the project's operational life) and compared against a pre-agreed minimum level. If actual levels fall below that threshold, an appropriate balancing payment is made by the authority.

Such structures can be regarded as diluting the transfer of traffic risk to a degree, but this may be preferable for some projects – it is capable, for example, of facilitating cheaper finance for the concessionaire and therefore a reduced reliance on grant funding (which is payable regardless of the traffic case and is arguably therefore less attractive to the authority).

*(c)* *Competing roads/zone of influence*

For each project where traffic risk is passed it will be necessary to consider the impact and likelihood of the creation of and amendments to other relevant transport links – for example:

- whether traffic volumes are capable of being materially reduced by the creation of a directly competing toll road or 'free to use' route;
- if so, whether the creation of such a route is in fact likely (especially given the cost involved and given the existence of the project road already performing the necessary function);
- whether there are any strategically important feeder routes via which a material proportion of traffic volumes will come;
- if so, what the effect of the imposition of tolling or, if they are intra-urban routes, some kind of traffic-calming on those feeder routes would be; and
- whether the creation of competition from another mode of transport (eg, light/heavy rail) is a realistic possibility.

Depending on this analysis, the concessionaire may seek some form of protection against such eventualities in the concession agreement. This might refer to specific items of concern (eg, the imposition of tolling on particular routes) or, perhaps more rarely, may give protection from any such events within a pre-agreed 'zone of influence' around the project road.

Some authorities can be reluctant to offer significant competing roads protection on the grounds that they have no more control over whether a competing route is constructed than the concessionaire. Whether or not this is the case will depend on the nature and powers of the authority in question.

If it is granted by the authority, such protection is typically effected by a contractual mechanic that compares traffic levels pre and post the relevant event. This is then used to calculate a balancing payment from the authority that puts the concessionaire in the same position it would have been had the event not occurred.

**4.3  Construction issues**

Like most project financings, payments under DBFO/PPP road projects do not generally commence until completion of the project road (although this may not be the case for refurbishment/upgrade projects utilising an availability-based payment mechanism).

Accordingly, the concessionaire and especially its funders will focus much of their attention on construction issues, including:
- an assessment of the complexity of the construction job itself (more complex projects such as those involving some types of bridge or tunnel, may attract higher construction prices and bigger risk premiums);
- if the design and construct (D&C) contractor is a joint venture (as is common), how the liability for cost overruns is to be divided between the joint venture partners; and
- the perceived capacity of the D&C contractor/its constituent joint venture partners to manage the resulting issues. Are they suitably technically qualified/experienced to handle the size and complexity of the job? Are their financial resources sufficient to withstand the potential liabilities that might arise? How liquid a market is it in that jurisdiction – that is, would they be easily replaced if things went wrong?

Even after all of the experience now accumulated in road DBFO projects, the so-called 'winner's curse' can still strike: because construction price is usually such a large part of the overall price, the consortium with the lowest construction price is often best placed to win the deal. Unfortunately (and for the same reason), that consortium can also be the most susceptible to cost overruns. Accordingly, funders in particular will closely scrutinise the abilities of the D&C contractor in the context of the requirements of the project road and the relevant terms of the concession agreement and its financial robustness in the context of the project as a whole. As noted above, there will also be a focus on the replaceability of the D&C contractor should it fail to complete the build and dissolve into insolvency or be fired from the job. The more these issues are a concern, the more funders will look to the level of the cap in the subcontract and to revenue support instruments such as parent company guarantees and performance bonds.

Due diligence will also be undertaken into the proposed treatment of certain key construction risks such as the following:
- Land acquisition costs and injurious affection claims – these are commonly left in the authority's domain since it controls the compulsory purchase process.
- Planning risk – what is the planning process applicable to the project road? What are the risks involved in each stage in light of the nature of the project. Who is to be responsible for each element of the planning process? How likely is a challenge to any planning decision? Is there a definite deadline for any such challenge after which this risk falls away?
- Latent defect risk – if the project relates to the upgrading or taking over of existing roads, a slew of issues arise as to the risk of defects in the existing road and the structures on it arising during the concession period. Will there, for example, be any right of recovery against contractors responsible for the existing assets? If so, by what means is this recourse to be affected? Will those contractors have the right to come on the project road and effect a repair? If so, how will this interface with the operation of the project road?

- Completion process – what must happen in order for payment under the concession contract (whether through the commencement of tolling or otherwise) to get started? How is completion measured – is the process sufficiently robust, clear and objective? Who measures completion – the authority, the concessionaire or an independent third party?
- Ground conditions/archaeology – will site condition risk be borne by the concessionaire (and passed down to the D&C contractor)? This is a reasonably common starting point unless there is a particular issue relevant to the project that makes this approach poor value for money. In some Scandinavian road projects, for example, geological risk can sometimes be shared outside agreed parameters. Archaeological/munitions risk[1] can also sometimes be shared, depending on the level of perceived risk for the project in question. Suitably detailed and reliable survey information will be key to accepting and pricing all of these risks.
- Protestors/trespassers – who bears the risk of unauthorised access to the site or of protesters preventing delivery of materials to the site? If, as is not uncommon, these risks will be borne by the concessionaire, the concessionaire is likely to insist that the authority at least commit to handing over the site free from such persons. What are the D&C contractor's proposals for keeping the site free from such persons in the future? Should the site, in fact, be handed over in stages to help mitigate the risk? Due diligence will be required into the local political environment to judge the scale of this risk (after all, some proposed roads are more popular than others) and as to the concessionaire's powers at law to deal with such persons.

### 4.4 Operational issues

There are many operational issues at hand in road projects and not enough space here to address them all in any detail. The following are noted in passing.

*(a)* *Long-term risk*

If the construction is under-priced by even a small percentage, it is a problem because of the relatively large cost of construction in proportion to total project cost. With operational risk, the difficulty is not so much sheer size but longevity – the concessionaire's key cover ratios could be affected for many years. In these circumstances, there may be relatively little headroom built into the concessionaire's financing and, accordingly, it can become brittle (ie, relatively susceptible to future problems) and at risk of overall failure. This problem can be exacerbated by the modern trend for increasingly long debt tenors (and correspondingly short 'tails') which can give the concessionaire relatively little time to recover.

*(b)* *Maintenance structures*

In accommodation sector PFI/PPP projects, 'hard FM' obligations are usually the subject of a more or less complete pass-down from the project company to one or more subcontractors for the full term of the concession period.

---

1 Munitions risk being the risk of discovery of unexploded bombs and suchlike on site, which can be an issue, for example, for ex-army land.

Joss Dare

This can be the case in roads concessions too, but it is also not unusual for maintenance/lifecycle obligations to be held in the concessionaire or let on, say, five yearly rolling contracts. Where this is the case, or where there is a concession-life maintenance contract with a market-testing provision, the concessionaire is exposed to pricing variations during the concession term and it may wish to sculpt the debt-repayment profile to give room to reserve against potential price increases.

*(c)* *Control over the road*
The sponsors and their financiers will undertake due diligence into the degree of control the concessionaire will have over the project road (which will largely be driven by the applicable local regulations/law). For example, do any third parties, such as existing road contractors already employed by the authority or statutory undertakers (eg, utilities companies), have a statutory or contractual right to enter onto the project road? Does any local, regional or national authority have the right to order or prevent works on the road (eg, as part of wider legislation designed to prevent congestion by coordinating roadworks, such as the United Kingdom's Traffic Management Act 2004)?

*(d)* *Change in law*
The concession contract is often specific about which party bears the risk of the various types of change in law commonly identified in PPP projects. The concessionaire will wish to obtain (but will not always succeed in obtaining) protection from the implementation of new safety regulations (eg, a new requirement that central reservation barriers should be built higher) introduced during the lifetime of the project.

Classically (like most sectors of PFI/PPP), so-called 'general changes in law' – that is, changes of general application that do not discriminate against the concessionaire or the PPP industry – are borne by the concessionaire (although there may be included some kind of sharing mechanism in relation to the resulting capital expenditure). The unintentional impact of such general changes on the cloistered world of PPP projects can sometimes be significant. For example, in the United Kingdom, the Housing Grants and Regeneration Act 1996, the Freedom of Information Act 2000, the Enterprise Act 2002 and the Insurance Mediation Directive (2002/92/EC) all created unexpected side-effects for PFI deals. This is generally considered a price of doing business in the industry, but the problems created can sometimes be significant.

4.5 **Events of default**
A key area of due diligence for the concessionaire and its financiers will be the provisions that can bring a premature end to the concession and, in particular, the concessionaire 'events of default'. They will be keen to limit these where they can, but also to introduce as much objectivity and clarity as possible and ensure there is always the ability to remedy the default (assuming it is capable of remedy).

This is particularly important if the compensation on termination regime for authority default is not as favourable as might be hoped for (see section 4.7).

## 4.6 Rights of step-in

Like any other PPP project, it is a key requirement in roads deals for funders to be able to step in to rescue a failing project before it is terminated by the authority (although, as noted above, in a project in which traffic risk has been transferred to the concessionaire, its ability materially to influence matters on stepping in to a project with below forecast traffic may be somewhat limited in practice). The mechanism by which this is achieved varies depending on the local law, but funders will generally prefer a separate direct agreement to be put in place between the authority, the concessionaire and the funders, clarifying these rights of 'step-in'.

## 4.7 Compensation on termination

Many roads concessions in a number of jurisdictions (eg, notably, the United Kingdom and Ireland) provide for zero compensation on termination of the concession for concessionaire default. As may be imagined, this is a serious concern for sponsors and financiers alike (as they stand to lose their investment) and raises the prospect of a windfall gain for the authority – the so called 'free road' scenario.

Perhaps history does not record why this position was originally accepted, but a market precedent, once set, can be difficult to change. In the United Kingdom, at least, the introduction of Standardisation of PFI Contracts Version 3 is beginning to spread into the roads sector – bringing with it the market value mechanism for compensation on termination for contractor default. One reason sometimes cited for the payment of no compensation is that, particularly following construction completion (and especially for non real-tolled projects), the risk of defaulting on a road should be quite limited: they do not, for example, have the complicated operational interfaces of, say, a hospital. Opinions divide as to the merits of this argument.

Other jurisdictions (eg, parts of Scandinavia and Greece) include express contractual compensation on termination provisions which seek to give a measure of comfort to the concessionaire (or more realistically, in this scenario, to its funders). This can take a number of forms. One possibility is a form of 'cost to complete' mechanism which seeks, effectively, to calculate and pay to the concessionaire the value of the construction work undertaken up to termination less the amount by which the expected cost to complete the build exceeds that planned for. In Spain, there have been projects using a book value calculation for the compensation payment (ie, effectively, the cost of the construction work carried out). Some civil code jurisdictions are silent as to the issue and funders take comfort from the application of the principle of unjust enrichment (ie, that it would be unfair, and therefore not permissible at law, for the government to take back an asset as large as a road without paying fair value for it).

Whatever mechanism is adopted, all parties – but particularly the funders and their advisers – will wish to examine the relevant contractual provisions in the context of the applicable law of that jurisdiction to determine the efficacy of the protection offered (if any).

4.8  *Force majeure*

Like most PPP sectors, the contractual application of *force majeure* tends to be reasonably limited in road projects. In some jurisdictions (eg, Ireland and, historically at least, the United Kingdom) there can be two categories of *force majeure*: eligible *force majeure* and the remainder, with only eligible *force majeure* attracting compensation on termination payments (which typically cover outstanding senior debt/subcontract breakage costs, but not equity or return on equity).

Sometimes no express list of *force majeure* events is set down in the concession agreement, which might simply refer to matters outside the control of the parties preventing performance of the contractual obligations. Alternatively, there may be a defined – and probably quite limited – list of specified qualifying events. Such a list might typically include terrorism, nuclear contamination, war etc, riot etc and, for UK projects (rather curiously) pressure waves from supersonic devices. The damage this latter event would do to a road is often not immediately apparent. Local factors can be relevant as well. For example, terrorism may be given slightly different treatment in some jurisdictions (eg, Northern Ireland, with the existence of the Criminal Damage Compensation Order); or earthquakes beyond a particular level on the Richter scale might qualify in projects in countries prone to such events.

## 5.  Jurisdiction issues

The private sector will consider a whole range of factors when deciding whether to invest in a region, including whether it fits with their overall strategy. Some such factors include the following:

- Proximity to other key regions – if a country's neighbours all have vibrant PPP or other relevant industries, this may help persuade investors to cross the border (especially if they already have a base nearby as a result).
- Local resource – is there sufficient local resource to build and operate the project road?
- *Vires*/covenant risk – does the authority have the necessary legal power to enter into the concession contract and sufficient covenant strength to meet its liabilities under it?
- Political will/acceptability – is the prevailing government serious about utilising private investment in public infrastructure? Is the local populace willing to accept it?
- Resistance to tolling – what level of consumer resistance is expected for real-tolled projects in the region?
- Population levels, population migration and the forecasted growth of car ownership/usage – what impact will these have on the traffic case?
- Stability – is the country sufficiently politically stable generally? More specifically, does PPP-related policy chop and change continuously? Is it likely to do so after the next election? Will the next government cancel the procurement or, even worse, the concession itself post-award?
- Transparency of process – is the PPP procurement process suitably fair and transparent? If bidders do not believe in the veracity of the process, why should they spend significant amounts of bid costs in competing in it?

- Deal flow – how many projects are proposed in the region? Projects of this nature require the creation and maintenance of significant resources – a load which is best spread over a number of transactions if at all possible.
- Central organisation – is there a central public sector organisation driving through the PPP agenda, bringing through a steady deal flow, enforcing standardised terms and ensuring fair play in the procurement process?
- Standard contract – does the jurisdiction have a tried and tested standard contract for the sector? If not, is it at least trying to create one? Is there a willingness to adopt internationally accepted terms and conditions?
- Language – in what language will the tender documents be written?
- Law – what law will apply to the concession? Which courts will have jurisdiction? Is this a suitable form for dispute resolution?
- Quality of tender documentation – what is the quality? Has the authority taken advice from suitably well-qualified international advisers? Does the bid document include unnecessary/unattractive terms such as bid bonds?
- Applicable regime – how favourable is it? Is there a PPP/concession law? Is it any good? Is there an appropriate regulatory framework?
- Taxation regime – is it favourable to inward investment in PPP projects? Are there repatriation of profit concerns?
- Procurement regime – what rules will govern the process? Will they be adhered to? What is the likelihood of a challenge (eg, by way of judicial review)?
- Insolvency/security regime – what are the rules governing the exercise of security and the implementation of insolvency in that jurisdiction? How will this affect the funder's ability to recover its investment in a termination scenario?
- The impact of accounting treatment – what accounting rules apply in the jurisdiction and how do they impact on the treatment of different types of project? To what extent is off-balance sheet treatment critical to the authority?

## 6. Specific issues for EU projects

If the road is to be within the borders of the European Union (or, potentially, the various accession countries currently positioning themselves for EU entry), it will be necessary to take into account the requirements of EU legislation – in respect of both the procurement of the project (see section 6.4) and its construction and operation. This section looks at the creation and implementation of the TEN-T and then examines two of the EU directives that are currently of key relevance for real-tolled road projects in the European Union.

### 6.1 The Trans-European Network – Transport

The fostering of the free movement of goods and people within its borders has long been a key objective of the European Union. More latterly, the advancement of economic and social cohesion has also become a priority in EU policy. As noted in section 1, properly developed transport links are a fundamental prerequisite to the achievement of these kinds of goals. This was recognised by the European Commission in 1990 when it first adopted an action plan with a view to creating 'trans-European networks' (for transport, energy and telecommunications). In the transport context, these are the arterial highways/railways/seaways that connect Europe – initially internally with itself and eventually with its neighbours and trading partners.

The creation of the TEN-T was given a legal basis by the Maastricht Treaty in 1993, and in 1994 the European Council identified 14 key strategic projects required to bring this vision into reality. However, 10 years later, few of the original goals of the TEN-T had been achieved. Indeed, in 2003 barely 30% of the network had been constructed and only three of the original 14 priority projects had been completed.

This raised, as a serious possibility, the prospect of the TEN-T not being completed in the medium-term future. Accordingly, in 2004 the commission compiled a new list of 30 trans-national 'axes' (which it describes as the backbone of the TEN-T) and key individual projects (mostly designed to cure localised bottlenecks on key strategic route) to be prioritised.[2] At the same time, the commission introduced new rules for the granting of EU aid in the field of trans-European networks. In addition, the TEN-T budget – which sits alongside the EU cohesion and structural funds and national budgets – was significantly increased (see section 6.5 for more detail on EU funding).

In 2004 the commission estimated that traffic between member states would double by 2020 and that by then the TEN-T would cover some 89,500 kilometres (km) of roads. According to the commission's literature, the completion of the TEN-T now involves the construction of 12,500 km of new roads and the upgrade of another 3,500 km. The commission estimates that the investment required to create a 'true' transport network (including all modes of travel, not just roads) across the enlarged European Union is now a staggering €600 billion. In 2005 the commission estimated that the cost of completing its priority list of 30 projects alone would amount to €252 billion.

Given the enormous cost of fully implementing the TEN-T, it is acknowledged that national government funding – and by extension the EU aid that is funded by those national governments – is incapable of funding all the required projects in the required timescale. There is therefore a growing belief that the increased use of private finance (eg, through DBFO/PPP structures), 'primed', where appropriate, by EU funding and supported by the increased adoption of road user charging, is both inevitable and desirable if the grand vision of the TEN-T is to be fulfilled.

## 6.2 The Eurovignette Directive

The Eurovignette Directive (1999/62/EC), which came into force on July 20 2000, concerns the charging of heavy goods vehicles[3] for the use of certain transport infrastructure.

Since the directive came into force, the commission has undertaken various consultations on this issue, eventually culminating in an amendment to the

---

2   See TEN-T Priority Axes and Projects 2005 on http://europa.eu.int/comm/ten/transport.index_en.htm.
3   In this context (and for the purposes of this chapter generally), being those vehicles that are intended or are used exclusively for the carriage of goods by road which have a maximum permissible laden weight of over 3.5 tonnes

Eurovignette Directive by way of Directive 2006/38/EC of May 17 2006 (the 'Amending Directive'). The Amending Directive was published in the *Official Journal* (and came into force) on June 9 2006.

The Eurovignette Directive is designed to eliminate distortions in competition between transport undertakings in the member states via the harmonisation of the various levy systems and the establishment of fair mechanisms for charging infrastructure costs to hauliers. The objective of the Amending Directive is to allow a fairer system of charging for the use of road infrastructure based on the 'user pays' principle and to afford member states the ability to apply the 'polluter pays' principle to users.

The Amending Directive is required to be implemented at a national level by no later than June 10 2008.

*(a)* **Tolls and user charges**

Together the two directives cover the tolls and user charges that may be imposed on heavy good vehicles using any route in the TEN-T. Member states are free, within the framework of EU law, to impose tolls and user charges on roads outside of the TEN-T, including routes which are parallel to and in competition with TEN-T routes, provided always that those charges do not discriminate against international traffic or result in distortions of competition between operators.

A 'toll' is defined as a specified amount payable for a vehicle travelling a given distance on the project road, the amount of which is based on the distance travelled and the type of vehicle. A 'user charge' is a specified payment which confers on that vehicle the right to use the project road for a given period.

The Eurovignette Directive does not require a member state to introduce tolls or user charges where none are currently imposed, but establishes guidelines for the calculation, level and collection of those already operative in the member states or any which might succeed them.

*(b)* **Conditions of charging a toll or a user charge under the directives**

Article 7 lists the conditions which must be met by member states wishing to introduce and/or maintain tolls or user charges for heavy goods vehicles using roads in the TEN-T. These conditions include the following:[4]

- By 2012 such tolls or user charges must be applied to all heavy goods vehicles, unless the member state considers that this would create significant adverse effects on the free flow of traffic, the environment, noise levels, congestion or health, or involve administrative costs which would be more than 30% of additional revenue generated.
- With the exception of bridges, tunnels and mountain passes, tolls and user charges may not be imposed simultaneously.
- There must be no discrimination on the grounds of the nationality or place of establishment of the haulier, the registration of the vehicle or the origin or destination of the vehicle.

---

[4] This is not a complete list – refer to the Eurovignette Directive for full details.

- Subject to commission approval, reductions of up to 13% may be offered to frequent users of the roads but arrangements for the collection of tolls and user charges must not place non-regular users of the road at an unjustified disadvantage, either financially or otherwise.
- User charges must be in proportion to the duration of the use made of the infrastructure and may not exceed the maximum rates set out at Annex II of the Amending Directive.
- Tolls shall be based on the principle of the recovery of infrastructure costs only. Specifically, the weighted average tolls to be charged on a road (being the total revenue divided by length of road) shall take into account construction costs and the costs of operating, maintaining and developing the infrastructure network and, significantly, may also include a return on capital or profit margin based on market conditions.
- Tolls may, however, be varied for purposes such as combating environmental damage, tackling congestion, minimising infrastructure damage, optimising infrastructure use or promoting road safety – which includes variations as a result of the vehicle's emission class, the time or type of day or season. Limits are imposed on the maximum permissible 'mark-up' of a toll against the non-discounted level.
- A member state must, when a concession contract is renewed (but no later, in any event, than 2010) have variable toll rates in place depending on the emission class of a vehicle, unless this would seriously undermine the coherency of the tolling system, is not technically practical or would lead to diverting the most polluting vehicles away from the TEN-T and, as a consequence, impact on road safety and public health.
- Other variations to toll rates may be permissible in exceptional projects of high European interest (in order to secure the commercial viability of those projects) and in relation to infrastructure in mountainous regions suffering from acute congestion and the use of which is the cause of significant environmental damage. Particular rules govern the use of the proceeds of an increased toll applied in a mountainous area.

Subject to the requirement that the revenue collected under both directives is to be used to "benefit the transport sector and optimise the entire transport system", it is for a member state to determine the use to be made of that revenue.

Article 8 of the Eurovignette Directive provides for the possibility of two or more member states cooperating to introduce a common system for user charges, subject to compliance with certain conditions such as the fair sharing of revenue among member states and allowing other member states to enter the common system.

*(c)* *Interaction with other taxes or charges*

The Eurovignette Directive (Article 9(1)) does not prevent a member state from applying:
- specific taxes or charges levied upon registration of the vehicle or imposed on vehicles or loads of abnormal weights or dimensions;

- parking fees and specific urban traffic charges; and
- charges aimed at combating time and place-related traffic congestion.

Member states that install electronic toll systems are responsible for ensuring that their systems are compatible (Article 11(3)).

### 6.3 The Interoperability Directive

The aim of Directive 2004/52/EC on the interoperability of electronic road toll systems in the European Union ('the Interoperability Directive) is to lay down the necessary conditions to ensure the interoperability of existing and future electronic road toll systems in the European Union and to create a European electronic toll service for all parts of the road network. The service will be based upon the principle of 'one contract per customer, one box per vehicle'. The commission has argued that by ensuring the interoperability of toll systems, the Interoperability Directive will facilitate the implementation of a Europe-wide infrastructure charging policy.

The commission suggests that it would be possible for existing systems to be maintained alongside the new European service until they are decommissioned, although there would presumably be an obligation on operators to make interoperable receivers available to users who wanted them.

The proposed new European electronic toll service will concern only the method of collecting tolls or fees, and not the level of charges or the purpose for which they are levied.

*(a)* *When does the Interoperability Directive apply?*

The Interoperability Directive applies to the electronic collection of all types of road fee on the entire EU road network, urban and interurban motorways, major and minor roads, and structures such as tunnels, bridges and ferries.

However, it does not apply to:
- road toll systems for which no electronic means of toll collection exists;
- electronic road toll systems which do not need the installation of onboard equipment; or
- small, strictly local road toll systems for which the costs of compliance with the Interoperability Directive would be disproportionate to the benefits.

*(b)* *Requirements as to technology*

If a toll collection system uses tags for carrying out electronic toll transactions, the operator must make available to interested users onboard equipment which is suitable for use (or at least interoperable and capable of communicating) with all electronic toll systems in service in the member states using one or more of the following technologies (suitable for use in all types of vehicle):
- satellite positioning;
- mobile communications using the GSM-GPRS standard; and/or
- 5.8 gigahertz microwave technology.

All new electronic toll systems brought into service on or after January 1 2007 must use one or more of these technologies (the commission has expressed a preference for the use of either of the first two technologies). The commission intends to draw up a report by December 31 2009 in relation to the possible migration to systems using satellite positioning and mobile communications technologies by systems using other technologies. The report will include a study of use and a cost-benefit analysis of each of these technologies.

(c) *The European electronic toll service*

The European electronic toll service will encompass all the road networks in the European Union on which tolls or road-usage fees are collected electronically. The European electronic toll service will be complementary to the national electronic toll services of the member states. There is, however, no guidance as to what the exact relationship between national services and the European service will be. In a preliminary discussion document issued by the commission it was envisaged that national toll systems should be maintained alongside the new European service until decommissioned. However, the text of the Interoperability Directive does not reflect this intention.

The European electronic toll service will be defined by:
- a contractual set of rules allowing all operators and/or issuers to provide the service;
- a set of technical standards and requirements; and
- a single subscription contract (irrespective of nationality or place of vehicle registration) between clients and the operators and/or issuers offering the service. The contract will give access to the service on the whole of the network and subscriptions will be available from the operator of any part of the network. It is not clear from the wording of the Interoperability Directive whether each customer must be offered a single contract designed by any toll operator or whether a single model contract is to be used by all toll operators.

(d) *Implementation timetable*

The current timetable is that, three years following the decisions on the definition of the European electronic toll service having been taken by the commission, member states are to ensure that operators offer their customers the electronic toll service for heavy goods vehicles or those which are allowed to carry more than nine passengers. Within five years this is to be extended to all other types of vehicle.

The commission envisages that by 2010, a uniform system will enable almost 80% of toll transactions to be carried out using electronic toll equipment and that the technological leap should bring the cost of equipping a vehicle down to about €100.

(e) *Non-discrimination issues*

The implementation of systems of electronic toll collection in the member states must be non-discriminatory in all respects between domestic road users and road users from other member states.

Automatic debiting of toll charges to bank accounts or credit/debit card accounts which are domiciled anywhere in the European Union and beyond is conditional on a fully operational EU payments area with non-discriminatory service charges.

*(f)    Other issues*
The introduction of electronic toll systems will entail the processing of personal data and all parties concerned will need to consider carefully the effect of applicable data protection laws on this activity.

The equipment for the European electronic toll service will also need to comply with all applicable laws on radio and telecommunications terminal equipment.

### 6.4    The impact of EU procurement rules

Road projects procured within the European Union will have to follow the relevant procurement rules. This section sets out a brief review of some of the issues that arise from this.

The first question which arises is whether the contract can be classified for public procurement purposes as a concession contract. The European Commission's communication on this issue (from 2000) indicates that key requirements for a contract to be a concession are:

- the transfer of the responsibilities of operation, including technical, financial and managerial matters relating to the construction. For example, the concessionaire will make the investments required so that the project road may be both available and useful to users, and is responsible for paying for the construction; and
- the transfer of a significant element of exploitation risk to the concessionaire.

The degree of risk which must pass for a contract to amount to a concession is unclear. A European Court of Justice advocate general has indicated that the concessionaire must bear the "principal, or at least the substantive, economic risk attaching to the performance of the service [or work] involved", and must "effectively obtain at least a significant proportion of its remuneration not from the granting entity but from the exploitation of the service [or work]".

As noted in section 3.6, some projects involve a mixture of payment options (eg, availability/grant payments/traffic guarantees supporting real tolls). Whether the test for a concession contract would be satisfied in such cases will turn on the facts of each case. UK PFI contracts, for example, are generally considered to involve sufficient risk on the contractor to be classified as concessions.

The next issue is whether the contract is properly classified as a works or a services concession. The concession will generally involve both the construction of the project road (works) and its operation (services). The commission has indicated that a contract will be a works contract if it is 'principally concerned' with the building of a structure on behalf of the grantor. Another view is that the value of the works and services must be considered in order to classify the contract (ie, are the works or services of greater value?). As regards the calculation of greater value, in the case of a transport asset where the contractor enjoys ownership during the lifetime of the contract but later transfers it to the authority, the test seems to be whether the residual value of the work after it has been used to perform the contract and been transferred is greater than the value of the performance during the period in which the service is provided.

Usually, a contract for the construction and operation of a road will be a works concession, whichever of the two tests is applied. The UK government takes the view that a contract should be classified according to its predominant purpose and, for example, the following contracts have been classified as works concessions: the Channel Tunnel Rail Link, the Skye bridge, the Second Severn bridge and the Dartford QE2 bridge.

On this basis (assuming the value threshold is exceeded and no exclusions apply), most DBFO roads contracts will probably qualify as public works concession contracts under the regulations enacted by the relevant member state to give effect to the new Public Sector Procurement Directive (2004/18/EC). In the United Kingdom, these are the new Public Contracts Regulations 2006, which came into effect on January 31 2006. This section considers the position under English law, but the law in other member states should be analogous given that it is designed to give effect to the same directive.

The distinction between works contracts and concessions is important because public works concession contracts are not subject to the full scope of the Public Contracts Regulations. In particular, under the regulations there is no explicit obligation to run a competition following the advertisement of the contract under Regulation 36 (see below). In particular, Regulation 12 (requiring the use of the open procedure or the restricted procedure in normal circumstances and the negotiated procedure or competitive dialogue procedure in relevant (limited) circumstances) does not apply. There is therefore no requirement for authorities to use the new competitive dialogue procedure in these circumstances (although in theory it could be used voluntarily).

The principal provisions that apply to the award procedure for public works concession contracts are Regulations 36 and 37.

Regulation 36 requires the authority to publicise its intention to seek offers in relation to the public works concession contract by sending the appropriate form to the *Official Journal* and to allow not less than 52 days from the date of despatch (or 45 days if sent by electronic means) for the receipt of tenders or of requests to be selected to tender for or to negotiate the contract, as the case may be.

Regulation 36 also imposes certain obligations on the authority in connection with the provision of contract documents and further information to economic operators (ie, potential concessionaires).

Regulation 37 imposes an obligation on the authority to take certain measures relating to the subcontracting of work by the concessionaire and also includes provisions relating to works subcontracts subsequently awarded by the concessionaire itself. So far as the obligations on the authority are concerned, it must require as a term of the concession contract that the concessionaire subcontract some or all of the work(s) to persons who are not affiliated to it. The amount of works subcontracted must be not less than 30% of the value of the project and may be a greater amount if specified in the contract (at the option of the concessionaire). Alternatively, the authority may simply request in the contract documents that potential concessionaires indicate the proportion of work(s), if any, which they would intend to subcontract to persons not affiliated to them were they awarded the concession contract. This latter alternative does not require that any works be actually subcontracted or even require the authority to take this possibility into account in its evaluation of tenders, and is usually the recommended approach.

As far as the obligations on the concessionaire are concerned, Regulation 37 requires it to advertise certain works subcontracts and imposes certain obligations on it in connection with the provision of contract documents and further information to economic operators (ie, potential subcontractors).

The award of all public works concession contracts is also subject to the general principles of the EC Treaty requiring fairness, transparency and equality of treatment. In order to meet these requirements, the authority will almost certainly need to run a formal competition process. In doing so, it would be free to elect to use the negotiated procedure, competitive dialogue procedure or an alternative procedure as long as, in each case, the structure and application of the chosen procedure complies with these general principles. It is relevant to note in this context the following quote from the commission's April 2004 green paper on public-private partnerships and EU law on public contracts and concessions:

*There are few provisions of secondary legislation which coordinate the procedures for the award of contracts designated as concession contracts in Community law. In the case of works concessions, there are only certain advertising obligations, intended to ensure prior competition by interested operators, and an obligation regarding the minimum time-limit for the receipt of applications [a footnote refers to the current and new EC Works/Public Sector Directives]. The contracting bodies are then free to decide how to select the private partner, although in so doing they must nonetheless guarantee full compliance with the principles and rules resulting from the Treaty.*

Finally, it should be noted that Regulation 11, which requires the publication of periodic information notices, does not apply to public works concession contracts.

## 6.5  EU funding

At the risk of oversimplifying a complex area, there are the following main opportunities for EU transport projects to access EU funding (not including for these purposes funding from multilaterals such as the European Investment Bank and the European Bank for Reconstruction and Development, which is outside the scope of this chapter).

### (a)  TEN-T funds

As noted earlier in this chapter, the European Commission has recognised the need to use central funding to prime and support the use of private finance in realising the completion of the TEN-T.

Accordingly, the dedicated TEN-T budget can now be accessed for TEN-T priority projects to assist in financing preparatory studies (up to 50% of the cost) and construction itself (previously this was capped at 10%, but since 2004 this can be increased to 20% in exceptional cases).

According to commission figures, it poured almost €5 billion into TEN-T projects up to 2004 – an average of €600 million per year since 2000. It is proposed that this should be increased still further – up to €3 billion per year, with the maximum EU contribution for cross-border priority projects being raised from 20% to 50%.

*(b)* ***Structural funds and cohesion funds***

These funds have contributed significantly to TEN-T projects since 2000 – around €20 billion in regions as diverse as Spain, Portugal, Greece and Ireland.

*(i)* *The structural fund[5]*

The structural fund is not dedicated to transport, having instead its own objectives that can sometimes include the development of transport links.

Structural funding is usually said to have three objectives:
- promoting the development and structural adjustment of regions whose development is lagging behind (generally regarded in this context as 75% of average EU gross national product (GNP) per capita);
- supporting the economic and social conversion of areas facing structural difficulties; and
- supporting the adaptation and modernisation of policies and systems of education, training and employment.

Structural funding for 2000 to 2006 is set at €195 billion and as such utilises around a third of the total EU budget. A further €15 billion has been allocated to the accession states during 2004 to 2006.

*(ii)* *The cohesion fund[6]*

Like the structural fund, the cohesion fund has its own agenda and is not dedicated to transport development.

Set up in 1994, it is a structural instrument designed to assist member states in reducing economic and social disparities and to stabilise their economies.

Only those member states whose GNP per capita is below 90% of the EU average are eligible for cohesion funding. According to the commission, since 2004 this has meant Greece, Portugal, Spain, Cyprus, the Czech Republic, Estonia, Hungary, Latvia, Lithuania, Malta, Poland, Slovakia and Slovenia.

Projects suitable for cohesion funding are those involving the environment and transport infrastructure which will strengthen cohesion and solidarity within the European Union.

Cohesion funding can meet up to 85% of eligible expenditure of the project.

Some €15.9 billion (in 2004 prices) of cohesion funding is available for the years 2004 to 2006. More than half of this (€8.49 billion) is reserved for the new member states.

---

5  For more details see *http://ec.europa.eu/regional_policy/funds/prord/sf_en.htm*.
6  For more details see *http://ec.europa.eu/regional_policy/funds/procf/cf_en.htm*.

*(iii)*    *Accession funds*[7]

Launched in 2000, the Instrument for Structural Policies for Pre-Accession is one of a number of means for the European Union to assist candidate countries in the preparation for accession.

It is based on the principles that govern the cohesion fund and provides assistance for infrastructure projects in the EU priority fields of the environment and transport.

One of its express objectives is "upgrading and expanding links with the trans-European transport networks".

According to EU literature, for the period 2000 to 2006 around €1 billion a year has been made available under the Instrument for Structural Policies for Pre-Accession (ISPA), assisting over 300 large-scale infrastructure investments in the 10 candidate countries of Central and Eastern Europe. After the EU enlargement in 2004, the remaining ISPA beneficiary countries were Bulgaria and Romania, the other beneficiary countries having become eligible to the cohesion fund. From January 2005 Croatia became eligible to benefits from the ISPA.

## 7. Recent developments and the future

Some recent developments that catch the eye and potential future trends are outlined below.

### 7.1 'Deep future'

The past two years or so have seen the development in North America of projects involving truly massive capital costs and correspondingly massive concession lengths. A new phrase, 'highly leveraged deep future projects', has recently been coined to describe these deals.

Instead of the low to mid hundreds of millions of dollars amortising over 25 to 35 years, these deals involve senior debt well in excess of €1 billion and have concessions of up to 99 years.

It is difficult to tell at this stage whether deals such as the Chicago Skyway, the Indiana Toll Road and Highway 407 in Canada represent a series of one-offs or the start of a trend.

### 7.2 Roads maintenance PPPs

The past few years have seen the emergence of roads maintenance PPP projects in the United Kingdom (one has been signed for Portsmouth and one is in procurement for Birmingham). These deals usually involve the concessionaire assuming responsibility for all roads within the designated area as well as for street lighting and so on in that area, and being paid on an availability/performance basis. These projects bring their own unique points for consideration. In particular, there are significant potential issues regarding the nature of the asset base taken on by the concessionaire. For example, not only will it be very large, it may also be difficult to ascertain the condition of it all with certainty (giving rise to potentially serious latent defect risk

---

[7]    For more details see *http://ec.europa.eu/regional_policy/funds/ispa/ispa_en.htm*

issues). The inter-relationship between the concessionaire and the various statutory undertakers who have rights of access over an entire city can also be complex and problematic.

7.3   **Congestion charging**

As noted above, it is now some years since Transport for London first introduced the Central London Congestion Charge and various expansions to its ambit are planned. This project was one of the first of its kind anywhere in the world and has been watched with interest by other major cities with similar traffic problems as London. Perhaps similar schemes will be brought to market elsewhere in the United Kingdom – and indeed the world – in the next few years.

7.4   **What next?**

While it can be foolhardy to attempt to predict the future (particularly in writing), at the moment the short-term future looks to be based upon real tolls and user charging. In the longer term, the imposition of the comprehensive distance-based charging systems that some developed economies have already acknowledged as the only realistic option for controlling escalating congestion (but to date have lacked the stomach to implement) may even become a reality. In the United Kingdom, this was again raised as a possibility by the government as recently as August 2006. However, this sort of major change to controlling congestion and funding road development and management is probably unlikely to happen any time soon.

For the moment, though, the global future for roads PPP generally looks reasonably rosy. There are extensive plans for the future use of private finance in road infrastructure in almost every corner of the globe: Europe (especially the accession states and future candidate countries), the United States, Canada, Australasia, India and Latin America (where Chile, Brazil and Mexico, to name but a few, all have active road programmes involving private finance).

# Railways

Tom Winsor
White & Case LLP

## 1. Introduction

Public-private partnerships (PPPs) in railways are significantly different from those in other industries, which makes them both difficult and special. There are two main reasons for this. The first is that railway projects are not as simple as schools, hospitals, prisons or even roads, tunnels or bridges. The difficulties and risks of work on the live, hot, operating railway put railway infrastructure works on a different plane from other types of infrastructure. The second is that, in the railway context, PPPs have a continuing political dynamic which places the industry on a different level of complexity.

Many commentators think of PPPs principally in the sense of the provision of public buildings or structures, frequently coupled with the provision of services relating to those assets. But there is a wider context and sense of the concept and it has particular relevance in the case of railways. It involves the partnership between the state and the private sector in the provision of essential services in which there is a heavy political interest, and probably a need for continuing public funding.

PPPs in railways are not only about building an asset and paying for it over time, although they are often certainly at least about that. They concern a long-term relationship which involves the delivery of complex, safety-critical services and where demand and other factors influencing their costs, stewardship and intensity of use will change over time.

## 2. Objectives

The most important thing for governments to decide when they embark on the design of a PPP is their objective. What do they want to achieve, and is it feasible on a sustainable, fair and affordable basis with private sector participation?

In many countries, railways are not economically viable without some measure of continuing public financial support. This is a function of their physical condition, their social importance in the national and regional economies which they serve, and the sometimes abstruse question of the structure of access charges. There will be ostensibly profitable parts of the railways, but their true economic health is sometimes obscured by other factors such as cross-subsidies or accounting treatment.

In many countries, networks and rolling stock have been neglected – sometimes severely – in the years of public ownership, with inadequate, usually annualised, financial settlements from cash-strapped governments. Operating losses have often reached a level which is simply no longer affordable. The years of decline in the condition, capacity and capability of the railway's physical assets must be paid for one day if the railway is not to close. And closure – or substantial reduction – is often politically and economically unfeasible, especially in countries whose manufacturing and service sectors are growing and which do not have adequate available capacity in other transport modes. Failures and lack of capacity in infrastructure lead inexorably to deterioration in performance, and poor-quality rolling stock deters patronage. It is a vicious circle of decline. These malfunctions are often major restraining or decelerating factors in the development of an economy, and when economies are growing – as in India and China – such shortcomings cannot realistically be tolerated.

Often, the uncomfortable fact of putting right the neglect of years must be faced and tackled at the point of the industry's restructuring and the prospective establishment of PPPs which are intended to bring private money and expertise into the railway. By that time, usually the national treasury is exhausted or severely stretched, and other means must be found for the repair, renewal and expansion of the railway.

The need for public funding of operators – in contrast to the infrastructure provider – in a vertically separated railway will also be a function of the structure and level of access charges which the infrastructure company is allowed to charge for use of its network. This is true even of the railways in Great Britain, where it is only because of the direct funding by the government of a large part of the infrastructure provider's revenue requirements that passenger franchise holders can promise premium payments for their franchises, rather than receive public subsidies.

There will therefore usually be a need to access sources of finance available to the private sector because of national funding limitations. This was the underlying premise of the white paper on railways published by the European Commission in 1996, which led to mandatory radical reform in Europe's railways. It was also one of the main driving forces behind the restructuring and privatisation of the British railway industry. The same was true in Germany, Sweden and South America.

Government may wish to introduce competition into the railway. Separating infrastructure, where there can be no competition, from operations, where there can, is a major step which can bring very significant benefits in railway efficiency and the efficiency of other transport modes which compete with rail. Competition can come in two forms: competition for the market and competition in the market. Competition for the market is essentially franchising: contracts for the provision of railway services either in exchange for subsidy or accompanied by the payment of a premium. Competition in the market can take place in both passenger and freight sectors. It has, of course, been much more prevalent in freight. In Europe, for example, significant on-rail freight competition has developed in Britain and Germany, and is developing strongly in other member states. On-rail passenger competition has been more sluggish, but breakthroughs in open access passenger operations in Britain may herald stronger growth in the future and in other countries when it is realised that it is not always necessary to have a franchise or contract with the state to run passenger rail services.

Private management can introduce efficiency and also find and grow new markets, unconstrained by public sector financial and other restraints. In turn, this can reduce the drain on national and regional budgets, and can contribute to them. If costs can be reduced while maintaining the necessary levels of service, there may be more money to spend on enhancing that service – for example, for small or medium-scale capacity enhancement schemes such as platform lengthening, crossovers, freight loops and even resignalling.

Bringing in private sector parties can also enable government to transfer risks to the private sector, although this can entail severe difficulties if the risks are not adequately identified, understood or quantified at the outset.

Frequently there will be disagreements within government and the wider constituency of opinion as to which of these objectives – which ones and which blend – should be pursued. Vested interests, such as organised labour, will resist some of these options being objectives at all. The chosen solution may be complex and a compromise. But when it is confused – because decision-makers will not face up to some of the issues; because they do not properly understand them and the implications of adopting or rejecting them; or because they simply have not thought of them – potentially severe problems will be stored for the future, when their resolution will be painful and expensive.

The choice of solution is dependent on the government's objectives. If these are uncertain, the solution may well turn out to be the wrong one.

3. **The political dynamic**

Designing a transport partnership is fraught with difficulty. It is a complex field, and that complexity is in large part a function of the fact not only that there is a significant continuing political dimension in the railway sector, but also that transport planning horizons are much longer than political ones. The politician will usually be more concerned with the next election or his next move within government. Yet railway projects, including major renewal schemes such as the West Coast main line in Great Britain, take years to plan and commission. Politicians like cutting the ribbon at the opening ceremony, and not, years before, explaining to disappointed parties why funds are not available for favoured schemes because they have been committed to a railway purpose which will not produce tangible benefits (for which credit can be taken) in what, in political terms, is the distant future. There are, of course, exceptions, but the political dynamic must be recognised. Cynics have been heard to remark that political honesty in transport planning is a concept of the future, and always will be.

So in designing a PPP for a railway, it is first necessary to have a clear understanding of the nature of the forces at work and how those players will behave not only at the beginning of the enterprise, but throughout its life, which may be many years.

Transport is the business of government. And, in a private sector industry, it is just as much the concern of business. It is both their jobs. That must be recognised immediately.

It is the role of government to make decisions about what kind of transport should be provided for the benefit of the community, including the wider community which benefits from transport links. It is the role of business to deliver transport services within that overall policy. Business will do this provided it can have the confidence and certainty necessary to come in and provide quality transport services at a fair and affordable price.

Getting the terms of that partnership between the public and private sectors clearly and properly established so as to meet the legitimate objectives and interests of both partners is essential. This is because when the partnership is not placed on such a secure foundation, it will become unstable and the partners will eventually fall out. Serious harm to the public interest and commercial interests may well follow, as was starkly apparent when Railtrack, the national railway infrastructure company of Britain, collapsed in October 2001 in the most controversial of circumstances.

So how do we establish a fair and sustainable partnership for the railways? To make a partnership work you must know, respect and, as far as possible, accommodate the essential objectives of both partners. It is no good the private sector complaining that governments are political. And it is equally pointless for government to complain that business wants to make money. If the public sector and the private sector are going to get along, each must acknowledge and accept the fundamental nature of the other partner in the relationship and work with that fact, not against it.

If the partnership is going to prosper and deliver its objectives, neither partner can be allowed to behave in an uncontrolled, arbitrary or destructive way which would do serious harm to the interests of the other partner. There must be some restraints, some ground rules, some fundamental precepts which must not be violated. And the way in which you establish those basic rules for living and getting along together is a compact or contract between the state and the private sector, sometimes policed by an independent institution which respects the terms of the contract and serves as a breakwater between the forces at work on either side to ensure stability. In the British railway industry, as far as infrastructure provision is concerned, the economic regulator does that job. In other countries, the state's relationship with the private sector is established in a contract, sometimes with special constitutional status. In the case of the operators of passenger and freight trains, the solutions are simpler, with franchising or concessioning of passenger services and often the outright privatisation of freight operations. In some systems there is a spectrum of models, reflecting the different circumstances and dynamics of each part of the railway.

Business wants to be able to make money. If the business in question is the monopoly provision of infrastructure services, then left to its own devices it will tend to abuse that position by charging unreasonably high prices, unduly discriminating against users, unreasonably denying access to the system and providing a poor quality of service. This is unacceptable, so the entity should be made subject to regulatory controls and accountabilities – the models of accountability vary, too – which hold in check the propensity to these excesses. Those accountabilities need to be strong and properly designed if they are to be effective. Insofar as they are monitored and enforced by a public authority, this must be done according to clear and conspicuous objective public interest duties. The issue of regulatory design and competence is discussed later in this chapter.

Governments want other things. They know that they cannot – or should not – run the operation in question. When government runs something, no one really knows what it costs. This is because governments do not manage according to profit incentives; they manage to administrative budgets. They often operate on unreliable information and, not knowing what something ought to cost, will usually decide to pay what they want and accept what comes back for that money. So, having given up on the idea of running the railway, government needs to know that its objectives – politically accountable and politically determined – will be respected.

In the contract between the state and the private sector, there must be clarity about what the state expects for its money. The contract between the two must be one in which the private sector can have confidence. Will it be honoured in all political circumstances? Will it withstand every political shock? Will government not try inappropriately to circumvent it, interfere with it or otherwise undermine or destroy it? It comes down to the sanctity of contract between the state and the private sector. That contract must be well designed so that both parties want to stay in the relationship and make it work. For that to happen, both parties must go into it with their eyes open and be good for the promises they make.

As discussed, governments work according to political cycles. Business does not want to, and proper and efficient transport planning and investment decisions find it extremely hard to. In the British railway industry, for a long time there was an absence of consistency or continuity of political thought and investment or business policy. That in turn prevented either any long-term planning or the completion of plans made in good faith. And so there is a need for long-term vision which outlives the political cycle. How can the system be insulated from this to the appropriate extent?

To put it another way:
- how do you give government the confidence that the public interest will be protected and promoted in decisions in the industry in question; *but*
- avoid an intensity of political intervention which will deter investment or drive its costs up; *and*
- allow long-term planning and consistency, so getting away from government's stop-start policies on direction, structure or funding; *and*
- prevent government from getting a disproportionate amount of blame when things go wrong?

Governments can so easily interfere to a damaging extent in the day-to-day affairs and operation of transport concerns, causing damage to confidence and raising the cost of finance. Yet when things are thought to be dysfunctional, or perhaps where there is simply a serious problem which is causing political trouble, governments often feel both so powerless and so afraid of the blame that they barge in, trying to impose their own solutions, sometimes ending up making the position much worse. In Britain, in the aftermath of the October 2000 Hatfield rail crash, caused by a broken rail, the integrity of the national network in large measure disintegrated. This led to a sudden rise in political intervention, when government mistakenly tried to supervise operational recovery. Then in April 2001, government publicly forced Railtrack to appoint a public interest director in return for an acceleration of government funding, causing the sharpest-ever fall in its share price because of the perception of the manifestation of severe political risk. A few months later, in October 2001, Railtrack collapsed into administration – a special class of insolvency for railway companies – at the instance of the secretary of state for transport, in the most controversial and damaging of circumstances. These sorts of intervention can have serious and unintended consequences.

The answer to these questions is to have a properly designed and functioning, stable and respected regime of accountability of the private sector to the public sector. Such a system is a source of stability and protection for all concerned, especially when the industry faces severe difficulties. Its absence deters private investment or makes it more expensive and, over time, will cause the industry to malfunction, bringing further unwanted and usually damaging political interventions.

## 4. Structural reform – separation

The most radical structural reform a railway can undergo is separation of infrastructure from operations. This change is complex and must be done properly; if it is done well, the benefits in improving the operational and financial efficiency of the railway can be very significant.

The European Commission, through a series of directives for the railway sector, has moved a long way towards vertical separation. It began in 1991 with a requirement for separate accounting for infrastructure and operations, and has moved steadily in the direction of greater degrees of separation. It has done this because it is correctly convinced that railways will not be efficient if they remain monolithic, with cross-subsidies, uncertain or obscure accounting arrangements for internal transactions, and the ability to deter or destroy any competitive service which dares to materialise. One of the fundamentals of the EC Treaty is the promotion and protection of competition, and competition is least likely to develop and thrive in the old railway structures. The European Commission has been proved right in this, since the most successful railways in Europe – those in Britain and Germany – are those which have embraced liberalisation to the greatest extent. The poorest-performing, most economically inefficient railways are those which have been slow to reform and embrace competition.

The European directives do not require member states to privatise their railways. Determining the ownership of railway assets is not part of the European Commission's remit. But the commission insists that there be transparency and objectivity in the operation of the market and in many of the decisions which affect it. In fact, as with most, if not all, public sector infrastructure assets, it does not matter whether railway assets are owned in the public sector or the private sector. They will be tied to the national railway and there will be physical or regulatory restraints on the ability of anyone to take them out of the jurisdiction. What matters most is how they are operated, and whether that achieves or facilitates the public sector's legitimate objectives. That is a function of the design of the railway PPP, and of the mechanisms and instruments of accountability which are put in place to protect both the public interest and the interests of private sector players which depend on fair treatment.

5. **Accountability**

A variety of accountabilities need to be properly established in a railway PPP. These are a function of the dynamics of the relationship between the public and private sectors, and between the industry's participants. All of them matter.

The interface between the public and private sectors is, of course, very significant. Striking the right balance between the power of the public and private sectors is essential. That not only means clarity about where the boundaries between the public and private sectors are drawn; it also means coming up with a division of roles which is going to be respected by both sides, not assaulted. If the dividing line is fuzzy, there will be territorial encroachments by both sides. If it is radically misplaced, it will eventually be subject to severe pressure. Brittle, fragile and significantly unbalanced structures will eventually break. When they do, it will be expensive. This applies with equal force to the relative jurisdictions of the agencies and institutions of government, particularly the ministry of transport and the regulatory body.

The propensity of the public sector to try to intrude into the proper domain of the private sector – political interventions borne of frustration and impatience – will be a direct function of the performance of the industry in the private sector. If things are going well, operational performance is as good as or better than projected, financial efficiency is on track and passenger satisfaction is at sufficiently high levels, political pressure should be next to non-existent and the partnership will be secure.

It is when things go wrong – especially when there is a severe failure – that the dividing line comes under strain. This happened in spectacular fashion in Britain when Railtrack's failures in its stewardship of the network led to the multi-fatality Hatfield crash and months of operational disruption afterwards because the company had inadequate knowledge of the condition of its assets. Railtrack was in a complex PPP established by licence, contract and regulatory oversight, but it was a PPP nonetheless. Despite that status, and the need for stability and predictability in the dynamic between the public and private sectors, politicians intervened immediately and did immense harm, eventually causing the company to collapse and necessitating financial rescues of a large proportion of the passenger train operators which suffered considerable losses as a result of the failures. This episode also involved a major threat to the independence and jurisdiction of the economic regulator for the railways, because politicians were intolerant of the ability of the regulator to advance additional funding to what they saw as a failing company. The British government at the time had never been in favour of rail privatisation, and certainly not of the model chosen by its predecessor, and some members of the governing party saw the severity of Railtrack's problems as an opportunity to renationalise the infrastructure without compensation. In short, the system was subjected to enormous adverse forces which necessitated the restructuring of the infrastructure provider – the creation of Network Rail as the successor to Railtrack as a company without shareholders – on a radically different and unforeseeable basis.

It also caused major difficulties in the capital and equity markets in relation to PPPs generally.

This shows that when things go badly wrong in a PPP, strong forces will collide violently and the system can fracture. It is essential that every possible step be taken to avoid this happening. And it can be avoided by ensuring that the remainder of the railway industry architecture – the matrix of economic, legal and regulatory instruments of accountability and incentivisation – is well designed and functions well.

In designing the accountabilities of the railway to the public interest and to one another, it is necessary always to bear in mind the risks which the industry faces and to ensure the efficient allocation of those risks.

If the condition of the infrastructure is either poor or uncertain (or both), it is unrealistic to expect the private sector to take the risk that it will require substantial, and possibly early, increases in maintenance and renewal. If the state is responsible for the assets' decline, it should assume the responsibility for putting this right, unless it is prepared to pay the private sector a handsome premium for doing so. If taxpayers have taken a maintenance holiday during the years of public ownership, they cannot expect the private sector to take on the consequences without complaint or compensation. That said, the costs can be very large indeed. In the case of Railtrack and Network Rail, the British rail regulator increased the company's five-year budget by 50% in October 2000 (from £10 billion to £15 billion) and in December 2003 increased it by a further 50% to £22.2 billion. This was principally to allow the company to recover the condition and capacity of the network from its decline during the years of nationalisation. Train operators needed the infrastructure provider to be fully and efficiently funded for this work because they depended on the proper performance of the network to run their trains. However, because of indemnities in their franchises with the state, they were financially neutral in the substantial increase in access charges payable to the infrastructure provider. If they had not been protected, it would have been impossible for the state to have let the franchises, since the private sector train operators were even less able than Railtrack to take the infrastructure condition risk.

In Eastern Europe, much of the rolling stock fleet is life expired and urgent investment is needed simply to maintain a reasonably functional service. In such cases the problem is easier to solve, because rolling stock replacement or refurbishment is a simpler and less costly concern than infrastructure renewal.

So the infrastructure provider must be assured of the necessary revenues so as to be able efficiently and economically to operate, maintain and renew the network on which everyone in the industry depends. When the infrastructure provider fails in its stewardship obligations, almost all parts of the industry – and the public interest – will suffer. That assurance of funding must come from the state, whether directly or through access charges paid by operators, which in turn will recover an appropriate proportion from public sources. The nature of the assurance can be in the form of a contract between the infrastructure provider and the national treasury or ministry of transport, or through the jurisdiction of an economic regulator with sufficient powers.

The contract model is favoured in most European countries, but it has its drawbacks. The infrastructure provider is at a negotiating disadvantage with the state because its leverage will often be weak – it cannot force the state to give it money, although it can point out the consequences of inadequate provision in terms of operational performance and network integrity. The alternative is to confer on the regulatory body the job of assessing what an efficient network operator should require for the operation, maintenance and renewal of the railway in light of the expected demands on the system, netting off its income from other sources such as property and advertising. The regulatory body may or may not have a budget to fund the infrastructure costs; in the British model, it did not, but it did have the power to set access charges at higher levels and, as explained, rely on the state's indemnity contracts with the train operators to secure the necessary funding for the higher charges payable to the infrastructure provider. Following the significant regulatory increases in the revenues payable to the infrastructure provider in Britain, in 2005 the law was changed to impose a financial limit on the regulator's jurisdiction. In future regulatory settlements, if the national treasury wishes to resist increases or impose cuts, the regulatory body will be required to determine where the railway will be reduced in its capacity, condition or performance.

Once the infrastructure provider has the financial settlement, it is important that it spends it wisely, and that it fully meets its obligations to its customers (the train operators) and to the public interest. The design and establishment of these obligations, and how they may be changed over time, are therefore crucial.

In Britain, at the time of privatisation, in several respects the matrix of accountability was deficient – in some cases, seriously deficient. The right approach in restructuring an industry in preparation for getting private sector skills and money into it – through PPPs of any variety – is to get the design right at the beginning and then avoid making material changes afterwards, when the private sector has come in. In 1993 to 1997, Britain did things differently. Through a combination of neglect, inability and political pressure, the railway industry was endowed with a contractual and regulatory matrix of extraordinary weakness. The company's network licence was made deliberately weak and was in no fit state for a private sector Railtrack. And the contracts and industry-wide codes were in too many respects unspecific in their requirements, lacking in their procedures and weak or uncertain in their remedies.

If a railway is to be able confidently and competently to do its job of operation, maintenance and renewal of the infrastructure, and the punctual and reliable provision of passenger and freight train services, it needs a sound framework which is capable of providing the answers and the remedies when questions arise or things go awry. Britain's original privatisation model did not have that. The system malfunctioned in many respects, and it was necessary to carry out major reforms.

In 1999 the British rail regulator set about improving and enhancing the accountability of the railway companies to the public interest and to one another, using the flexibility and utility of the existing system: the mechanisms for evolutionary change built into the matrix by its architects 10 years previously when they saw the shortcuts which were being taken and the weaknesses which were being established in the initial regime. In 2004, that reform programme was virtually finished, and the results – in terms of operational performance, financial efficiency, network quality, safety and passenger and customer satisfaction – have been spectacularly good.

The principal focus of the reform programme was on the monopoly provider of infrastructure services – Railtrack, now Network Rail. In the original blueprint for the railway, Railtrack was meant to have been the powerhouse of the railway industry. It squandered that role. In the years after privatisation, it underperformed in too many respects. Track quality declined and rails broke. Its investment in new capacity was sluggish, and its performance on infrastructure-caused delays and cancellations to passenger trains was poor. Its relationships with its dependent customers – train operators, local authorities, freight facility developers and others – were marred by frustration and unresponsiveness. That record and culture needed to be turned around quickly, in order to make the company respons0ive, competent and effective. Although there were some encouraging signs that progress was being made in the way Railtrack managed its business, the company fell back after the Hatfield crash and the struggle was lost.

The financial framework of a railway industry needs to provide the companies concerned with a stable and sound environment for investment. That means improving the incentives to invest in new capacity and better services, and ensuring that they have certainty and predictability in how that investment will be treated in future regulatory reviews. This is essential if the industry is to raise the finance needed to deliver the required level of investment in the network. The 2000 regulatory review of access charges established a much greater degree of incentivisation of the interested party to grow the capacity of the railway to meet projected demand, and to attract traffic and improve the condition of its assets.

The 2003 regulatory review of access charges built on that regime of incentivisation, and determined that Network Rail should deliver significant improvements in network outputs and sharp falls in delays caused to passenger and freight train operators. At the same time, Network Rail was required to ensure that asset condition improved across a broad range of measures contained in a new asset stewardship index. The index includes measures for broken rails, temporary speed restrictions, signalling, structures and track geometry.

The interested party's licence – enforced by the rail regulator and its principal means of accountability to the public interest – was not fit for its purpose. The reform programme amended the licence, introducing nine new conditions which established obligations on the infrastructure provider in relation to the proper and timely use of access charges and taxpayers' funds, with the ability to check on the progress and quality of spending and work, and to correct shortcomings before they become serious. The reforms involved the use of independent reporters on Network Rail's stewardship of the network, restraints on the disposal of its assets (including land) which may be needed for railway uses in the future, and the establishment of a reliable and comprehensive register of the condition, capacity and capability of the company's assets. They also involved much better, clearer and stronger relationships between Network Rail and its train operator and other customers, to ensure clarity, stability and empowerment, with mutual interest and a clear drive for success.

The reforms also dealt with the most important interface of all – the track-train connection. New forms of freight and passenger track access contract were devised and have now been implemented across the industry. In both cases, the objective of the work was clarity, simplicity, streamlining and strengthening. Operating a multi-user railway on which capacity is full or near to full is no easy matter. There are many interdependent things which need to be done to ensure that the railway operates well on a day-to-day basis. This is especially so for one which is having to cope with both current and future demands, including those associated with considerable maintenance and renewal programmes. The new contracts between Network Rail and its train operator customers acknowledge this fact and the need for railway companies to work together, not against one another. They recognise the intensity of the interdependence of the infrastructure provider and the infrastructure user, and create a true joint venture of aligned objectives, clarity of specification and simplicity of remedies so that, when things go wrong, recovery can be achieved as quickly and efficiently as possible.

Long-term relationships of this kind which are properly established and clearly understood, with a fair balance of risks and responsibilities between the parties, are far more likely to succeed than those which are one-sided or inequitable.

Railways need operational rules which, in some respects, are the same for all players. In Britain, the common rules are established in the network code, which is the central instrument incorporated into every access contract dealing with:

- timetable development;
- the handling of operational disruption;
- changes to the network (both enhancements and deteriorations);
- changes to rolling stock and the introduction of new trains onto the system;
- local accountabilities;
- the provision of information; and
- changes to access rights themselves, to prevent ossification of the timetable.

In 2004, the network code was substantially reformed to correct many of the deficiencies of the original privatisation settlement and is now contributing to an intensification of a true joint venture spirit in an interdependent railway.

With increasing harmonisation of Europe's railways, it may be speculated that in perhaps 10 years' time Europe will have a single network code and a single economic regulatory body, to ensure legal and economic as well as technical interoperability.

These reforms were not about command and control of the industry. Nor did they contemplate any transfer of management responsibility of the companies concerned. They were concerned with establishing a better, clearer and fairer balance of responsibility and obligation in the industry, to allow the companies to deal with one another from positions of broad equality of bargaining position, in a cooperative and mature way, as interdependent commercial companies do in other fields of activity. They created a virtuous circle of effective incentive-based regulation, strong and empowered management, clear contracts and sound accountability. They focused on empowerment of both sides of the track-train interface relationship, so as to ensure cooperative working and shared understandings. With empowerment comes the need for commercial maturity and competences.

In designing a PPP for the railways, the correct design of these interfaces is essential. It is the best way to avoid undue interventions from the public sector partner.

## 6. Regulatory design and competence

Some railway PPPs will be established purely or principally on the basis of a contract between the state and the private sector. That will be the constitution of the partnership and, as a long-term contract, will require considerable flexibility so that it can be adapted over time to meet changed circumstances. That is a very difficult thing to do, and means must be established for the resolution of differences when the unforeseen happens. That may involve resort to mediation, arbitration or some other neutral tribunal. In some cases, it will involve a separate, independent regulatory body.

In Europe, the railway directives require the establishment of a regulatory body with appropriate powers to deal with abuses of monopoly power, anti-competitive behaviour, capacity allocation and charging. Some regulatory bodies – such as those in Britain – go further than that and invest in the regulator powers in relation to the stewardship of the network.

In every PPP in the railways, the regulatory regime must be flexible enough to deal with changes in circumstances in a predictable and objective way. Ideally, the regulatory body will have a large measure of operational, perhaps even legal, independence from central government. The greater the degree of regulatory independence, the happier business will be because that autonomy provides a high degree of insulation of regulatory decisions from political criteria and undue political intervention.

If the regulatory body is to be independent of central government, that independence needs to be sustainable. If politicians will not tolerate substantial power in the hands of the regulator – for example, the power to determine public sector spending on the railway – it would be far better if those powers were denied to the regulatory body in the first place. The greatest harm is done when the juggernaut of government later tries to withdraw such powers from the regulator after the private sector has come into the market on the faith of the regulator's jurisdiction.

The pivotal role of the regulatory body is often underestimated, or misunderstood, by government, by industry and, in some EU countries, by the infant regulatory bodies themselves. A sound and durable regulatory regime is a protective measure for everyone in the industry, including the infrastructure manager. European directives provide supranational stability for the regulatory regimes of member states, provided they are honoured. It is fundamental to the development of the European Union's railways that networks are operated, maintained and renewed in a timely, efficient and economical manner. To ensure sustainability, this means that infrastructure managers must be assured of fair remuneration for their efficiency and competence. When infrastructure is subsidised from public funds, access charges can be lower than the system's long-run sustainable cost. When there is no subsidy, there is no alternative to access charges which meet the total efficient cost of the system. Anything lower will inevitably cause the network to deteriorate, contrary to the fundamental purposes of the directives. Regulatory bodies which do not respect and implement that basic part of the regime, which side with vested interests and allow improper and extraneous pressure to prevail, serve only to pervert the system and deny its primary purpose. And in doing so, they forfeit their integrity and do great harm to the system they are supposed to nurture and protect. The European Commission has powers to investigate any such failures, and the European Court of Justice can correct them.

As well as being properly empowered, regulatory bodies must discharge the very important roles entrusted to them with professionalism, competence and courage. The best way for a regulatory body to secure and then hold onto the trust and confidence of industry players is to establish clear and objective criteria for decisions which match and promote its policy and legal remit, and then to apply them consistently and fairly in accordance with processes which are demonstrably fair. This means consulting first on the criteria, and then on individual decisions, hearing all sides of the argument with a truly open mind, ensuring that viewpoints are properly and fully understood and that everyone has a proper opportunity to make representations and objections. In major cases, a draft decision should be made available to the affected parties, and when the final decision has been made it should be accompanied by full, published reasons. If all this is done, while there will always be some who dislike the decision, they will know that they have been listened to and understood, and that full weight has been given to their arguments. The importance of this in establishing regulatory legitimacy, and therefore confidence, in the system cannot be overstated.

*Certain passages of this chapter are adaptations from speeches delivered by the author in 2004 while he held office as the UK rail regulator.*

# Health

**Paul Smith**
CMS Cameron McKenna LLP

At a time when the reform of public health services is high on the agendas of many European governments, it is timely to examine the extent to which the private sector is participating in bringing such reforms into effect through public-private partnerships (PPPs).

This chapter examines:

- the nature of some of the public health service reforms across Western Europe and the extent to which the private sector has participated; and
- examples of some of the legal/commercial arrangements that have been developed in the United Kingdom to facilitate the private sector's participation in the provision of public health services.

## 1. Health service models and reforms, and private sector participation, in Western Europe

Healthcare systems vary widely across Western Europe, where both public and private facilities co-exist. The systems tend to fall into one of two differing forms of public insurance model. The United Kingdom, Italy and Spain use an integrated model, where the insurance provider also provides the services; in contrast, France, Germany and Belgium use a contract model where there is a separation between the services and the insurer.

Set out below is a brief synopsis of the healthcare systems and the most recent reforms in the United Kingdom, Italy, Spain, Holland, France, Belgium and Portugal, together with some examples of where the private sector has participated in effecting those reforms.

### 1.1 The United Kingdom

| Proportion of gross domestic product (GDP) spent on health | 8.0% (2003) |
|---|---|
| Annual expenditure on health per capita (average exchange rate $US) | $2,428 (2003) |

*Source*: World Health Organisation, Core Health Indicators

*(a)* **The National Health Service**

The United Kingdom's National Health Service (NHS) was established on July 5 1948 following the enactment of Nye Bevan's National Health Service Act in 1946. The NHS took control of over 2,500 hospitals and was organised broadly into three parts (hospital services, family doctors and local authority community care), involving the creation of 14 regional hospital boards and 147 local health authorities.

The underlying principles of the NHS then were that it was funded predominantly from taxation and that it would in general be free at the point of use, comprehensive and available to all, regardless of means to pay. Many of those principles remain true today.

Since 1948, the NHS has undergone some notable reforms relating both to organisation and to intensive capital investment. One of the more significant organisational changes was implemented by the Conservative government in the late 1980s and early 1990s, following its paper "Working with Patients" and later the NHS and Community Care Act 1990. The objectives of the reforms were fairly familiar: improvements in efficiency, quality, equity, choice/responsiveness and accountability. It was hoped that these objectives would be satisfied by the creation of the so-called 'internal market', whereby health authorities ceased to run hospitals directly and instead became purchasers of healthcare services from providers which, in theory, could be from the public or private sector. Public sector providers (eg, hospitals, organisations providing care for the mentally ill and ambulatory services) became self-governing NHS trusts with certain responsibilities and powers to enable them to fulfil that provider role. It was hoped the changes would enable health authorities to focus on assessing the health needs of their resident populations and purchasing health services necessary to meet those needs, while leaving the providers to focus on delivering services efficiently in competition with others.

In addition, primary care providers (eg, general practitioners (GPs)) were encouraged to hold a devolved budget used to purchase certain health services directly ('GP fund holders'). The intention was that this would create an alternative purchaser to the health authorities and improve the quality of secondary care, given the direct relationship between the GP and the hospital.

Not all expectations of the reform were realised. The internal market did not really become a true market at all, as real competition was often not possible or expected. The cost of administration was also higher than perhaps expected, opening the government to criticism for diverting valuable resources away from front-line health services into management, when in fact improvements in the management of the NHS were long overdue.

New Labour was elected as the governing party in 1997 and quickly set about putting into effect a key manifesto promise: the abolishment of the internal market. Its white paper entitled "The New NHS – Modern, Dependable" set out a challenging timetable of further reform which, in practice, built upon the Conservatives' "Working with Patients", evidenced by the retention of:
- the capitation-based budget allocation to health authorities (budgets based on population size, age structure and deprivation);
- the devolved powers for NHS trusts; and
- the purchaser/provider split.

However, there was an emphasis on cooperation between participants in local health economies rather than competition, which manifested itself in the new government seeking to reduce management costs through simplifying the contracting process.

In July 2000 the government published its NHS Plan, a 10-year plan of investment in infrastructure and reform of the NHS.

The key elements of the NHS Plan (and subsequent documents supporting the original NHS Plan) are:
- major investment in new hospitals, modern IT systems and additional consultants, GPs and nursing staff;
- the creation of patient choice;
- the reduction of waiting times for outpatient appointments to three months and for inpatient appointments to six months;
- the introduction of practice-based commissioning;
- the creation of foundation trusts;
- new contracts for GPs and consultants;
- the introduction of payment by results; and
- improvement of primary care in deprived areas.

Given that we are six years into the plan, much of it has already been put into effect. For example, over £5 billion has been invested in health projects using the Private Finance Initiative (PFI) alone; independent sector treatment centres (ISTCs) are now an alternative source of treatment for patients; the Local Investment Finance Trust (LIFT) Programme has delivered over 50 primary care schemes at a capital value of over £500 million; and 40 NHS trusts have successfully converted to foundation trust status. That said, while the £12 billion National Programme for Information Technology in the NHS is up and running, it is the subject of much criticism due to delays and increases in costs; and the introduction of payment by results (leading to a lack of certainty in income forecasting) is causing many trusts to re-examine their investment plans, including scaling back their plans for PFI projects.

(b)  *Private sector participation*

For the private sector, the implementation of the NHS Plan has impacted on a number of areas, including:
- the development of the PFI, creating £5.3 billion of deals in construction and/or operation, £6.1 billion of deals awaiting financial close and £5.8 billion of deals still planned to be released to the market in the secondary care sector;
- the creation of LIFTs in relation to the provision of facilities and certain facilities management services for the primary care sector, creating 51 deals that have reached financial close and nine (the rest of the fourth wave) yet to be released to the market; and
- the development of ISTCs whereby the private sector has, to date, provided around 250,000 procedures and is forecast to provide a further 145,000 procedures in 2006 and 250,000 procedures per year as part of the Phase 2 procurement, once operational.

Each of the above is examined in more detail in Part 2.

## 1.2 Italy

| Proportion of GDP spent on health | 8.4% (2003) |
|---|---|
| Annual expenditure on health per capita (average exchange rate $US) | $2,139 (2003) |

*Source*: World Health Organisation, Core Health Indicators.

*(a)* **The Italian National Health Service**

The Italian National Health Service (*Servizo Sanitario Nazionale* (SNN)) was created in 1978 with the initial intention that it would be financed from taxation. In reality, until the late 1990s the SNN was financed by a combination of compulsory employer/employee/self-employed contributions, tax and patient co-payments. This was amended in 1998 when compulsory contributions were replaced by regional corporation tax. Since 2001 and the reform of the Italian Constitution, the state and the regions have shared responsibility for healthcare.

The state has exclusive power to define the basic benefit package, which must be uniformly provided throughout the country. The 20 regions have responsibility for organising and administering the healthcare system. Most recently, central government has surrendered a share of the revenues from value added tax (VAT) to the regions. The central government contribution is calculated on the basis of the estimated cost to provide all citizens with 'uniform' levels of care. Each region receives a central grant equal to the *quota capitara* (amount of money per person), less the revenues raised by regional taxes. Further changes to move away from central government contributions to regional contributions are planned to take effect from 2011.

In comparison to much of Western Europe, patients in Italy enjoy great flexibility in their healthcare. To obtain medical care there are only two limiting factors:

- Patients must use healthcare facilities in the area in which they reside; and
- They must have a doctor's prescription for most forms of care.

However, patients can choose their own provider, as long as it has a contract with the SNN and possesses the necessary capacity.

This method of providing healthcare does not exclude private sector participation. However, all private providers serving SNN patients must be accredited by the region. The individual regions also maintain the choice of which private sector participants they are prepared to negotiate service agreements with. Among private sector participants in the health sector in Italy, there is growing concern as regards the role of private providers within the regions that have large private health sectors, particularly Lazio (Rome), Lombardy (Milan) and Campania (Naples). Private sector healthcare providers in these regions view the regulations that are aimed at governing the private sector, including the need for accreditation, as a scheme to give an unfair advantage to the public providers and this point is supported by the Italian Competition Authority.

*(b)*   *Private sector participation*

In recent years Italy has introduced PFI-style procurement within the health sector for the provision of hospital buildings. Italy's first hospital PFI project, the Ospitale di Mestre, worth €210 million, reached financial close in 2005. The Ospitale di Mestre deal represents the first example in Italy of a PPP project financed to international standards in compliance with the Italian project finance legal framework. The procurement process for the project was complicated by the need to apply international PPP practices within Italian law and by the use of English law for the finance documents. However, the eventual success of the project may well pave the way for further projects to follow.

Since the culmination of the Mestre project, the Italian PFI sector has been quietly building a pipeline of projects. The Merloni Law is now in place and while it is seen as initially confusing by those outside Italy, it appears to be working successfully for local contractors.

## 1.3   Spain

| Proportion of GDP spent on health | 7.7% (2003) |
|---|---|
| Annual expenditure on health per capita (average exchange rate $US) | $1,541(2003) |

*Source*: World Health Organisation, Core Health Indicators

*(a)*   *Spanish healthcare system*

Spain's healthcare system is tax based and during the past 20 years the responsibility for care has largely been devolved to Spain's 17 regions. Private insurance companies provide complementary healthcare coverage and increasingly play a role in covering services not included in the basic package, which are designed to avoid waiting lists. In 2003, 18.7% of the population purchased private insurance policies. The autonomous regions decide how to organise or provide health services and implement the national legislation.

The Inter-territorial Council (*Consejo Interterritorial del Sistema Nacional de Salud*) is composed of representatives from the independent communities and the state administration, and is in charge of promoting the cohesion of the health system. The healthcare system is financed by general taxation, including VAT and income tax, and also from regionally raised taxes. Private healthcare financing complements public financing with out-of-pocket payments to the public system as well as the private sector (eg, private outpatient care) and contributions to voluntary insurance.

Spain's healthcare system has undergone major reform in recent years. Key changes include the development of a new reformed primary healthcare network and the evolution of financing and management structures. The government has devolved the health services to 17 autonomous regions across the country and has implemented a tax-funded system similar to other countries across Western Europe. However, there remain limitations in the form of a central government that continues to provide the majority of the funding for healthcare and coordination of national policy.

## (b) *Private sector participation*

February 2006 saw the financial close of Spain's first PFI hospital project, worth €250 million, in Madrid. As the first such project to close in Spain, the hospital in Majadahonda serves as a pattern not only for seven further planned projects in Madrid, but also for other regions in Spain contemplating PFI projects. The Majadahonda deal is notable in this regard as it effectively opened the Spanish market to healthcare PFIs using a model similar to that used in the United Kingdom.

A key difference between the approach adopted for the procurement and closing process in Spain is the speed of procurement and the lack of a best and final offer stage. In the case of the Majadahonda project this ensured that the project progressed quickly to selection of a preferred bidder.

A further difference is the distinction between commercial and financial close. While the Majadahonda project was not project financed until February 2006, commercial close had occurred with the sponsors earlier and construction works had commenced in June 2005. Although not uncommon in some jurisdictions, this approach can leave more risk with the sponsors, such as the ability to obtain finance, after the project documents have been signed.

The apparent success of the Majadahonda PFI project has increased activity and appetite for PFI in the health sector in Spain, driven by the market experience that Spanish companies have to offer. Spain has half of the world's top 10 concessionaires including ACS, Ferrovial/Cintra, FCC, Abertis plus Sacyr, Acciona and OHL.

## 1.4 The Netherlands

| Proportion of GDP spent on health | 9.8% (2003) |
|---|---|
| Annual expenditure on health per capita (average exchange rate $US) | $3,088 (2003) |

*Source*: World Health Organisation, Core Health Indicators

## (a) *Dutch healthcare system*

The Netherlands has three different categories of health insurance, governed by different bodies:

- public insurance for 'exceptional medical expenses';
- compulsory social health insurance for those on low incomes and voluntary private health insurance for high earners; and
- voluntary supplementary insurance – open to all.

The first includes the expenses associated with long-term care or high-cost treatment under legislation that covers everyone living in the Netherlands, with very few exceptions. The majority of treatments are covered by the Exceptional Medical Expenses Act, which applies to everyone resident in the Netherlands and all non-residents employed but subject to Dutch income tax. The second category comprises normal, necessary medical care, while the third includes forms of care regarded as less necessary (eg, dental care, prostheses, hearing aids); supplementary private medical insurance largely covers the costs of these services. In recent years, there has been a shift in the Netherlands from the government to the private sector, as well as a transfer of services from central to local government.

Insured persons are free to register with the GP of their choice. Rather like the NHS in the United Kingdom, the GPs act as gatekeepers in the healthcare system. Patients receive a referral card or letter depending on whether they are covered by sickness funds or are voluntarily insured. Such referrals name the speciality but not the individual specialist.

A prominent trend over the last decade has been the shift of responsibility from government to insurers and towards more competition among healthcare providers. Most recently, discussions have begun as to whether the different types of health insurance should be merged into one system. The reform of the health insurance system, with a per-capita, risk-independent premium instead of a percentage contribution, has also been discussed. The new health insurance scheme, which integrates both statutory and private (voluntary) health insurance into one single compulsory scheme, came into effect on January 1 2006.

*(b)* *Private sector participation*
Unlike in France, Italy and Spain, development of PFI in the Netherlands has been not been particularly successful in terms of PFI healthcare projects. The Netherlands' pilot health PFI project, the Groene Hart Hospital in Gouda, failed to get off the ground and the decision not to proceed was based on the reasoning that a PFI approach would delay the delivery of a new hospital. A replacement pilot is being still being sought, but given that the Dutch Knowledge Centre is keen to use a large project in order to achieve best value for money, it could be some time before a suitable project is found to trial the implementation of PFI in the healthcare sector in the Netherlands.

1.5    France

| Proportion of GDP spent on health | 10.1% (2003) |
|---|---|
| Annual expenditure on health per capita (average exchange rate $US) | $2,981 (2003) |

*Source*: World Health Organisation, Core Health Indicators

*(a)* *French healthcare system*
France's health system is centrally controlled and based on a national social insurance regime. It is regulated by the state and funded mainly by social health insurance contributions that cover 96% of the population. The remainder is paid for by taxes and voluntary health insurance. All legal residents of France are insured under the state system.

In order to obtain treatment under public health insurance, the relevant treatment or service must be prescribed by a healthcare professional. Patients have to pay for services upfront and are partially reimbursed later. The French health system is rated for its high degree of flexibility. Patients are able to choose their own GP and can bypass him if the need arises. The French health system is gradually becoming

Health

more decentralised from a national to a regional level. At the same time, there has been a shift in power from the health insurance funds to the state.

Since the 1970s financial sustainability has been a key issue for the French health system. Major reforms took place in the late 1990s that aimed to remove financial barriers to accessing healthcare. In May 2004 the government proposed a series of reforms to reduce costs and improve efficiency, which would purportedly save €15 billion by 2007. The government proposed to introduce the following changes:

- charging all patients €1 per visit to a physician;
- requiring pensioners who can afford it to pay substantially more than they do currently;
- raising healthcare levies on firms;
- reducing waste and excessive consumption (particularly of pharmaceuticals);
- reducing reimbursement for expensive pharmaceuticals;
- preventing fraud with national health insurance cards; and
- establishing a computerised, personal medical record accessible by any French healthcare professional to prevent patients from 'shopping around'.

The success of these policies remains to be seen; however, the focus on reducing costs and establishing centralised records mirrors some of the proposals put forward in relation to the NHS in the United Kingdom.

*(b)* *Private sector participation*

Since the reforms of 2004, France has seen significant development in the private sector. In particular, May 2006 saw a competition between construction companies Eiffage and Bouygues for France's largest hospital PFI worth €250 to 300 million near Paris. If successful, the project (known as the Sud-Francilien Hospital PFI) will be France's most important health PFI to date and the first to comprise the construction and operation of a complete hospital.

Indeed, since 2005 there has been significant focus on construction and maintenance in French healthcare PFIs. As of October 2005 over 30 PFI projects were launched in the healthcare sector on the basis of the 2003 hospital PFI legislation, including four major projects valued at between €100 and €300 million each (the €100 million Caen Hospital PFI, the most important French hospital PFI to date; the €250 to 300 million Southern Ile de France Hospital PFI; the €150 to 200 million Saint Nazaire PFI; and the €120 million Bourgoin-Jallieu Hospital PFI). However, these include very few services (except heat, water and electricity). Services including catering and laundry remain excluded. Currently, the majority of the project sponsors are construction contractors or financial institutions.

The development of the Hôpital 2007 healthcare investment programme aims to advance cooperation between the private and public sectors. In addition, the change in public healthcare laws is anticipated to increase private sector interest in France's rapidly developing PFI programme.

## 1.6 Portugal

| Proportion of GDP spent on health | 9.6% (2003) |
|---|---|
| Annual expenditure on health per capita (average exchange rate $US) | $1,348 (2003) |

*Source*: World Health Organisation, Core Health Indicators

*(a)* *Portuguese healthcare system*

In 1979 a national health service was created in Portugal whereby healthcare was made available to the population that was free at the point of use and was funded predominantly out of taxation. Since then, the Portuguese health system has seen a variety of reforms, the most recent of which was announced in 2002 in the new national healthcare system. The most recent reform was to be effected from 2002 to 2006 and, according to the Ministry of Finance, was to direct the health system into a mix of health services, where public, private and social entities co-exist and act in an integrated manner, directed towards the needs of healthcare users.[1] The plans included:

- the creation of partnerships between the public and private sectors;
- the reduction of waiting lists;
- the provision of each person with access to a family doctor;
- the transformation of public hospitals into companies;
- the introduction of alternative management tools;
- the development of a continuous care network;
- the creation of *Entidade Reguladora da Saude*, a body to regulate the introduction of the private sector in the provision of public health services;
- improvement of the information systems network;
- changes to pharmaceutical policy; and
- reorganisation of the emergency services.

Although the plans have been implemented in a number of different ways, it remains to be seen how successful they will be; for example, the PPP market in Portugal has not developed at the rate hoped for and future projects have recently been put on hold.

*(b)* *Private sector participation*

The introduction of the new national healthcare system in Portugal created an opportunity to develop PPP projects within the health sector to develop new or replacement facilities and the provision of health services to the public. Recently, however, the Portuguese government suspended the seven deals not yet out to tender, while the three deals in procurement have been criticised by the PPP industry due to delays and objections from unions, which believe that the PPP structure will result in a degradation in the quality of care standards and the conditions for healthcare workers.

Even by early 2006, Portuguese hospital PPPs had not made a great deal of progress. While the first wave of hospitals has been tendered, as at the date of writing

---

[1] Page 10, Ministry of Finance quoted in the "University of York Department of Management Studies Working Paper Number 5" [www.york.ac.uk/management/research/working_paper_series.com].

only one has made it to best and final offer stage (Cascasis), and of the five hospitals in the initial wave, one is soon to be re-tendered as the first time it came to market the bids varied so greatly that no effective comparison could be made between the bidders.

## 2. Legal/commercial arrangements developed in UK healthcare PPP projects

The implementation of the NHS Plan has created a variety of opportunities for the private sector, including:
- the continued use of the PFI;
- the creation of LIFTs; and
- the development of ISTCs.

This section examines the legal/commercial arrangements of each (albeit with only an overview of the PFI), and considers the extent to which those arrangements will continue as the current health reforms reach a conclusion.

### 2.1 The PFI

*(a) Overview*

Norman Lamont, the Conservative chancellor of the exchequer in John Major's government, introduced the PFI in 1992. While opinions differ on what motivated the government to support this method of procuring improvements in public services, the success of projects in the transport sector which had developed to allow user charges to be used by the private sector to raise private finance to construct public infrastructure was certainly a key factor. It was also felt that, given the then accounting standards, private sector investment in public infrastructure would not be counted towards public sector borrowing (ie, it would not be accounted for on the public sector's balance sheet), thus assisting the government in achieving its public sector borrowing requirement targets in the context of the Maastricht Treaty. Publicly, the government has denied that accounting treatment was ever a factor and has preferred the view that support for the use of the PFI would be given where it represented good value for money.

Much has already been written about risk allocation under a PFI contract, so we will not go over that ground again. However, by way of a very brief overview, the essential elements include the following:
- While regarded as a 'contract for services', a typical PFI contract involves the creation of an asset (eg, a hospital, school or road) and the provision of services to maintain that asset for around 30 years.
- In return, the public sector purchaser of the 'service' pays a service charge from the date on which the asset is available for use (ie, completion of construction). It is critical for risk transfer that no payments are made by the public sector until such time as the asset is complete and available for use. The service charge is subject to adjustment if the asset is not subsequently available for use or the performance of the service falls below defined standards. Other than

termination for default, these adjustments are the public sector's principal sanction against the private sector for poor performance.
- Long-term risks, such as changes in law, tax, inflation, the insurance market, the price of providing construction and other services, are allocated between the parties. Given the maturity of the PFI market, the allocation of such risks is fairly standardised.
- The contract can be terminated early by either party. In most cases, the public sector pays a compensatory payment ranging from lost income and profit to an amount that effectively represents the private sector's outstanding liabilities to its senior funders (through re-tendering the remaining term of the project in the open market or, in the absence of a market, by a market value calculation). The amount depends on whether the project terminates through public sector or private sector default.

The familiar typical PFI structure in health is outlined below.

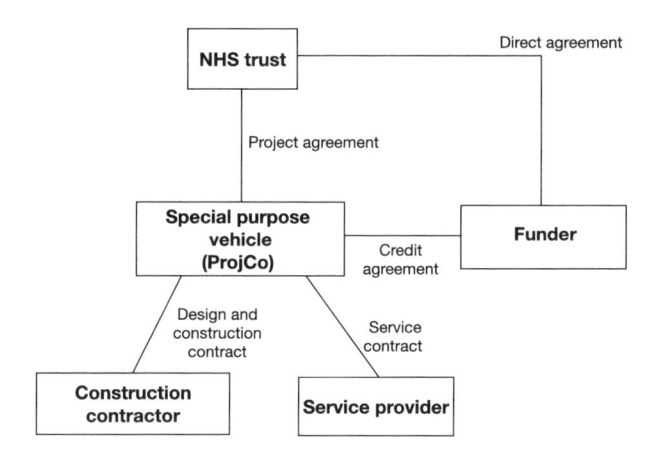

```
              NHS trust ─────────────── Direct agreement
                  │
              Project agreement
                  │
          Special purpose
             vehicle      ── Credit ──  Funder
            (ProjCo)       agreement
           /       \
    Design and    Service
    construction  contract
    contract
       /            \
 Construction    Service provider
 contractor
```

The development of the PFI as a procurement tool has been greatly assisted by government and government-sponsored organisations preparing guidance for the benefit of the public sector on good practice procurement methods, including required risk allocation in PFI project agreements. A government body called The Treasury Taskforce issued the first edition of the standardisation of PFI contracts in 1999 and this has since been updated, first by the Office of Government Commerce in 2002 and most recently in April 2004 (with amendments in December 2005) by Her Majesty's Treasury. The most recent edition of the guidance sets out a number of mandatory provisions for inclusion in all PFI project agreements in an attempt to streamline further the procurement process.

Since its inception, on average, 10% to 15% of annual investment in public services has come through the PFI, and in March 2006, in a report entitled "PFI:

Strengthening Long Term Partnerships", the UK government reiterated its commitment to PFI where it continues to represent good value for money.

*(b)* *Initial barriers to development of the PFI market in health*

The PFI health market has developed alongside the use of PFI generally in the United Kingdom since the Conservative government in 1994 announced that the use of private sector finance was to be investigated in relation to all public infrastructure projects. Although this directive was abandoned in 1997, the health sector had already begun to procure projects using a PFI model, albeit with some quite fundamental barriers to progress.

The problems in the health sector were twofold. First, there was concern that NHS trusts (the procuring authority) did not have the necessary authority to enter into contracts of the nature of PFI project agreements and direct agreements with senior funders. This is because when NHS trusts were created and given their powers (eg, to enter into certain contracts) by statute in the 1980s, the PFI could not have been contemplated. Second, the way in which NHS trusts were funded meant that investors (and particularly senior funders) were concerned that NHS trusts may at some stage be unable to meet their debts (eg, where a significant termination compensation payment fell due).

Both problems required primary legislation to solve them, thus causing delays to those projects that, other than these two issues, were ready for financial close. The authority issue was solved by the introduction of the NHS (Private Finance) Act 1997, which specifically clarified that NHS trusts had the power to enter into PFI contracts and direct agreements with senior funders. The covenant issue was solved by the introduction of the NHS (Residual Liabilities) Act 1996, which obliged the secretary of state for health to satisfy undischarged liabilities of an insolvent NHS trust or transfer such liabilities to another public sector health body, including another NHS trust.

Having enacted the legislation necessary for PFI projects in health to be closed, it was felt necessary to bring some order to procurement management.

*(c)* *Role of the NHS Private Finance Unit*

Private sector sponsors and contractors were initially quite critical of the organisation of the procurement of PFI projects in health. It was considered that, too frequently, tenders were being invited on projects that were not affordable and/or did not have a robust business case supporting them. The resultant delays, abortive design and other development costs linked to uncertainty as to the programme of projects being offered to the market generated a response from government in the form of the creation of the NHS Private Finance Unit (PFU). In addition to assisting in organising procurement timetables and deal flow, the PFU promoted a consistent approach to risk transfer across all health sector PFI projects and produced essential practical guidance to NHS trusts involved in procuring PFI projects. Today, the PFU has a key role in policing the use by contracting parties of its NHS Standard Form Project Agreement and has certain powers in relation to the approval of projects.

Examples of PFU publications include the following:
- The NHS standard form project agreement – this is to be used by NHS trusts and NHS foundation trusts when procuring a PFI project. The use of these forms is monitored by the PFU and any derogation therefrom is allowed only for project-specific reasons.
- Output specifications – the output specifications are applicable to PFI projects and also to other in-house PFI projects. The objective is to save both time and cost for both the NHS and the private sector. The specifications set out a framework for the individual service requirements of the NHS trust or NHS foundation trust, which must then be tailored by the trust in order to reflect its particular needs. If the needs are outside of those covered by the standard output specification, they must be discussed more fully with the PFU.
- Pre-qualification questionnaire – in order to ensure transparency of approach to pre-qualifying tenderers for NHS health projects, the PFU has supplemented the NHS standard form and standardised approach to output specifications with a standard form pre-qualification questionnaire. The intention behind the introduction of this document was to standardise documentation and to speed up the procurement process by avoiding the need for trusts to develop further documentation themselves.
- Guidance – in 1999, the Department of Health published comprehensive guidance for NHS trusts to be followed in the procurement of PFI hospital projects. The original 1999 guidance manual was suspended in 2005 to enable it to be updated to reflect the Department of Health's own guidance on implementing the new value for money guidance published by Her Majesty's Treasury in August 2004, and also to reflect developments in the general guidance on PFI projects published by Her Majesty's Treasury. The new Department of Health guidance is comprised of two phases: the first is an interim document that will be used to test the new principles contained in the guidance, while the second and final version will reflect the lessons learned during the first phase. The introduction from January 31 2006 of the new EU Competitive Dialogue Directive has meant that more chapters of the 1999 manual are now out of date. While the new guidance is being prepared at the time of writing, the original guidance has now been modified to permit use during this time and has been supplemented by further guidance in relation to design quality and methods of financing PFI schemes.

(d)   *Effects of implementation of the NHS Plan*

For the private sector, the implementation of the NHS Plan has impacted on a number of key areas, namely:
- the need to revisit the scale of PFI health deals yet to reach financial close, given financial pressures on NHS trusts arising out of the implementation of payment by results;
- the creation of foundation trusts;

- the focus on primary care and community-based health facilities; and
- the policy of reducing waiting times.

*(e)* **The PFI revisited**

The introduction of payment by results in particular has led to a re-evaluation of a number of PFI health schemes. This section:
- identifies the reasons for re-evaluation of planned PFI hospital deals within the context of the NHS reforms;
- examines the effect of the NHS reforms and Treasury reviews; and
- identifies changes that could be made to the NHS standard form PFI model to accommodate the requirements of the NHS reforms.

*(i)* *Reasons for the re-evaluation of planned PFI hospital deals*

Following publication of the various proposals for NHS reforms, it became apparent that there were a number of potential inconsistencies between the outcomes proposed in the revised government policies and the standard form PFI hospital approach.

*(ii)* *Secondary healthcare v primary healthcare*

The January 2006 health white paper entitled "Our care, our health, our say – a new direction for community services" signalled a policy shift towards the provision of healthcare from district general hospitals to local community facilities and primary care providers through primary care trusts. The change in focus of health policy has caused many trusts procuring new developments through the PFI to evaluate their business cases to take into account a potential loss of business and commensurate income to other healthcare providers in the public and private sectors.

*(iii)* *Fixed priced/availability-based service payments v payment by results*

Even where an NHS trust or foundation trust has achieved an acceptable level of certainty in relation to its service model, the introduction of payment by results means that there is less certainty in its income forecasts. Where trusts enter into long-term, fixed-priced contracts with an availability-based service payment such as PFI, such lack of certainty causes serious concerns over the ability to afford its own services as well as payments to the private sector provider.

*(iv)* *Long-term contracts v flexibility in service provision*

The uncertainties created by the above mean that the focus has shifted again to ensuring that arrangements with private sector service providers include some flexibility – a factor that has so far proved difficult to accommodate in the PFI, given its project finance structure. There is in fact a fundamental inconsistency. To provide an affordable solution, projects tend to be long term (between 25 and 40 years) and geared according to the traditional project finance risk profile. Flexibility tends to have an adverse effect on that risk profile, thus increasing the price; if that price is too high, the government may have to rethink its investment plans promised in the NHS Plan.

The combined effect of the tensions between the PFI structures and the requirements of the NHS reforms, along with general value for money and affordability considerations at Her Majesty's Treasury, led to a number of PFI hospital schemes being called in for Treasury review.

(v) *Effect of NHS reforms and Treasury review on PFI hospital schemes*
A number of PFI health projects procured during 2005/2006 have been the subject of review and these have been widely reported in the press (often along with reports of budget deficits and wide-scale redundancies).

One scheme that has not been the subject of Treasury review but has decided itself to reconsider its plans for a PFI is the Essex Three Rivers Healthcare NHS trust. The trust decided not to go ahead with the proposed PFI scheme, citing the following four main reasons:

- "Our health, our care, our say" – key features of the proposed PFI hospital scheme related to the provision of outpatient and diagnostic services. These services are specifically mentioned in the January 2006 white paper as services that could be provided in the local community, thereby removing a potential source of income from the trust.
- Payment by results – the trust was concerned about its ability to predict with sufficient certainty patient numbers and thereby its income following the introduction of payment by results.
- ISTC – the trust estimated that a planned ISTC in the Essex region could reduce its elective income by 20%.
- Supporting people with long-term conditions – consistent with the government's white paper on community care, there is likely to be a shift from hospital care to community care for those with long-term conditions, again removing a potential source of income.

The chief executive of the trust is quoted in the press release announcing the withdrawal of the PFI scheme as follows: "We need to be sure that the future plan for the hospital is the right one for the long term. The plan we have now needs to change to make it more affordable and the 'best fit' with the rapidly changing healthcare system."

What is clear is that, as the reforms begin to take hold, careful consideration will need to be given to procurement planning by the NHS and to market selection by the private sector. For as long as it has been around, the PFI has been the subject of criticism for its development costs, and the private sector will not be able to tolerate too many instances of projects aborting while procuring authorities seek to meet the challenges of reform.

(vi) *Potential developments for standard form hospital PFI schemes*
Although Treasury reviews of previously approved PFI schemes are continuing,[2] a number of PFI hospital schemes have reached financial close following completion

---

2  Although on August 17 2006, the Department of Health reported the approval of six of those PFI health projects.

of review. Some of these schemes have been subject to slight modification, while others have been subject to more radical re-appraisal or re-definition, or have even been aborted. However, the fact that a number of schemes have progressed to financial close following the reviews shows that there is still a place for PFI hospital schemes within the NHS. The challenge for both the public and private sectors is to ensure that any proposed PFI scheme stands up to financial and operational scrutiny in the light of and having regard to the proposed NHS reforms and the required flexibility for the future.

Given the effect of the NHS reforms, it is likely that a number of modifications to the NHS Standard Form will be required or proposed to address some concerns arising. A selection of these issues are considered below.

**Reduction in scope of services:** Trusts may wish to explore a reduction in the scope or type of services to be provided under the PFI contract. For example, there may be a business case to support the provision of new buildings with certain physical facilities (particularly if the space provided can be converted to a different use without destroying clinical functionality) over a period of 25 to 40 years; however, flexibility may be retained in respect of other services.

The possibility of the trust retaining responsibility for the provision of certain services raises interface issues between the trust and the PFI contractor and its subcontractors; for example, there could be a split responsibility in relation to looking after the building. Trusts and the PFU are likely to be reluctant to accept risk transfer back to the public sector while being similarly reluctant to accept a risk premium to cover the risk.

**Public sector break options:** There has been discussion in a number of sectors about the inclusion of public sector break options in PFI contracts. A break option would be structured to allow a trust to terminate the PFI contract at specific points in time and pay pre-determined levels of compensation to the private sector.

Public sector break options were included in the recent Docklands Light Railway project and are currently being introduced in some Ministry of Defence PFI projects. The inclusion of break options may provide trusts with a degree of flexibility to manage any future changes in health service requirements. However, the issue of how funds will be sourced to pay any compensation payable may make this option less desirable for trusts in comparison to central government departments.

**Flexible change mechanisms:** The need for NHS trusts and foundation trusts to be able to adapt to changing circumstances, as well as potential changes in revenue caused by payment by results, means that a high degree of flexibility within PFI contracts will become more important. Although the current standard form NHS PFI contract contains variation mechanisms, a number of potential developments to this mechanism could be considered to enable changes to be instructed and accepted within a more streamlined manner. Various alternatives that may be considered are:
- increased use of the small works and small services procedures;
- the introduction of periodic 'contract reviews' to review the services provided and any changes required as a result of changes to the NHS;

- the ability to make certain changes which do not affect the 'risk profile' or payments to the PFI contractor without reference to funders; and
- increased use of 'call-off' style arrangements under which the trust or foundation trust can receive certain services for limited periods of time or on a limited or per-use basis.

As mentioned earlier, changes of this nature are likely to come at a price.

*(vii)* *Refinancing issues*

In addition to the NHS reforms and the Treasury focus on the development of PFI as a procurement tool and means of infrastructure provision, the Select Committee on Public Accounts has, during 2005 and 2006, turned its attention to PFI contracts, in particular the refinancing of the Norfolk and Norwich hospital project. The findings of the select committee in relation to this specific project may have wide-reaching implications for private sector investors wishing to invest in PFI projects in the health sector with a view to refinancing.

The benefits of refinancing of PFI projects for both the private sector and the public sector are clear, but reports such as the "Update on PFI Debt Refinancing and the PFI Equity Market" released by the National Audit Office in April 2006 highlighted some concerns with the mechanisms that apply to refinancing. There are currently two alternatives that may apply where a refinancing is to take place:
- specific contractual arrangements, more recently in accordance with Office of Government Commerce/Partnerships UK/PFU guidance or, for earlier projects, as agreed between the parties; and
- the voluntary code for refinancing that applies to any projects which do not contain specific contractual provisions governing the sharing of any refinancing benefit.[3]

The National Audit Office report was generally not critical of the amounts obtained by the public sector or the private sector as a result of refinancing or of other financial implications for the public sector. However, it did identify a number of concerns with the ways in which the mechanisms operated.

In contrast to the National Audit Office report, the Select Committee on Public Accounts summarised its findings on the Norfolk and Norwich refinancing with the following damning sentence: "We would not expect to see another Accounting Officer appearing before this Committee defending what we believe to be the unacceptable face of capitalism in the consortium's dealings with the public sector."

The Norfolk and Norwich project agreement did not contain specific contractual provisions relating to refinancing and therefore the parties applied the voluntary code, which provided for a 30% share of any refinancing gain to be apportioned to

---

[3] "Update on PFI Debt Refinancing and the PFI Equity Market", National Audit Office, www.hm-treasury.gov.uk/media//924E0/PPP_Refinancing_Code_of_Conduct.pdf.

the trust. Despite the parties applying the voluntary code, the select committee identified a number of particular criticisms:
- the significant increases to the internal rate of return for the investors in the project;
- the public sector's share of the refinancing gain being unacceptably small relative to that of the private sector;
- the extension of the contract term, notwithstanding uncertainty regarding the services required from the NHS over the next 30 years; and
- the provision stating that the increase in debt arising from the refinancing would be covered in any termination payments payable by the trust following a voluntary termination of project agreement; this would reduce the trust's ability to terminate if (for example) it wanted to change fundamentally the service specification.

The last two reasons set out above link back to general issues arising in relation to the flexibility of PFI hospital projects following the introduction of the NHS reforms and discussed above. The other criticisms link specifically to the financial implications of the trust of the refinancing, either because (in the eyes of the Public Accounts Committee) the trust did not obtain sufficient benefit or because the trust's potential liabilities on a termination had increased to an unacceptable level. The position requiring repayment of any increased debt on a termination is consistent with current indications from the lending market that, were a refinancing to occur and the level of debt to increase, it would expect that any additional sums would be covered by termination payments in all circumstances that senior debt is paid out in full.

To some, the extent of the criticism levelled by the select committee appeared excessive, particularly given that the trust benefited by around £34 million when there was no contractual entitlement for it to do so and the opportunity to effect the refinancing was, perhaps, possible only given the successful performance of the project.

It may well be that the increase to 50% of the public sector share of refinancing gains applicable in projects signed post-July 2002 will satisfy the criticism of the level of benefits obtained by the public sector. However, this is not yet clear. The head of the PFU was asked, shortly after publication of the select committee report, where the Department of Health stood in relation to the refinancing of PFI projects in light of the select committee's criticisms. His response was that the Treasury view of refinancing was very robust, in that PFI contracts post-2002 contain mandatory refinancing provisions and contracts entered into prior to that date that do not address refinancing in their provisions are governed by the code. He also indicated, however, that while Her Majesty's Treasury took this robust view, it would not be appearing before the select committee and that therefore the PFU was reflecting on potential next steps.

The criticism levelled at those appearing in front of the select committee has led, at the date of writing, to an apparent paralysis of the refinancing market. It is clear that NHS trusts are keen to secure the financial benefits (either upfront or through a reduced unitary charge) that a refinancing can offer, particularly given the existence of deficits at many NHS trusts. A number of refinancing options are being considered in the health sector, but the Department of Health is not publicly rushing forward to conclude any potential deals.

## 2.2 Foundation trusts

*(a) Creation*

The basis for the creation of foundation trusts is in the Health and Social Care (Community Health and Standards) Act 2003. A foundation trust is a 'public benefit corporation' controlled locally by members and a board of governors rather than through central control. The policy objective following the introduction of foundation trusts was that all trusts should convert to foundation trust status by 2008 to 2009.

In order to become a foundation trust, an existing trust must have a three-star rating from the Healthcare Commission and have support from the secretary of state. Support for an application from the secretary of state is dependent on his satisfaction with a five-year business plan, a human resources strategy and the governance proposals for the foundation trust. The Department of Health has published guidance to assist trusts in the preparation of an application to become a foundation trust, such as "Applying for Foundation Trust Status" and "NHS Foundation Trust Sourcebook for Developing Governance Arrangements". Foundation trust status is granted as a 30-year licence from Monitor, the independent regulator of foundation trusts.

*(b) Structure*

Foundation trusts are governed by 'members' made up from local residents, patients and carers and staff. Members of the foundation trust elect a board of governors, which is responsible for the appointment of the board of directors. The board of directors is responsible for day-to-day management of the foundation trust and operational matters.

Foundation trusts are regulated by the Healthcare Commission, which has the power to carry out investigations and produces an annual performance rating for each foundation trust. Monitor also regulates the financial performance of foundation trusts and has extensive powers to intervene in foundation trusts in the event of poor management or financial difficulties.

A key concern, from a PFI perspective, in relation to foundation trusts is that the provisions of the NHS (Residual Liabilities) Act 1996 do not apply. The effect of this is that the secretary of state does not pick up responsibility for the liabilities of foundation trusts following insolvency. This has created a number of issues for both future and existing PFI projects, which are discussed below.

*(c) Impact of foundation trust status on PFI*

The introduction of foundation trusts caused some initial uncertainty in the PFI market and questions arose as to how any PFI deal with a foundation trust as a counterparty would be fundable, given that foundation trusts were not afforded the protection offered by the NHS (Residual Liabilities) Act. In order to solve this problem for the private sector, the secretary of state has agreed to enter into a 'deed of safeguard' in relation to all PFI health deals where a foundation trust is the counterparty. Effectively, the government has agreed to stand behind the obligations of a foundation trust under a PFI contract in the event of insolvency of the foundation trust.

The introduction of the deed of safeguard appears to have cleared the way for deals with foundation trusts to achieve financial close. That said, given the autonomy enjoyed by foundation trusts, some commentators believe that the risk of insolvency is greater, given that government may allow poorly performing foundation trusts to fail. This change in risk profile may cause investment in projects involving foundation trusts to be less attractive.

2.3 **Focus on primary care and community-based health facilities**
The NHS Plan sets out the government's plan to improve the provision of primary care services in deprived areas. The PFI was considered not to be an appropriate procurement method to develop primary care facilities, given that each facility requires only on average a capital requirement of around £5 million, and instead the LIFT programme (aimed at improving all primary care facilities) was initiated in 2001.

(a) **What is LIFT?**
LIFT is a central government initiative to revitalise primary care premises. The scheme is focused primarily on areas where traditional mechanisms for funding GP (and other primary care providers, such as pharmacists, opticians and dentists) buildings have proved unsuccessful.

The intention of the LIFT scheme is to enable primary care trusts and LIFT companies to re-house GPs and other healthcare providers in new, purpose-built, more spacious facilities or to develop existing premises to meet modern standards, including a drive towards the possible co-location of health and social care professionals in one building together. The Department of Health has suggested that in the present health climate, GPs are put off practising due to poor-quality premises and restrictive, long-term leases. LIFT seeks to resolve this through buying GPs out of existing premises and offering them instead flexible leases.

(b) **LIFT structure**
Partnerships for Health (PfH) is a joint venture between the Department of Health (50%) and Partnerships UK (50%) to provide central procurement advice to the primary care trusts through the establishment of a local joint venture company, a LIFT company. The LIFT company is given geographic exclusivity to provide certain services and initiate primary care projects over a period of time. For primary care trusts within the LIFT scheme, there is extensive guidance on how the selection of a LIFT private sector partner should be managed.

The structure of LIFT deals is outlined in the following diagrams.

[Diagram: LIFT structure showing Strategic partnering board, Private sector partners (60), Local stakeholders (20), PfH (20), Shareholders' agreement, Scheme approval, Strategic partnering agreement, SHA/PCT/MHT/LA, LIFTco. Second diagram: LIFTco 100% wholly owned subsidiary → Fundco, with Funder/Loan, Lease plus agreement to End users (GPs, PCTs, MHTs, Las, Pharmacists), rent £, Sales agreement (surplus land) → External developer, Supply chain agreement → Supply chain members → Construction, Hard FM, Sales agreement (existing and future sites) → Site owner, Build/maintain.]

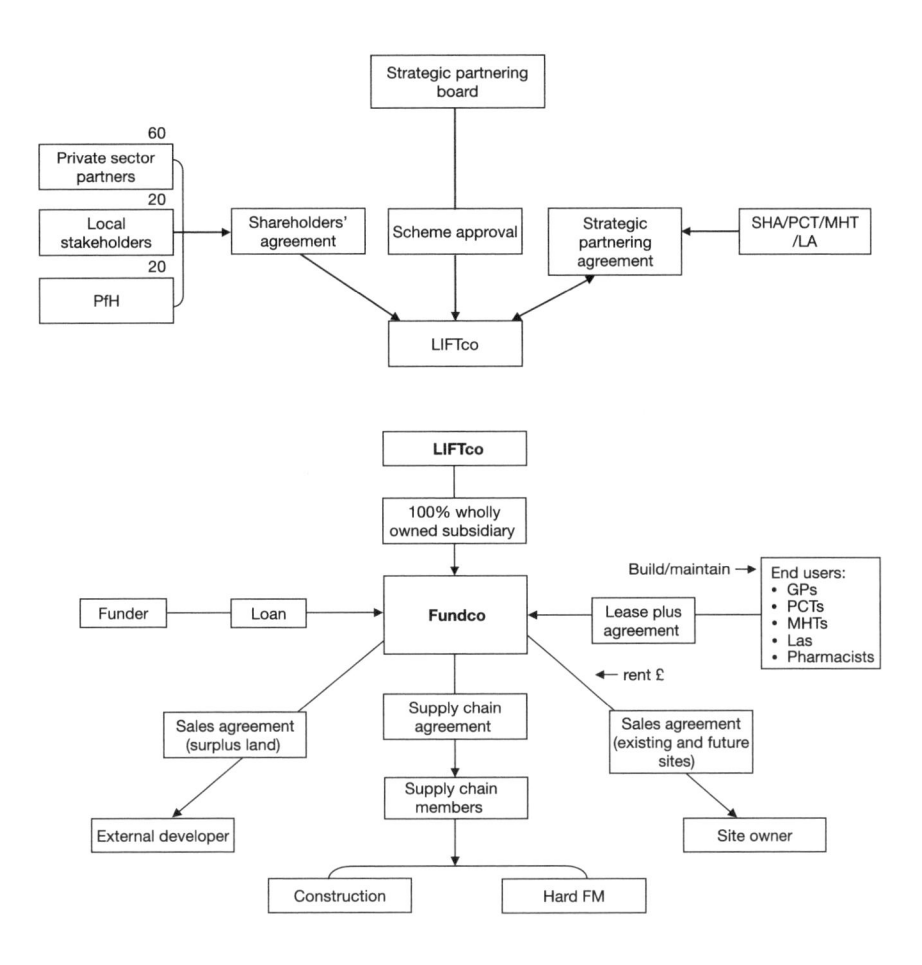

Following selection, the LIFT company will have the exclusive right to procure schemes (which the primary care trust, LIFT company and other public sector bodies put forward), subject to satisfying a value for money test evaluated by a strategic partnering board. This permits long-term investment projects to be prioritised according to local needs and through the utilisation of private sector expertise.

This structure fits with the government policy to use the private sector to increase healthcare investment. The primary care trust can take shareholdings within the LIFT company, usually in the form of a 20% stake. The private sector partner takes 60% and PfH the remaining 20%. The public sector benefits from profits made by the LIFT company and gains significant control through a shareholders' agreement. This is intended to ensure that the LIFT company does not prejudice the interests of the public sector.

(c) *Key issues – exclusivity and cost of procuring new deals*

Primary care developments are relatively small scale in PFI terms, costing approximately £5 million. In theory, these are unsuitable for PFI due to high transaction costs and Treasury guidance stating that PFI should not be used for projects under £20 million. However, the benefit of LIFT is that schemes can be 'bundled' together. Applying this 'batched' approach, the total capital value for each tranche of schemes will assist in the creation of value for money savings while simultaneously procuring new developments. This method also promotes a standardised procurement process. The priorities of the projects are determined by the strategic partnering board. The LIFT company can also set up individual special purpose vehicles to carry out specific projects. These are financed on a property finance basis.

In a traditional lease position, the tenant assumes most of the risks, particularly the risk that defects may appear in the building or that maintenance is more costly than expected. The LIFT approach uses a 'Lease Plus' form, which operates from a different perspective, combining the traditional fully repairing and insuring leases with aspects of the PFI standard form. The LIFT company and/or special purpose vehicle (as landlord) are responsible for all aspects of construction and maintenance of the development. The tenant will pay a higher rent but, importantly, the rent is indexed by the Retail Price Index rather than being dependent on the amount of repair work needed. In contrast to the traditional fully repairing and insuring lease, Lease Plus is more likely to achieve favourable VAT treatment for the public sector. Moreover, Lease Plus gives the tenant rights to take action if the landlord fails to carry out maintenance; the tenant can carry out the necessary work itself and deduct the cost from the rent. This system is rarely seen in traditional property leases and would appear to offer great advantages to the development and subsequent maintenance of healthcare units.

As a further transfer of risk to the private sector, it is argued that LIFT has genuine 'residual value'. In traditional PFI, the cost of the asset and its maintenance is recovered by payments made by the recipient of the service (eg, the NHS trust). The current view promoted by the primary care trust/government is that the units are more likely to be used for alternative uses after their role as an NHS facility has ended. The LIFT company takes the risk that it can recover further capital/income from the property after the end of the initial lease term. All tenants have a statutory right to remain after the lease term, with the main public sector body having the right to purchase the property at the end if it chooses to do so.

Consistent with the NHS Plan, the first LIFT schemes focused on deprived inner city areas (and isolated rural areas) across the United Kingdom. The first scheme to reach financial close was in East London and contains a flagship one-stop centre that includes a pharmacy, dentist, radiology and transfer of cardiology outpatients.

(d) *LIFT as a focus on community care*

The white paper entitled "Our care, our health, our say – a new direction for community services" presented an opportunity for the private sector further to develop the LIFT model. The paper promotes an overall aim of shifting resources away from district general hospitals into community hospitals. From 2008, primary care trusts will be examined against a new strategy for the development of preventative services, including setting goals for the shift of resources towards prevention. As a direct consequence of this objective, the government is proposing to develop the necessary infrastructure through the generation of community facilities.

The focus on community facilities procured by primary care trusts offers an opportunity for current (and future) LIFT companies to develop community hospitals using a PFI-type risk allocation and funding structure with a separate (perhaps ringfenced) arrangement relating to the provision of clinical services. For participants in the private sector with experience in LIFT structures and the provision of ISTCs, the opportunities that this element of the reforms brings are significant.

The white paper also included a proposal for the establishment of a social enterprise unit within the Department of Health to coordinate social enterprise policy including private-sector providers and ensuring that a network of support is put in place to encourage the wider use of social enterprise models. The Department of Health will also establish a fund from April 2007 to provide advice to social entrepreneurs who want to develop new models to deliver health and social care services.

## 2.4 Policy to reduce waiting times

### (a) Introduction of private sector treatment centres

One of the core objectives of the NHS Plan was to ensure that by 2005, no patient should wait more than three months for an initial outpatient appointment and no more than six months (reducing to three months by 2008) for any inpatient treatment required. Increasing the capacity of the NHS, particularly in targeted clinical specialities, was seen as fundamental to achieving this aim of reducing waiting times while also ensuring treatment in accordance with clinical need. At the same time, the NHS plan also sought to provide choice to patients in terms of the hospital or healthcare facility to which they will be referred to receive their treatment. The stated objective was to have four or five healthcare providers available to each patient by December 2005.

The ISTC programme was, ostensibly at least, born out of these core objectives. In addition, the ISTC programme is also stated to have as its objectives:

- the expansion of plurality of provision in the NHS (this is really shorthand for 'competition');
- the promotion of innovative service models (it is hoped not only that the private sector will introduce innovative techniques, but also that its business model will result in the standardisation and promulgation of those techniques); and
- the end to spot purchasing (private sector provision at a premium) by the NHS to cover shortfalls in capacity during times of high healthcare need.

In order to achieve these objectives, ISTCs differ fundamentally from existing procurement methods, such as PFI and private sector healthcare. They involve the provision of clinical services by the private sector to NHS patients – crucially, they do not typically involve the treatment of private patients. NHS patients continue to experience healthcare that is free at the point of delivery, but the primary care trusts and other bodies within the NHS that are responsible for purchasing clinical services are able to refer patients to the private sector-run ISTC facilities to deliver the clinical services as well as (or instead of) the local NHS hospital. The procedures offered by the ISTCs therefore supplement and overlap with the NHS infrastructure that is already in place, thereby providing additional capacity and patient choice.

The ISTCs deliver this additional capacity and patient choice in both diagnostic and elective (surgical) clinical services, but only in respect of a limited range of relatively straightforward procedures. The precise range of procedures offered depends on the requirements of the local area and these are specified during the procurement led by the Department of Health.

*(a)*     *Core characteristics of ISTCs – Phase 1*

The ISTC procurements have included a set of standard form documentation. The provider's primary obligation is to deliver the clinical services to the necessary standard and within a prescribed period (counted from the date when a patient is first referred to the provider). Where the provider fails to do so, it faces immediate financial sanctions and, ultimately, termination of its contract for persistent default.

The services agreement is for five years, with an opportunity to extend the contract if the parties agree. While the payment arrangements are based on the number of referrals made to the ISTC, the provider does not take volume risk as it benefits from a guaranteed minimum income. Given the short-term nature of the arrangement, albeit with a guaranteed income, some regard the ISTC procurement as a government-sponsored start-up opportunity to create businesses that can compete with other health providers in the longer term.

The 'additionality' provisions within the services agreement are another challenge to which the provider will need to develop its own innovative operational solution. 'Additionality' refers to the core NHS Plan-derived objective that ISTCs should provide additional capacity to the NHS. Providers are prevented, therefore, from using staff that are currently employed by the NHS or have been employed by the NHS in the previous six months. Providers will need to staff their facilities from alternative sources – most obviously, from abroad. The exception to this restriction is that the provider is entitled to make use of NHS staff through secondments or through subcontracting clinical services to NHS trusts. However, these agreements are strictly controlled by the Department of Health. In particular, there is an explicit policy that there should be no 'reverse risk transfer' achieved through these agreement – that is, the provider should not seek to transfer to the NHS trusts risks that it has been required by the Department of Health to accept itself under the services agreement.

The provider is not required to accept clinical negligence risk. The Department of Health has determined that it would not represent value for money for the private sector to accept this risk, and therefore the provider is required to participate in the Clinical Negligence Scheme for Trusts, which provides a centralised fund to address clinical negligence claims. However, the provider is required to make a contribution to the fund where its poor procedures cause the premium charged to the public sector to be increased.

Finally, the provider is not required under Phase 1 to accept the risk of a shortfall in funds to meet its debt services obligations upon termination. If a Phase 1 scheme were to be terminated early, the provider would be paid sufficient compensation by the authority to ensure that it could meet any outstanding liability to its senior funders. In addition, such compensation is ringfenced from deductions in respect of any liability owed by the provider to the authority. This arrangement is acceptable to the authority as it is entitled to recover undischarged liabilities of the provider from the provider's parent company subject to an appropriate limit on liability.

(b) *Development of characteristics in Phase 2*

The evolution of the ISTC programme can already be seen in the Phase 2 procurement. A number of key changes have been introduced into the contractual arrangements, apparently seeking to address problems encountered in Phase 1.

Foremost among the alterations is a relaxation of the additionality provisions. Restrictions on recruitment of NHS staff now apply only in respect of certain 'shortage professions', a list of which is developed in respect of each scheme. The provider remains unable to entice particular staff away from the NHS, but is entitled to recruit an NHS or recent ex-NHS employee who is not a member of a shortage profession through a general advertisement.

A second key difference is the extent to which the authority can exercise greater control over the provider through a range of sanctions for failure and extensive reporting obligations. For example, the authority can take steps itself to provide clinical services at the provider's expense where the provider fails – for example, where a facility is not completed on time.

The covenant strength of the provider has also been re-examined, resulting in the requirement for uncapped parent company guarantees and liquid support (eg, a bank bond) to cover the liabilities of the provider arising out of any termination of the services agreement.

Phase 2 also sees the tightening of the compensation on termination arrangements including the effective removal of the ringfencing of senior debt. We are yet to see how sponsors and senior funders will react to this. On the one hand, it may lead to more innovative bespoke financing solutions. On the other, it may merely increase the cost of finance and put pressure on the affordability of the projects.

(c) *Characteristics and developments considered in the wider context of the reforms*

The relaxation of the additionality provisions in the Phase 2 procurement raises issues as to the extent to which the ISTC programme is aimed at providing true additional capacity. It may be that the recent recruitment drive in the NHS has overcompensated and that there is now a surplus of healthcare staff in the market. It may be that additional capacity is not necessary, but that the creation of ISTCs is necessary to generate plurality (competition) to improve quality and reduce prices. The concern is whether this is short term. If the procurement is to kick-start public sector service providers into improving the quality of the service they provide, then this will be a major disappointment to the private sector investors which plan to be in the market for the longer term – that is, benefit from the start-up opportunity and compete with other healthcare providers for NHS referrals.

This development begins to make more sense in the context of government encouragement for successful NHS trusts to convert to foundation trusts. With control over its own budget and resourcing, it will be for each NHS trust to act to stem the loss of referrals (and, consequently, income) to the local ISTCs or to make the necessary cutbacks to accommodate such losses.

*(d)    Issues to be resolved*

In spite of the evolution of the ISTC programme in Phase 2, there remain a number of criticisms of the schemes that some commentators argue will need to be addressed if the programme is to find long-term success. Key among these criticisms is that as NHS trusts lose patients to ISTCs, cash is diverted to ISTCs and NHS trust budgets fall, which in turn results in the closure of wards and facilities. The effects of this process can already be seen, even on proposed PFIs – for example, the Colchester (Essex Rivers) Hospital PFI project discussed earlier.

A second criticism is that complex procedures are still performed by trusts, while the ISTCs enjoy the easy, high-volume procedures and effectively cherry-pick the profitable work. Loss of this effective subsidy makes it harder for trusts to continue to fund the high-complexity procedures.

It also makes it harder for trusts to fund the research and teaching that form an important part of their function. ISTCs, at present, have limited teaching or research obligations. The future of a truly competitive healthcare market may require ISTCs to take up their share of these obligations in order to ensure a level playing field.

Finally, does the volume-based 'rewards by results' system under which ISTCs function pose a risk to patient care? Some have argued that ISTCs are incentivised to maximise patient throughput rather than to ensure that patients are discharged only when ready. Such opinions should be viewed against the backdrop of strict contractual provisions surrounding patient care, the scrutiny of the Healthcare Commission and the fact that ISTCs will need to trade in large part on their reputation when it comes to patient choice of which facility to be referred to.

## 3. Conclusions

Reforms in the United Kingdom have provided significant opportunities for the private sector. Other European countries are experiencing similar reforms, but with variable growth in opportunities for the private sector.

In the United Kingdom, reforms will inevitably require contractual arrangements between the public and private sectors to be flexible enough to cope with change. This is likely to come at a price and may adversely affect the ability of procuring authorities to afford projects necessary to achieve the objectives of the reforms.

The government may need to deal with concerns expressed by the private sector that it is being used to kick-start improvements by the public sector, effectively acting as a 'stalking horse'.

While reforms are being implemented, the government will need to manage the inevitable disruption as projects are put on hold, changed or even cancelled. In particular, investors and contractors may need to be given comfort that some or all of their development costs will be reimbursed if projects are cancelled.

The government will also need to deal with the political sensitivities associated with refinancings if it is to unlock significant gains for the public sector and not dissuade investors from investing in health deals.

Additionally, the government may need to take stock of its procurement strategies to ensure that it is achieving the most effective solutions to the issues raised by the reforms; if community-based services are the way forward, then existing procurement strategies ought to be revisited to avoid disruption and even cancellation of any further projects.

Meanwhile, European governments that are developing procurement strategies to deal with health reform ought to look to the experiences of the United Kingdom and, where applicable, learn from its successful (and less successful) arrangements.

*The author gratefully acknowledges the assistance of Managing Associate Rob Gray, Associate Phil Duffield and Trainee Solicitor Kristen Houghton, all in the CMS Cameron McKenna infrastructure and project finance group, in the preparation of this chapter.*

# Prisons

Cameron Smith
Ashurst

## 1. Introduction

### 1.1 Overview

This chapter focuses on the custodial sector and, in particular, on the use of public-private partnerships (PPPs) to procure the development and management of prison facilities by the private sector.

While the chapter examines prison projects in the broadest sense (from pure management contracts for the operation of existing establishments to the development, financing and operation of new-build facilities), it focuses primarily on the most complex form of these projects which involve the design, construction, management and financing of prisons (colloquially referred to as 'DCMF' projects).

This chapter also seeks to provide an overview of PPP prison projects globally, identifying those countries in which PPP procurement methods and associated risk management tools have been adopted to deliver and manage prison infrastructure. However, the principal focus is on the UK prison sector,[1] the world's second most active private prison sector after that of the United States.

Distinctions are often drawn between projects developed under the UK government's Private Finance Initiative (PFI) and those developed as public-private partnerships. Although there are various technical differences between PFI and PPP projects,[2] this chapter uses the term 'PPP projects' to cover any activity carried on jointly by the private and public sectors, and treats PFI projects as a subset of PPP projects.

By way of introduction, the prison sector has not been as fertile an area for PPP development of public infrastructure as the transport sector (eg, roads, light and heavy rail and bridges), the health sector (eg, hospitals and healthcare facilities), or the education sector (eg, schools and universities) in terms of deal volume.[3]

However, UK prison PPP projects are the best example of output-based projects delivering outsourced services with full risk transfer to the private sector, as the

---

[1] The principal focus of the chapter is, in particular, on those prison PPP projects carried out in England and Scotland, as no such projects in this sector have yet been carried out in Wales or Northern Ireland.
[2] A review of the differences between PFI and PPP projects is beyond the remit of this chapter. However, PFI projects are generally considered to involve the provision of private sector financing to deliver key infrastructure assets and the contracts for the delivery of these assets will usually be required to conform to the latest version of Her Majesty's Treasury's Standardisation of PFI Contracts. All other projects involving the management or delivery of public infrastructure or public services are generally referred to as PPP projects (which may or may not require the provision of third-party financing).
[3] In the United Kingdom, only 11 prison projects have reached financial close. Nine of these were awarded in England and two in Scotland.

involvement of the public sector in the operation of the completed facility is negligible. It has been more common, therefore, in this sector, compared to any other sector, for consortia to be led by the operators, rather than construction contractors or financial investors.

## 1.2 The role of private prisons in the public sector

As prison populations in all countries have risen substantially in recent times, governments have sought to develop further prison facilities to house prisoners.[4] In addition, changing social attitudes have required the upgrading of prison infrastructure and the provision of more purposeful activities within prisons, much of which requires the development of more modern prison facilities than are currently in place. The private sector is able to deliver these facilities as capably as the public sector.

Although private prisons are designed, constructed, managed, operated and financed by the private sector, these prisons nonetheless fit within the public sector prison community and are subject to a degree of public sector control through a variety of mechanisms. In the United Kingdom, contracted-out prisons are still being run in accordance with the Prison Act 1952 and the regulations made pursuant to that legislation (the Prison Rules 1999).

Under the Prison Act 1952, public prisons (as compared to private prisons) have a governor, who has legal custody of all the prisoners in his prison and is also responsible for the transport of prisoners to and from the prison. The governor has wide-ranging powers under this act, which include the imposition of limited punishment for disciplinary offences.

On the other hand, under the Criminal Justice Act,[5] a contracted-out prison or private prison is required to have a director as well as a controller.

The director is appointed by the private sector contractor and must be a prison custody officer approved by the Home Office. The director exercises all of the powers of the day-to-day running of the prison that are given to that person under the enabling legislation, but has no power to impose punishment on prisoners. The director must also act within the terms of the contract with the Home Office and the Prison Rules.

The controller, however, is a crown servant appointed by the Home Office who reports to the home secretary in relation to the running of the prison. As well as reviewing the performance of the private sector contractor under the terms of the contract, the controller will also investigate any allegations made against prison custody officers and will exercise disciplinary powers under the Prison Rules within the facility.

Prison custody officers within private prisons are employed either by the private sector contractor or by the operating subcontractor, whereas prison officers within public prisons are employed by the Home Office. Prison custody officers must be

---

[4] Data provided by the Home Office Research Development Statistics office indicates that prisoner numbers in England and Wales have risen from approximately 45,000 in 1993 to approximately 76,000 in 2006.
[5] Criminal Justice Act 1991, Section 85.

certified by the secretary of state as fit and proper persons, and must have received training to a standard approved by the secretary of state.

Private prisons, however, fulfil a similar role to public prisons in providing accommodation for any prisoners convicted by the courts and must operate like any other public prison in managing their prisoner populations. In the event that any incidents occur which require the provision of mutual aid, staff from a private prison may be required to assist in a public prison and vice versa. In addition, prisoners will occasionally be moved between public and private prisons, depending upon availability of prisoner places.

Private prisons are also subject to the same degree of scrutiny as public prisons (if not more, due to increased attention for political reasons) by bodies such as Her Majesty's Inspectorate of Prisons and the National Offender Management Service.

### 1.3 The rationale for a PFI/PPP approach

Various reasons are often cited for adopting a PPP approach for the development of prison facilities. The reasons which are most often given are to:

- reduce costs;
- ensure the delivery of services of a high standard;
- facilitate risk transfer from the public sector to the private sector; and
- improve the performance of the public sector and assist in public sector reform.

*(a) Cost savings*

The most compelling reason for using a PPP approach to developing and delivering prisons and prison services is to reduce the cost of incarcerating prisoners or, in the lexicon of PPP, to improve value for money from the government's perspective. The prison sector is no different from any other sector in this respect, but the potential cost savings in the prison sector are somewhat more noticeable, given the extent to which the private sector is involved in all aspects of the design, construction and operations.

The various consortia which bid for prison PPP projects generally comprise a construction contractor and a prison operator, each of which will need to coordinate activities in order to deliver the most economically efficient proposal, calculated on a net present value basis.

Traditionally, prison infrastructure has been designed and built by a construction contractor and then operated by the public sector, with only minimal consultation between the two. Often, this consultation has been driven by a desire not to reduce costs, but instead to maintain security and meet public policy consideration without reference to other critical criteria. However, the tender process adopted for PPP prison projects requires each consortium to engage at an early stage in value engineering and design development in order to ensure that the construction, operating and financing costs are all taken into account in delivering a solution which represents the best overall value for money solution.

By focusing on delivering a high-standard design and construction solution, it is often possible to reduce the prison operating costs over the life of a project, thereby reducing the net costs of the project as a whole. These types of efficiency savings arise as a result of the holistic approach taken in delivering PPP prison projects.

Cost savings are also experienced as a result of better private sector project and service delivery skills, and the more rigorous and disciplined approach to project management.[6]

(b) *Service delivery*

The second reason for adopting a PPP approach to delivering prison infrastructure and services is due to the need to improve service delivery. It is often said that the delivery of services under a PPP approach results in a better overall quality of service as a result of the design, construction and operational activities being interdependent, and due to the sponsors and funders having to adopt a long-term approach to the development of infrastructure and provision and costing of services.

Although part of the reason for the service delivery in private prisons being of a higher standard is due to the adoption of more rigorous private sector project management techniques,[7] often the reason for the enhanced service quality is due to the strict contractual requirements which are enforced through the various contractual mechanisms. Such mechanisms ensure that a private sector contractor which reduces the volume of quality of services will suffer a significant financial penalty. The public sector is not subject to such a restrictive regime and therefore service quality may at times be allowed to suffer where budgetary constraints justify a reduction in the quality or quantity of services being provided.

The evidence so far in the United Kingdom suggests that the best PFI/PPP prisons out-perform most public sector prisons, although the lowest-performing PFI/PPP prisons can be among the worst in the prison estate. In addition, PFI/PPP prisons tend to be better than public prisons in areas relating to decency and regimes (eg, the purposeful activities available to prisoners). However, private sector prisons perform less well in areas such as safety and security.[8] This is to be expected, as there is a trade-off between the two competing sets of criteria.

(c) *Risk transfer*

A further reason cited for adopting a PPP approach to the delivery of prison services is due to the degree of risk which can be transferred to the private sector. A corollary of this risk transfer is that these projects can be accounted for off the government's balance sheet and therefore need not be taken into account in assessing the public sector borrowing. While the requirement to account for these projects off-balance sheet for the government is no longer a critical requirement in structuring these projects, the general degree of risk transfer is nonetheless highly attractive to government authorities.

---

6     See the Thirty-Fifth Report of the Public Accounts Committee Session 2002-2003 entitled "PFI Construction Performance".
7     See footnote 6.
8     See "The Operational Performance of PFI Prisons" report by the controller and auditor general, dated June 18 2003 (HC 700 Session 2002-2003: June 18 2003).

The overriding principle of project finance and PPP project structuring is that risks should be allocated to the party best able to manage such risks and, in the context of prison projects, this principle results in the private sector bearing all design, construction, operation, maintenance and financing risks, with few risks remaining with the public sector authority. The natural result of this transfer of risk from the public sector is that the public sector can budget more accurately on a long-term basis for the delivery of such essential public services and will not become liable for any cost or time overruns which may occur at any stage during the contract period.

*(d)* *Public sector reform*

Finally, the use of PPP delivery techniques has also assisted the UK government, in particular, in reforming public sector work practices. As private prisons form an integral part of the overall prison estate, there is a natural cross-fertilisation of ideas and developments which may ultimately be adopted by the public sector in running its own prisons.

By adopting the practices and learning from the lessons of the private sector (which is often seen as being more innovative in approach than the public sector), the public sector in the United Kingdom has been able to reform its own procedures in relation to the treatment of prisoners, training, education programmes, rehabilitation, care for vulnerable prisoners and in various other ways. The use of PPP techniques therefore has wider implications than for the development only of the private sector establishments.

The reasons set out above are cited commonly as providing a rationale for a PPP approach to the development of prison infrastructure and the delivery of prison services.

Over time, however, it is likely that governments will appreciate that there are also certain drawbacks to adopting a PPP approach. One of these is the lack of flexibility which is inherent in fixed-term, fixed-price contracts for the provision of these services. Nonetheless, in a carefully controlled environment, the rationale for a PPP approach to the delivery of prison infrastructure and services appears compelling.

## 1.4 Political considerations

There is probably far more sensitivity associated with the delivery of prison PPP projects than with the delivery of any other PPP facilities.

As the prison population rises in the United Kingdom and most other Western countries, and the calls for the incarceration of offenders increase, the need for more prisoner places grows weekly. In addition, legislation such as the Human Rights Act[9] and a trend towards more open government[10] force an improvement in living standards for prisoners and have made the respective authorities focus more on the provision of education, rehabilitation, recreation and health services within prison facilities.

---

9   Human Rights Act 1998.
10  Note, for example, the impact of the Freedom of Information Act 2000.

The focus within prisons has therefore shifted slightly away from the provision of secure accommodation towards the rehabilitation and training of prisoners – an area in which the private sector has traditionally had greater experience.

Nonetheless, there is still concern surrounding the involvement of the private sector in the deprivation of liberty of prisoners, which has traditionally been seen as the sole right of the state. These concerns range from slight unease to outright hostility, especially in the case of bodies such as trade unions (which are primarily concerned with the wage rates and pension rights of prison employees) and bodies such as the Prison Reform Trust[11] (which has a broader social agenda).

The political considerations fall into a number of categories. The more general concern is whether the private sector should ever be entitled to deprive individuals of their right to liberty or whether this should be the sole preserve of the state. Put another way, should a party motivated by profit have the right to make money out of depriving a citizen of his freedom?

The more specific concerns relate to the accountability of the private sector operator and the perceived lack of control by the public sector in managing what would otherwise be a public facility. The issue of public sector control over prisons is dealt with in section 3. In addition, the UK Home Office is usually quick to point out that private prisons are still subject to review by:

- Her Majesty's Inspectorate of Prisons, which carries out thorough investigations of prisons on a regular basis;
- the ombudsman, who acts as an impartial investigator in the event of complaints; and
- the relevant board of visitors, which safeguards the rights and wellbeing of all prisoners within an individual establishment.

Many of these concerns relate to perception and whether it is correct in principle for the private sector to profit from the imprisonment of prisoners.

However, supporters of private sector involvement in the prison sector are keen to point out that:

- private prisons are run very strictly in line with detailed service-level agreements, with harsh penalties imposed for failing to meet these requirements;
- the state retains responsibility for sentencing, justice and punishment, and the operator has no responsibility for these functions;
- the state maintains a close watch over the activities of the operator – in the United Kingdom, this involves the appointment by the Prison Service within the prison of a controller; and
- the state has quite extensive step-in rights which may be exercised in a number of scenarios.

In short, supporters of prison PPP projects argue that the state decides who is sentenced and for how long: the sole responsibility of the private sector is to provide

---

11   See Prison Reform Trust report "Private Punishment: Who Profits?" of January 2005.

facilities within which this sentence can be carried out. The private sector in no way influences or benefits from the length of the sentence imposed by the state.

The nature of the opposition to private sector involvement in the prison sector and the political environment in which prison PPP projects are carried out should also not be discounted. The very structure of these projects has, in a number of jurisdictions, been dictated by these political considerations.

In the United Kingdom, where the opposition is more muted, the private sector provides all services including design, construction, financing, maintenance and operation. However, in France, where the public would not accept the outsourcing of purely 'public' services, the provision of surveillance, security, operation and registration is kept out of the contracts. Such functions cannot be validly delegated to the private sector, since the delegation of certain public services to the private sector (eg, police services, public education services and security in prisons) is strictly prohibited under French law.[12]

To understand these concerns, it is necessary to appreciate the reasons for the different contractual structures set out below.

## 2. Structure of PFI/PPP prison projects

### 2.1 Overview

PPP prison projects are carried in a variety of ways, ranging from a simple outsourcing of the management of the facility to full private sector provision of a new prison infrastructure.

A number of factors will be taken into account by the relevant authority in determining the structure to be adopted. The principal factors which are likely to be taken into account by the authority will be:

- the needs of the authority and the reasons why the private sector is being chosen to provide such infrastructure (eg, is the private sector involvement required in order to source off-balance sheet financing or to utilise the more innovative and efficient private sector project management skills?);
- the political considerations and the political environment which applies in the relevant jurisdiction (as described under section 1.4); and
- the constitutional powers of the authority and the types of structure which are permitted by law or regulation.

The UK model, which involves the design, construction, financing, maintenance and operation of new prison infrastructure, is at one end of the spectrum. Other jurisdictions (which are described below in section 7) have adopted other contractual structures incorporating one or more of these elements.

The most commonly used contractual structures are described below.

---

12     The delegation of certain key functions within the French prison system (eg, custodial services, security, surveillance and so on) are, in accordance with the jurisprudence of the *Conseil d' Etat* (the French Administrative High Court of Justice), strictly prohibited.

## 2.2 Common contractual structures

### (a) Full services model

The full services model is the model favoured by Her Majesty's Prison Service in England and the Scottish Prison Service in Scotland.

This structure involves the contractor taking on the design, construction and financing of a single-site prison facility and assuming responsibility for the operation and maintenance of the facility for a further 25 years, enabling the contractor to pay all outstanding debt as well as providing an equity return to the sponsors. The contractor will also take responsibility for obtaining planning approval, although the authority will generally have chosen the site to be used for the facility.

Under this model, the contractor does not usually take responsibility or bear any risk in relation to the usage of the prison, but instead will be paid for making available the required number of prisoner places, whether or not these places are used. Usage risk will therefore remain with the authority, which is responsible for allocating prisoners to the facility.[13]

As the authority has very little involvement in the running of the prison, the authority's scrutiny is managed through the role of the controller. The controller is the authority's representative within the facility, who is responsible for monitoring the performance of the contractor and ensuring compliance with all operational requirements once the facility is operational.

The principal advantage of this model is the extent of the risk transfer to the private sector, which is responsible for managing all service provision. As a result, the design and construction of the facility will be dictated by operational and maintenance requirements, and the management of these responsibilities will lead to a greater degree of efficiency within the design and the operational regime.

The disadvantage from the public sector perspective is the lack of control and flexibility with respect to the operational regime and the political sensitivity of this model. In addition, adoption of this model places a significant burden on the authority to specify its design and operational requirements at the outset, to ensure that the terms of the contract are appropriate before the project commences.

### (b) Full services (except custodial services)

This model, which involves the contractor taking responsibility for the design, construction, financing and maintenance of the facility, but not the provision of custodial services, security or operations, has been adopted in a number of the French prison projects. This model leaves the operational aspects and custodial services (including the provision of prison guards) within the control of the public sector and therefore avoids the implication that this essential public sector service has been outsourced to the private sector.

---

13  In Scotland, there is no central administration of prison usage, as this function is managed by the prisons themselves and prisoners can be sent directly to a prison by a court without central coordination of resources. Nonetheless, under this model, the contractor still does not take usage risk.

The advantage of this structure is that it benefits from all of the design, construction and operational synergies as the model outlined in section 2.2(a), but provides greater operational control and flexibility for the public sector. This is also less politically sensitive than adopting a full services model.

However, as both the public and private sectors will be performing services within the one facility, this model gives rise to issues relating to the interface between the operation, maintenance and design of a facility and loses any benefit of single-point responsibility being borne by one party during the operational phase. For example, it may not be clear who bears responsibility for maintenance cost increases, as the need for higher levels of maintenance within the facility may be due to:
- the operational regime within the facility, as managed by the public sector;
- the poor design of the facility, which is the responsibility of the contractor; or
- the low quality of construction and/or materials used during the construction or operational phases.

*(c)*    *Design, build, maintain and operate*
This model is similar to that used in the United Kingdom, Australia and the United States, but instead utilises funding from the public sector and therefore takes advantage of the lower public sector borrowing costs.

This particular contractual model involves payment being made:
- during the construction phase – by way of monthly or milestone payments, similar to a design and build contractual payment mechanism; and
- during the operational phase – by way of monthly payments for providing the services.

This model has been used in the United Kingdom in developing immigration detention facilities.

One of the advantages is that this model results in the authority taking the benefit of all synergies of the full services model, but with far more control over the construction and operating regimes, given that there is no third-party funder with a power to veto any authority changes or exercise control over the terms and conditions set out in the project agreement. As there is no funding requirement, the overall negotiation process is often far shorter, as there is no need for an extensive funder due diligence process and issues such as the calculation of compensation on termination are not as critical, as compared to the adoption of a model which utilises third-party financing. As there is no third-party financing in place which needs repayment, the authority also has the benefit of being able to determine the optimal duration of the project.

From the public sector's perspective, the lack of scrutiny from third-party funders (which will usually carry out their own thorough due diligence investigations) results in the authority having to exercise greater control and scrutiny over the design, construction and operational regimes.

## (d) Design, build and maintain

Contracts for the design, construction and maintenance of facilities are, in many respects, merely extensions of a design and build contract.

The authority exercises a far greater degree of control over the development of the prison, particularly because it is responsible for providing the finance and then operating the facility once it is built. Given that the contractor is not responsible for the operation of the facility, the authority will usually specify the design criteria to be met, leaving the contractor with the responsibility of determining the quality and nature of materials to be used in order to meet the design life requirements and maintenance obligations.

As the contractor is not responsible for operation of the facility, the authority has a greater degree of flexibility with respect to the operation of the prison. On the other hand, the scope for value engineering is diminished, as the contractor will not share in any benefit of operational cost savings as a result of any enhanced construction techniques or materials. Lines of responsibility during the operational phase are also likely to be less clear, given that maintenance and operations are split between two separate entities.

## (e) Design and build

Strictly speaking, design and build contracts are not considered to be PPP arrangements, as there is little public-private partnership involved in developing prison infrastructure on this basis. However, for the sake of identifying all potential contractual models for the development of prison infrastructure, they have been included in this chapter.

A design and build contract is likely to be the cheapest means of developing prison infrastructure, from the public sector's perspective, although the authority will ultimately take full responsibility for all operational and maintenance requirements and the financing of the development, as well as for identifying and incorporating all operational requirements at the outset of the project. As a result, there is little risk transfer to the private sector, save for design and construction risks.

As the contractor has no vested interest in ensuring the operational viability or maintaining the design life of the facility on a long-term basis, there is little scope for value engineering or identifying synergies between design, construction and operations, and therefore a design and build contract is one of the least 'efficient' models for developing prison infrastructure.

## (f) Escort arrangements

Although the escorting of prisoners from prison facilities to courts, hospitals or for other purposes is not an inherent part of providing prison infrastructure, a number of prison contracts in the United Kingdom and elsewhere also include the provision by the contractor of prison escort services.

This has little impact upon the development of the prison or the operation of the facility, but constitutes an additional service to be provided under the terms of the principal project agreement. Escort services can be provided on a regular basis or only on an emergency basis (ie, where there is a separate escort contract which has been let to a third party).

In any case, payment is usually made for these services on the basis of prisoner miles covered or individual escort trips arranged.

## 3. Key areas to be addressed in project agreements

As indicated above, the summary of the key contractual provisions set out below is based on the UK model of developing PPP prison projects, which involves the design, construction, maintenance, financing and operation of a new-build prison facility.

Although all contractors will take a slightly different approach to the management and allocation of various risks and responsibilities, there is nonetheless a great degree of consistency between prison operators and construction contractors as to the way in which risks should be analysed and managed under the terms of these prison contracts. The involvement of third-party funders also dictates, to a great extent, the way in which risks may be managed and those which the funders will expect to be assumed by the authority.

The summary of how these key risks are likely to be managed on a prison PPP project is therefore based on the UK PPP projects which have been carried out to date.

### 3.1 Planning

Before the relevant authority commences the tender process for a prison project, outline planning permission is usually obtained once the site has been identified. Until such time as outline planning permission has been obtained (which will confirm that, from a planning perspective, the development of a prison on that site is acceptable to the planning authority), there is little purpose in conducting the tender process.

The obligation to obtain detailed planning permission will usually be passed to the contractor. In order to obtain detailed planning permission, the contractor will need to provide the planning authority with all appropriate plans, designs and drawings of the proposed facility, and this can only therefore be achieved once the design has reached a sufficiently detailed level.

While planning permission is the responsibility of the contractor, the funders will normally insist upon detailed planning permission being in place (and any judicial review or other appeal process having expired) before any financing will be provided under the terms of the financing agreements. Detailed planning permission is therefore usually a condition precedent to financial close on a prison PPP project.

### 3.2 Property

In order for the contractor and its subcontractors to obtain access to the site so as to carry out the construction and then the management of the facility, the contractor will usually require either a lease or a licence over the site. The decision as to whether the authority should grant a lease or a licence will depend on a number of considerations, including:
- the nature of the access rights required by the contractor from a practical point of view;

- any relevant laws which may determine the nature of the interest to be granted;[14]
- any tax considerations;[15]
- any other financial considerations, such as any potential stamp duty land tax liability; and
- the structure of the financing package proposed.

The majority of UK prison projects have been carried out on the basis of a leasehold interest being granted from the authority (or other government department) to the contractor and (in some cases) the operating subcontractor.

### 3.3 Design

All responsibilities relating to design are invariably passed to the contractor, and are then subcontracted down to the construction subcontractor.

The authority will usually establish a protocol for the submission of designs throughout the construction phase, as well as a protocol for the management and security of design documentation (given the particular sensitivity to such documents in the context of a secure prison facility). The initial design documentation therefore often does not form part of the project agreement, but will be in an agreed form at the time of financial close and will therefore be included by reference into the project agreement.

### 3.4 Construction/works

All construction-related obligations are borne by the contractor and subcontracted down to the construction subcontractor on a full turnkey construction basis, in a way which is consistent with all other PPP sectors.

Given the nature of the facility being developed, security on site is usually paramount and the authority will also require prior notice of the identity of all individuals likely to be involved in the development of the prison, in order to carry out preliminary security checks.

### 3.5 Completion/certification of works

As on any PPP project, it is critical that there is a clear process for completing the construction phase and demonstrating that the services are ready to be provided before the operational phase may commence and the contractor is able to begin earning its revenue.

On a prison project, there is usually a two-stage process involving:
- the physical completion of the prison infrastructure; and
- demonstration of availability of prisoner places.

---

14   Under legislation passed in 2002, prison projects in France may be implemented on the basis of a long-term administrative lease and therefore the enabling legislation governs the form of access rights required.

15   In the United Kingdom, a leasehold interest is usually required in order for the contractor to claim capital allowances for tax purposes.

On the UK prison projects, physical completion of the prison is evidenced by the issue of a declaration by an independently appointed engineer. The issue of the engineer's declaration signals the completion of construction only.

Appointment of the independent engineer has traditionally been the responsibility of the authority, which itself undertakes to procure the certification of the works, when such works are complete in accordance with the project agreement.

The certification of the works is only one of several preconditions to opening the prison, however.

3.6     **Preparation for operation of the prison**
Before the prison may be opened and available prisoner places and additional prisoner places provided by the contractor, there are a number of conditions to be satisfied, in addition to demonstrating physical completion of the prison facility (see section 3.5). The various other conditions to be satisfied before opening the prison include:
- approval by the authority of the contractor's operational proposals and operating manuals;
- appointment of all necessary trained and certified staff;
- certification by the authority of all staff;
- the issue of 'cell certificates' in respect of each prison cell to be used;
- demonstration by the contractor that the key requirements have been met in respect of each prisoner place which is to be made available (eg, clothing, catering, education, recreation and health services are all available).

Unusually for a PPP project, the authority has a significant degree of discretion in approving the operational proposals and certifying the fitness of staff members to work within the facility.

The contractor will also need to appoint a director of the prison, who will need to be appointed several months in advance of opening and whose appointment will need to be approved by the authority.

Given the onerous requirements to be met before the prison may be opened, there is usually a period of time between the issue of the engineer's declaration (signalling that physical construction is complete) and the actual opening date (demonstrating that the prison is ready to provide services).

3.7     **Certification of cells**
In order for a prison cell to achieve cell certification, the relevant prison cell and other living accommodation to be occupied by a prisoner must comply with those parts of the construction specification, equipment schedule and maintenance schedule as relate to the prison cell and such other living accommodation. Cell certification is usually carried by a representative of the authority or (in the case of one of the Scottish prisons) the contractor itself.

In the event that any cell ceases to meet the requisite standards, the contractor is obliged to notify the authority and thereafter the cell certificate will be withdrawn until the cell has been repaired or upgraded to meet the necessary requirements.

Certification of a prison cell is one of the conditions needed to provide an available prisoner place.

## 3.8 Phase-in arrangements/liquidated damages

For operational reasons, available prisoner places are provided on a staggered basis in accordance with an agreed timetable, which commences with a small number of available prisoner places in week one and then increases to full accommodation over a period of several months.

This phase-in timetable has a dual purpose. First, it enables the operating subcontractor to maintain control of the facility during this critical period and ensure that prisoners are carefully initiated into the prison environment on a gradual basis. Second, it ensures that the authority does not pay for all prisoner places from the commencement of service provision, given that the authority is highly unlikely to be able to fill all available prisoner places at the outset. It therefore protects the authority from having to pay for unused prisoner places.

In the event that the contractor fails to make available the requisite number of available prisoner places in accordance with the phase-in timetable, it is usual in this sector for the contractor to be liable to pay liquidated damages to the authority at a predetermined rate. The rate of liquidated damages will typically depend on the number of prisoner places per day which have not been provided in accordance with the phase-in timetable.

Although the authority effectively 'saves' the fee per available prisoner place per day, nonetheless this saving is unlikely to meet the authority's full financial exposure. Therefore, liquidated damages are designed to ensure that the authority covers all of its additional costs incurred in housing prisoners in alternative facilities during the period of any delay. In this respect, prison PPP projects differ from accommodation projects in other sectors, where the contractor's exposure in the event of delay is limited solely to the revenue loss under the payment mechanism.

Such liquidated damages are usually passed down in full to the construction subcontractor, in addition to any other liquidated damages calculated on the basis of revenue forgone by the contractor.

## 3.9 Provision of prisoner places and additional prisoner places

The principal obligations during the operational phase are to provide:
- the required number of available prisoner places specified in the project agreement; and
- such other additional prisoner places as are required by the authority, up to a specified limit.

As the contractor is paid on a 'per prisoner place, per day' basis, a failure to provide the requisite number of available prisoner places will result in a loss of payment by the contractor, which can be viewed as an 'availability deduction'. Accordingly, if the contractor on any day fails to provide *any* available prisoner places, then the contractor will receive no payment for that day.

In respect of the additional prisoner places, however, the contractor is generally paid on a usage basis. Therefore, the authority is obliged to pay for such additional prisoner places only as and when they are requested by the authority and provided by the contractor. Given that there is no guarantee of any revenue in respect of these additional prisoner places, the costs of financing the facility are not spread across additional prisoner places and therefore the price per additional prison place per day is significantly less than that payable by the authority in respect of the 'base' number of available prison places.

In order to provide available prison places and additional prisoner places, the contractor is required to demonstrate that:
- the engineer's declaration has been obtained;
- all of the operational proposals and operating manuals have been approved by the authority;
- all staff have been trained and certified;
- the relevant prison cell has received a cell certificate; and
- the prisoner place has complied in all respects with the minimum requirements for that day.

The minimum requirements relate to:
- clothing;
- food;
- exercise/recreation;
- access to health services;
- access to education services; and
- access to various other services, including counselling and so on.

## 3.10 Provision of services

The operational requirements and the provisions relating to the carrying out of the services are very much output based in nature and therefore do not specify in detail the way in which the prison services are to be provided.

The authority does, however, have a degree of control over the way in which the services are provided and the prison is operated, by exercising its influence over the operating proposals which will need to be agreed prior to the opening of the facility.

A great deal of the operational regime is dictated and controlled by the payment mechanism and the minimum requirements which need to be met by the contractor in order to provide available prisoner places and additional prisoner places.

## 3.11 Maintenance

Although maintenance is less of an issue in the prison sector than it would be for a hospital or school PPP project (due to the robust nature of construction and the materials used in building the facility), the authority nonetheless retains a right to carry out surveys in the event that it believes that the contractor has failed to meet its maintenance obligations. The maintenance regime on a prison PPP project is similar to that in various other sectors. The principal difference is that the payment mechanism and maintenance regime are not particularly concerned with the aesthetic appearance of the prison or its furnishings.

## 3.12 Relief from performance/compensation events/*force majeure* events

It is usual in project agreements for PPP projects to include a discrete list of events for which the contractor will be entitled to relief from termination. In addition, a small number of *force majeure* events are usually included within the contract, entitling the contractor to claim relief from its obligations; should the *force majeure* event continue for a significant period of time, either party will be entitled to terminate.

On a number of the earlier UK prison projects, the UK government took the view that the inclusion of relief events was not appropriate in the context of a prison PPP project, as the inherent nature of a prison facility required the contractor to provide for all contingencies within its design, construction and operating regimes. Whereas a contractor on an accommodation-style PPP project might be entitled to relief from termination in the event of general industrial action during the operational period, this would not be appropriate in the context of a prison project where the continual operation of the facility was critical in order to preserve the security of the facility. As a result, the contractor was made responsible (on the earlier prison projects) for having in place contingency arrangements to address these circumstances.

The most recent UK prison project, however, has adopted an identical regime to that reflected in the UK government guidance on PFI contracts.[16] As a result, a similar relief event, *force majeure* event, compensation event mechanism was implemented to afford the contractor limited relief in certain circumstances in a form which is consistent with that used in other sectors on projects of this nature.

## 3.13 Change of law

The early UK prison projects provided the contractor with only limited change of law protection. This mechanism afforded protection to the contractor in the event of a change in prison legislation which was not foreseeable at the date of entering into the project agreement.

The most recent prison PPP project has, however, adopted the same change of law regime outlined in the most recent UK government guidance on PFI.[17]

As a result of this recent development, the contractor is entitled to protection in the event of:

- discriminatory changes in law (as defined in the project agreement);
- specific changes in law (ie, those specifically relating to prisons); and
- any general changes in law coming into effect during the operational phase which require capital expenditure in excess of an agreed amount.

As a result of the limited or (in some cases) non-existent benchmarking/market-testing regime which applies on prison PPP projects, all other changes of law during

---

16  See Chapter 5 of Her Majesty's Treasury's publication titled "Standardisation of PFI Contracts – Version 3", published in April 2004.
17  See Chapter 13 of Her Majesty's Treasury's publication titled "Standardisation of PFI Contracts – Version 3", published in April 2004.

the operational phase will need to be accommodated within the payment mechanism indexation regime (which is addressed in section 4.1).

This is one of the key operational risks in this sector.

## 3.14 Role of the director/controller

As indicated above, public prisons or directly managed prisons (as compared to private prisons or contracted-out prisons) have a governor, who has wide-ranging powers under the Prison Act.[18] The governor is responsible for the operation and running of the prison, as well as the imposition of limited punishment for disciplinary offences. The powers and duties of the governor are laid out in the Prison Rules 1999.

On the other hand, a contracted-out prison or private prison has a director as well as a controller.[19]

The director will be appointed by the contractor and must be a prison custody officer approved by the Home Office. The director exercises all the powers of the day-to-day running of the prison that are given to him under both the Prison Act 1952 (as altered to take account of the position of the controller) and the Prison Rules 1999. The director does not have any power to impose punishment on prisoners and must also act within the terms of the project agreement.

The controller, however, is a crown servant appointed by the Home Office who reports to the home secretary in relation to the running of the prison. As well as reviewing the performance of the private sector contractor under the terms of the project agreement, the controller will also investigate any allegations made against prison custody officers and exercise disciplinary powers under the Prison Rules within the facility. The controller is not therefore an employee of the contractor.

The project agreement will often make the controller responsible for checking the reports prepared by the contractor and investigating any allegations of performance failure in the first instance.

## 3.15 Staffing

Where the contractor bears responsibility for providing custodial services, all staffing within the prison is the sole responsibility of the contractor. Where custodial services are not provided by the controller, however (eg, as under the French model), the contractor is responsible only for those staff members needed to provide the services being carried out under the project agreement.

Due to the nature of the facility and the direct correlation between the quality and performance of the staff and the effectiveness of the rehabilitation regime within the prison, the authority generally is afforded additional control over the contractor's staff than would be considered usual on PPP projects. In particular:
- the authority will have the ability to require the removal of a staff member from the facility at any time for any reason;

---

18  Prison Act 1952 (1952 c52).
19  See Section 85 of the Criminal Justice Act 1991 (1991 c53).

- the authority will be required to approve the form and content of any training provided to custody officers by the contractor;
- all staff (whether construction, operational or otherwise) will need to be security-checked by the authority; and
- all custodial staff will need to be certified as prison custody officers by the authority following the carrying out of the approved training.

## 3.16 Performance monitoring

From the perspective of monitoring performance of the contractor, there is nothing unique about prison PPP projects. Most of the early UK prisons required monitoring and certification of cells to be carried out by the authority, with the contractor under an obligation to disclose instances of performance measures occurring or failures to meet the minimum requirements in respect of prisoner places.

The most recent UK prison projects, however, adopt a similar mechanism to that used in other sectors, where the contractor bears responsibility for disclosing and recording performance failures and actively monitoring performance across all services. Significant penalties apply in the event that the contractor fails to carry out such monitoring or omits to record or disclose any performance failure.

## 3.17 Benchmarking/market testing

Benchmarking and market testing are mechanisms which have been adopted across a range of PPP projects and sectors to enable price adjustments to take place on a regular basis to the unitary charge.[20]

Benchmarking generally involves the contractor preparing a benchmarking report on the price of providing the services against the price of providing corresponding services in comparable facilities. Following review of this report, the parties negotiate and agree (if possible) an appropriate price adjustment.

Market testing aims to rebase the price for the services after 'testing' them in the market. This is achieved generally by re-tendering certain services against the original performance standards, although there are several variations on this process.

Benchmarking and market testing on PPP projects are generally carried out on a regular basis (usually every five years during the operational period). They are usually carried out only in relation to 'soft' facilities management services, rather than 'hard' facilities management services (eg, maintenance), although this is not always the case.

Broadly speaking, benchmarking and market testing fulfil a number of purposes:
- They enable the authority to take the benefit of any general market reductions to the cost of providing services; and
- They afford the contractor partial protection in respect of increases in the cost of providing the services not otherwise addressed through the indexation mechanism (eg, as a result of general changes of law or increases in employment and pension costs).

---

20   See Chapter 14 of "Standardisation of PFI Contracts - Version 3" dated April 2004, published by Her Majesty's Treasury.

In the prison sector, this common PPP technique of rebasing part of the unitary charge has not been adopted. Instead, the UK government has preferred to use the indexation mechanism in the payment mechanism for its prison PPP projects, to address increases in the contractor's costs which might exceed the Retail Price Index (RPI) over the life of the project. This is addressed below.[21] This indexation mechanism is imperfect, as it will not fully protect against significant or one-off changes to the contractor's cost base as a result of general changes in law, for example. However, contractors appear to have been comfortable with this mechanism insofar as it applies to prison projects.

In addition, over the last few years the UK government has proposed and adopted on various prison projects a range of other quasi-benchmarking and market testing mechanisms, including:
- allowing the contractor to ask for a rebasing of its unitary charge every five years where changes to its operating costs reduce its rate of return by an agreed percentage;
- permitting the authority unilaterally to call for a market testing of the entirety of the operating subcontract services at certain agreed points throughout the life of the project; and
- permitting the authority unilaterally to call for a retendering of the whole of the project agreement, with the incoming contractor paying off all outstanding debt and compensating for loss of the outgoing contractor's equity investment.

The most recent UK prison project,[22] however, contains no benchmarking or market-testing procedure. The contractor is therefore reliant on the payment mechanism to meet all existing and future operating costs.

## 3.18 Change of control restrictions

Due to the politically sensitive nature of the prison sector, prison authorities will usually require more control over the transfer of any equity investments in prison PPP projects.

For this reason, the change of control mechanisms on the UK prison PPP projects usually include:
- an obligation on the contractor to obtain prior written approval from the authority to any direct or indirect change in control of 25% of the issued share capital;
- an obligation on the contractor to notify the authority of any transfer of 5% of more of the shares in the contractor;
- a right for shareholders in the contractor to transfer their shares to affiliates without restriction; and
- carve-outs for transfers occurring on recognised stock exchanges.

---

21  See section 4.1.
22  The Addiewell Prison Project, awarded by the Scottish ministers on June 20 2006.

Where a PPP project does not involve the provision of custodial services, often the restrictions on changes in control and on shareholdings are more relaxed.

### 3.19 Termination

The termination provisions for prison PPP projects are broadly similar to those found in other sectors and, in the most recent UK prison project, the termination provisions have been brought into line with the UK government's standardisation of PFI contracts guidance.[23]

The only additional termination right usually required by the authority is triggered when the contractor is in breach of a material obligation under the project agreement and this casts serious doubt on the contractor's ability to provide the services.

### 3.20 Compensation on termination

The mechanism for calculating and determining the compensation payable on termination has, on the most recent UK prison PPP project, been brought into line with the UK government's standardisation of PFI contracts guidance.

Earlier prison projects differed from other sectors in that:
- compensation was not generally payable on these projects in the event of termination during the construction period prior to the engineer's declaration being issued; and
- the authority had the right to terminate unilaterally following contractor breach, without affording the contractor or its funders the ability to rectify the breach, but compensation was payable on a 'no fault' basis in these circumstances.

### 3.21 Insurance

The insurance regime applicable to prison PPP projects is similar to that which applies across all other sectors in which PPP projects are carried out.

The contractor will therefore take responsibility for effecting and maintaining a range of project 'umbrella' policies during both the construction and operation phases, which will include:
- construction all risks insurance and property damage insurance;
- delay in start-up/business interruption insurance;
- public liability insurance;
- employers' liability insurance;
- motor vehicle insurance; and
- where applicable, medical malpractice insurance (to the extent that the contractor is responsible for dental and medical services).

As the insurance market is still not entirely comfortable insuring custodial facilities, and due to the lack of depth in the insurance market for projects of this nature, contractors in the United Kingdom have typically asked for additional

---

23   "Standardisation of PFI Contracts - Version 3" dated April 2004, published by Her Majesty's Treasury.

protection from the relevant authority in the event of insurances becoming unavailable during the duration of the project and where insurance costs increase above those experienced in other sectors.

3.22 **Indemnities**

As in any sector, the indemnities given in favour of the authority by the contractor will be structured in light of the services being provided.

In circumstances where the contractor is providing all design, construction, maintenance and custodial services in their entirety, where the authority has very limited involvement (if at all) in the operation of the facility (as with the UK PPP prison projects), the indemnities normally sought by the authority will be extensive and are likely to cover any liabilities incurred or suffered by the authority in relation to the project, whether arising out of the performance, non-performance, acts, omissions or breaches of the contractor.

The political sensitivity of these projects is usually given as the reason for the breadth of such indemnity protection sought by the authority.

In addition, the contractor is usually under an obligation to provide 'mutual aid' to other prison facilities in the event of riots or other disturbances at those facilities. The indemnities given by the contractor would usually also extend to any liabilities arising as a result of the involvement of the contractor's own staff or officers during the provision of such mutual aid.

The indemnities are almost invariably limited by reference to monetary caps and the level of insurance available to the contractor and its subcontractors.

3.23 **Authority/government step-in**

In other sectors, it is usual for any step-in rights of the authority to be heavily circumscribed and limited, so as to ensure that the contractor always has the ability to remedy any deficiency in service before step-in by the authority occurs (save in respect of matters which jeopardise health and safety).

It is notable on prison projects that the authority will usually have more extensive step-in and rectification rights, due to the critical nature of the services being provided and the consequences of failing to rectify any deficiency and service.

There is typically a degree of tension between:
- the authority's desire to exercise control in the event of any service deficiencies or where there is concern relating to the operation of the prison; and
- the interests of the contractor and the funders in seeking to ensure that their investment is protected to the greatest extent possible.

In particular, the contractor and funders will be concerned to ensure that the authority takes responsibility for any consequences of its actions. The issue is far more acute where such step-in occurs as a prelude to, or immediately following, a termination or rectification notice being given, as any such step-in may interfere with the funders' ability to exercise their own step-in rights under the direct agreement and to remedy any breaches which may continue.

A number of the early prison projects in the United Kingdom gave the authority the right to terminate the project earlier, without affording the funders any rectification opportunity. Where such rights were exercised, the funders would have the ability to recover all outstanding amounts under the financing agreements as part of the compensation payable by the authority following termination. In the most recent UK prison PPP project, the authority's step-in rights have been carefully structured so as to avoid any conflict with the funders' own step-in rights following a rectification notice or termination notice being given.

In addition to any contractual rights of step-in which are available to the authority, the authority will usually also have a statutory right to appoint a crown servant to take control of the facility in the event that the secretary of state believes that the director has lost or is likely to lose effective control of the prison, or where such a step is necessary in the interests of preserving the safety of any person or preventing any serious damage to any property.[24]

These statutory rights of the authority are usually acknowledged and accepted within the terms of the project agreement.

### 3.24 Dispute resolution

The project agreement will always contain detailed provisions enabling resolution of disputes, enabling parties to elevate disputes from a stage of mutual negotiation, through expert determination or adjudication to arbitration.

On UK prison projects, the authorities have been very reluctant to allow disputes to be resolved by litigation, as there is a concern that highly confidential information (eg, designs and operational procedures) may enter the public domain.

However, the dispute resolution mechanism on French prison projects (which do not involve any operational services being provided) contains dispute resolution clauses permitting disputes to be referred to the relevant competent court.

## 4. Payment mechanisms

### 4.1 Outline of payment structures

The following is a summary of a typical payment mechanism for a prison PPP project, based on the UK model, in which the contractor provides full services to the prison facility.

Payments are made on a monthly basis from the actual opening date.

The monthly payments are calculated as follows:
- available prisoner place payments;
- plus additional prisoner place payments;
- minus performance deductions;
- plus escort payments;
- plus/minus other adjustments (eg, insurance cost sharing payments).

---

24   See, for example, the Criminal Justice Act 1991, Section 88 (in respect of English prisons) and Section 111 of the Criminal Justice and Public Order Act 1994 (in respect of Scottish prisons).

*(a)* *Available prisoner places*

The 'core' payment made to the contractor is based on the number of available prisoner places provided by the contractor on each day during the relevant month, up to the maximum specified number. The payment per prisoner place per day comprises various components, including:
- the availability fee (which is not indexed);
- the indexed cost fee (which is indexed by reference to RPI); and
- a separate indexed cost fee (which is indexed by reference to RPI plus a fixed inflator).

In addition, a number of English (as compared to Scottish) prison projects also have a separate component of the payment per prisoner place per day relating to utility charges.

If the contractor provides all of the required prisoner places on each date during the month, the contractor will be paid the core payment, regardless of whether such available prisoner places are used by prisoners.

*(b)* *Additional prisoner places*

In addition to being paid for the specified number of available prisoner places, the contractor will also be paid for any additional prisoner places which are used by the authority. The contractor is typically obliged to provide a specified number of additional prisoner places, if and when required by the authority, and the contractor will be paid for these prisoner places only in the event that they are used from time to time. The payment for each additional prisoner place provided will be based on the marginal costs of providing such additional prisoner places.

*(c)* *Performance deductions*

The contractor will receive a reduced monthly payment in the event that it fails to provide available prisoner places when required. In addition, the project agreement will contain a performance measurement system which will specify a number of performance measures. In the event that any performance measure occurs, the contractor will incur performance points. If, in any quarter, the number of performance points incurred exceeds a base level, then further performance deductions will be made from the next monthly payment based on the number of performance points arising.

Performance points are calculated on a quarterly basis and a certain degree of tolerance is built into the payment mechanism by including an allowable 'base level' of performance points. If the number of performance points does not exceed the base level in any month, no Performance deduction will be made. Performance deductions are typically capped at a level equal to 5% of the overall unitary payment.

*(d)* *Escort payments*

In the event that the contractor also provides escort services, the contractor will be paid for these services separately under the payment mechanism. These payments for escort services will be calculated by reference to a unitary charge per mile travelled or per prisoner escorted.

*(e)* ***Adjustments***
Finally, the payment mechanism will also contain a number of adjusting payments. For example, in the event that insurance costs fall outside agreed parameters, an adjusting payment in respect of any excess insurance savings or excess insurance costs will also be made.

## 4.2 Availability v usage payments

On the UK prison PPP projects, where the contractor provides the requisite number of available prisoner places, the contractor is entitled to be paid for those places, regardless of whether the authority is able to supply prisoners to occupy the relevant cells. This position applies in respect of the base number of cells to be provided by the contractor, and therefore it can be said that the contractor is being paid on an 'availability' basis, rather than on a 'usage' basis.

In addition to being required to provide the base number of available prisoner places, the contractor is also required to provide additional prisoner places. The number of additional prisoner places is usually between 10% and 15% of the base number of available prisoner places. The contractor is typically paid for these additional prisoner places on a usage basis, as and when the authority uses these cells. The payments for these additional prisoner places are not generally taken into account in the base case financial model, as these payments are not guaranteed and therefore cannot be relied upon to meet debt service obligations.

Several of the UK prison projects have introduced a small element of demand risk (in respect of up to 5% of the available prisoner places), although this is usually resisted by the sponsors and funders for both financial and political reasons. It is therefore believed unlikely that demand risk will be passed to the private sector in the future.

## 4.3 Penalties/deductions

There are various deductions which can be made from the monthly payments to the contractor, as follows:
- availability deductions;
- performance deductions; and
- specific contractual deductions.

As the contractor is paid on the basis of each available prisoner place provided, there are no separate availability deductions under the payment mechanism. Instead, a failure by the contractor to provide an available prisoner place results in a loss of payment for that prisoner place. This therefore acts as a form of availability deduction.

Performance deductions are calculated on the basis set out under section 4.1 and cover matters such as:
- failure to submit reports by the due date;
- disciplinary infringements;
- assaults;
- self harm;
- drug offences; and
- breaches of security.

These deductions are capped at 5% of the overall contract fee and there is a degree of in-built tolerance of certain disciplinary offences through the use of an acceptable 'baseline total' of performance points.

Escapes from prison or from escort are penalised by means of specific monetary penalties payable by the contractor to the authority.

In addition, where the contractor fails to provide an additional prisoner place after being required to do so, separate monetary financial penalties will usually apply.

## 5. Key risks and issues

### 5.1 Overview

This section highlights a number of key risks which are of particular concern in the prison sector. In addition to the risks described below, prison PPP projects also involve analysis and management of critical risks which are also found across a variety of other sectors on projects of this nature. Such risks include those relating to:
- access and title issues;
- site and site conditions;
- contamination;
- maintenance and lifecycle works;
- utilities/rates;
- all financing risks, including interest rate hedging risk;
- insurance (including solvency of insurers, depth of the insurance market and recovery risks); and
- solvency and performance of subcontractors.

These risks are typically managed on prison projects in the same manner as they would be addressed in other sectors. Accordingly, these risks are not specifically addressed in this section.

### 5.2 Planning

Planning risk is particularly acute in this sector, due to the politically sensitive nature of these projects and the reluctance of local communities to accept the development of a prison in their neighbourhood. On the other hand, prison projects provide significant employment opportunities and are therefore generally situated in undeveloped or deprived areas of the country.

Due to concerns over planning risk, funders will generally require detailed planning permission and all planning conditions to be satisfied prior to financial close and, where appropriate, any judicial or other review process to have expired, before financial close takes place and financing is made available for the project.

### 5.3 Design and construction interface

Although the design and construction risks are very similar to a number of other sectors in which PPP projects are carried out, the interface between design and construction is particularly acute on prison projects.

The design of prison facilities is operationally driven and therefore the involvement of the operator in developing the design of the prison, and in approving and determining the materials and equipment to be used in the construction of the facility, is critical to ensure that the facility can be operated and maintained in the manner intended.

While wear and tear and damage to other facilities (eg, hospitals, schools and other government accommodation) is generally accidental, in the prison sector the design and construction needs to take account of the potential for deliberate damage and misuse of the prison facilities and equipment. Accordingly, the manner and timing of operational input into the design and construction process must be carefully managed by all project participants.

It is for this reason that many of the consortia which bid for prison projects are led by operational companies.

## 5.4 Custodial services

The provision of custodial services is a particular risk unlike any other encountered in other PPP sectors.

The usual approach taken by the private sector is that contractors, subcontractors and funders are prepared to accept risks which are able to be managed and controlled. As a result, contractors and funders are normally reluctant to take responsibility for third parties outside their control. This would normally include patients and clinical staff (on hospital projects), students and teachers (on schools projects) and public transport users (on transport projects).

It is therefore unusual for a contractor to take responsibility for the actions of prisoners, although this is a critical risk which is always borne by the contractor on prison projects of this nature.

These risks are normally managed by:
- building in a certain resilience in the physical prison infrastructure, through the design and construction process;
- ensuring staff are trained to manage prisoners and provide the right level of support;
- drafting the operational requirements in such a way that the contractor takes responsibility only for those actions of prisoners which are manageable in some way; and
- ensuring that any potential liability or deductions are kept to a minimum by, for example, ensuring a certain tolerance within the payment mechanism.

## 5.5 Security

The provision of security services is a critical area of prison operation. Security risks are managed throughout the design, construction and operation phases, by ensuring effective coordination of all of these activities so as to minimise the risk of any security lapses and manage the exposure in the event that a security lapse does occur.

## 5.6 Operating costs

Cost fluctuation during the operations phase is perhaps the biggest risk, given the lack of effective benchmarking or market testing during the life of the project.

As indicated above (see section 4.1), the payment mechanism divides the price per prisoner place per day into three (or on some projects, four) components, each of which is subject to a different indexation formula.

The contractor's ability to index that part of its fee which is referable to employment costs at a rate which exceeds RPI provides a certain degree of revenue protection in respect of employment and pension costs, which typically rise at a level above RPI. However, as the benchmarking/market-testing arrangements on prison projects do not operate in the same way as in other sectors and do not provide the contractor with the ability to re-price the services on a regular basis, the contractor will be exposed to risks such as:

- general changes in law affecting the cost of providing the services;
- changes to laws or regulations affecting tax rates, employment or pension costs;
- inaccurate estimation of the proportions of operating costs represented by wages, as compared to non-wage costs;
- any mismatch between RPI and the actual cost of providing services; and
- changes in the costs which are not passed down to the operator (eg, insurances, administration and management costs).

## 5.7 Demand risk

Funders and sponsors on prison projects have typically shunned demand risk on the basis that it would be politically unacceptable for the private sector to have a vested interest in the incarceration of prisoners and conviction rates. Accordingly, with several limited exceptions the payment mechanisms on prison PPP projects are based solely on payments being made in return for the contractor providing available prisoner places, whether or not such places are used.

The only demand risk taken by the private sector is in relation to additional prisoner places which are required from time to time by the authority. Where such places are needed, the payment in respect of such places is structured so as to cover the marginal costs of housing such prisoners. Any such revenues are not taken into account in establishing the base case financial model.

## 6. Financing arrangements

### 6.1 Types of financing available

Although capital markets financing is fairly common for PPP projects generally, prison projects have not to date been financed in the United Kingdom through bond issues. This is due partially to the less conventional risk profile of these projects as well as the requirement for greater flexibility, which is not generally a feature of bond financed projects.

All of the prison projects carried out in the United Kingdom to date, with one exception,[25] have been financed through the use of bank financing.

The size of the PPP prison projects carried out to date means that the amount of debt required is still at the lower end of what would be acceptable for a bond issue, although there is no particular reason why prison projects cannot be financed through the capital markets at some stage in the future.

## 6.2   Key financing concerns

*(a)   Limited market for contractors/operators*

Funders will always want to ensure that mechanisms are in place to enable subcontractors to be replaced if and when required due to insolvency or poor performance. However, the market for prison operators is relatively limited, which makes it more difficult for the funders to replace a construction subcontractor or operator where this is necessary in order to remedy any default and ensure the project remains viable.

Funders will therefore need to ensure that the balance sheet and financial viability of any key subcontractors are sufficiently robust to underpin the financing of these projects, and that appropriate contingency plans are in place in the event that a key subcontractor needs to be replaced.

*(b)   Restriction on step-in rights*

Funders on PPP projects have a limited ability to secure their interest and need to rely primarily on their ability to step into the project (under the terms of the direct agreement) and remedy any default which has occurred. While this is relatively straightforward in most PPP sectors, the willingness of the authority to step into the project following an operating default on a prison project interferes with the funders' own step-in rights.

The authority's step-in rights (either immediate prior to termination or pursuant to its statutory rights during the operations phase) need to be carefully drafted to ensure that these do not interfere with the funders' ability to manage any defaults which arise.

## 6.3   Refinancing

In the United Kingdom, only one 'traditional' refinancing has been carried out to date.[26] This was the subject of a report carried out by the National Audit Office and, as a result, it has been more difficult in this sector to refinance the senior debt due to the political sensitivity surrounding this first refinancing.

While the media is generally comfortable with contractors enhancing their returns through refinancing accommodation projects, the ability of sponsors to earn above-market returns from providing prison facilities appears less politically palatable.

---

25   One of the UK prison projects was financed by one of the sponsors through use of its corporate financing facility, although the project was subsequently refinanced.
26   See the National Audit Office report titled "The Refinancing of the Fazakerley PFI Contract", published on June 29 2000.

As a result, the market for refinancing prison projects is still fairly limited.

## 7. International perspective

### 7.1 Overview of private sector involvement in prison infrastructure
As indicated under section 1.4, the particular structure adopted by various different countries will be dictated by a variety of factors, including political considerations.

As a result, in the international context a variety of models have been adopted for the development of private prison infrastructure, ranging from mere operation and maintenance arrangements to full service models, such as that which has been adopted by the UK government and is described in this chapter.

It is not possible within the scope of this chapter to give specific details of the various models used in each country which has decided to use the private sector to assist in the development of prison infrastructure. However, we have attempted to outline below the various models that are common and the jurisdictions in which these are found.

### 7.2 Full service model
The full service model, involving design, construction, financing, maintenance, operation and custodial services, has been adopted primarily in the United Kingdom, Australia, South Africa, the United States and, to an extent, Israel.

In the United States, there are a large number of private prisons, only some of which have been developed on a PPP basis. Many other private prisons have been developed by prison operators without the benefit of a long-term concession or PPP arrangement. In these cases, facilities have been built on a speculative basis and then prison places provided to the relevant state authorities for use on a 'call-off' basis as and when required.

In the United Kingdom, Australia and South Africa, however, a similar full services model has been adopted, with the appropriate authorities awarding long-term PPP contracts to the private sector.

### 7.3 Full services (save for custodial and operational services)
This model involves the contractor carrying out all design, construction and maintenance obligations as well as financing the development of the prison. The relevant agreement does not require the contractor to provide custodial services or security.

This model has been adopted on a number of prison projects in France, in particular, where political considerations and the prevailing legal framework would effectively prevent the government involving the private sector in the provision of custodial services. In France, this model also involves the contractor providing utilities, cleaning, waste management and gardening services; however, the contractor is not responsible for soft facilities management such as provision of health services, catering, laundry, training, custodial activities or transport.

In France, there is an ongoing programme for the development of new prisons, which are typically let in batches.

The provision of key functions within the prison (including security and custodial activities) is strictly prohibited from being delegated to the private sector under French law.

It appears that the first Irish prison PPP project will also adopt a similar model to that used in France, although the tender process for this project is ongoing. It is expected that various other European countries may adopt a similar model.

## 7.4 Hybrid models

The development of private prison infrastructure is still in its infancy in a number of European and other jurisdictions. It is therefore expected that a number of hybrid models will emerge, depending on the political and financial objectives of the relevant authority.

One hybrid model being considered is the design, construction and financing of a prison, together with the operation and maintenance (but with operation and maintenance being provided only for a five-year period). The theory behind such a hybrid model is that the structure achieves the same efficiencies by combining design, construction and operations within the one contract, but without the contractor having to price and manage long-term operational risk. As a result, the authority would re-tender the services every five years, so as to obtain the most economic price for these services and rebase this price on a regular basis.

## 7.5 Operation and maintenance only

Although it is strictly outside the scope of a chapter on PPP structures, a number of prison authorities have also let short-term (eg, five-year) contracts for the operation and maintenance of former public sector prisons. The intention behind such structures is to encourage private-sector management techniques within these facilities and to capitalise on efficiencies which this may bring to the operation of these facilities.

Many private sector operators have, however, expressed certain reservations regarding the operation of outdated prisons, given the difficulty of efficiently and effectively operating such institutions without the benefit of having designed such facilities and given the physical state of these prisons.

## 8. Conclusion

Although the involvement of the private sector in the development of public infrastructure is always of some political interest and often controversial, the use of PPP procurement and management techniques and structures to develop prison infrastructure is one of the more controversial areas which has been considered by politicians across a number of jurisdictions.

The structure and negotiation of these contracts require an understanding of the political, financial and operational drivers behind the projects.

As these factors differ from country to country, the models which have been adopted in each such country vary and there is no 'correct' model for the development of prison infrastructure. The success or otherwise of private sector involvement in the provision of prison places is likely to become apparent only over the next 10 or 15 years, as more such facilities are developed and the various models which have been adopted can be compared and contrasted. Inevitably, however, some models will be more successful than others.

# Education

Frank Suttie
Giles Taylor
Beachcroft LLP

## 1. Introduction

This chapter is concerned with education public-private partnerships (PPPs) in all their shapes and forms.

First, it considers the provision of education in the United Kingdom, which will help to give an understanding of the framework within which UK education PPPs operate. The urgency of the need to modernise education facilities is not unique to the United Kingdom and the position in other parts of the world is briefly noted. The chapter then considers schools Private Finance Initiative (PFI) projects in the United Kingdom, the differences from accommodation-based PFI projects in other sectors and the impact of the new Building Schools for the Future (BSF) programme. Finally, it looks at education PPPs outside of UK schools PFI and BSF.

## 2. Background to UK education PFI and PPP projects

### 2.1 Introduction

Attempting to describe, in detail, the entire education system in the United Kingdom is well beyond the scope of this chapter. Discussion of England alone would involve the split between the state and independent sectors, at least six different stages of education through which a student may pass and, within just the state system, upwards of seven different types of school. Add the differences that exist within the school systems in Scotland, Wales and Northern Ireland and the task becomes Herculean. Even if the system were to be comprehensively set out, this would be an ephemeral achievement: successive governments have routinely tinkered with, overhauled and added to the UK education system, and no doubt this will continue.

Instead, we look at the basics of the English system, focusing on compulsory education up to the age of 16 where most of the education PFIs/PPPs have taken place. Where appropriate, major differences from Scotland, Wales and Northern Ireland are noted.[1] The aim is to give a participant in the UK education PPP market a firm grounding in the basic terrain in which he is working, if not the exact conditions underfoot. There is an emphasis on the legal framework and how that may impact on PPP arrangements.

---

1   However, these are only very briefly dealt with and would need to be considered separately. By and large, the schools system in Wales is most similar to the English system, although even there important differences exist.

Education

Throughout a person's life, education and learning shapes his wellbeing and opportunities. Early on, education is compulsory and more structured. However, as children grow older they are exposed to a wider range of educational opportunities, many of which are voluntary. Increasingly, there is a focus on continuing education throughout adulthood and a wider role to be played within the community by the education system.

As we are concerned with PPPs, we will largely ignore the traditional independent school sector and concentrate on state-provided education, and in particular the provision of compulsory education. However, this distinction is increasingly hard to identify. For example, universities are today much more like private sector companies and the move towards giving more independence to schools, as manifested by the advent of foundation schools (including trust schools) and academies, has further blurred the distinction.

**Overview of the education system in England[2]**

| Age | Institutions | Stage |
|---|---|---|
| 3 | Nursery schools | Pre-school |
| 4 | Primary schools | Primary school |
| 5 | | |
| 6 | | |
| 7 | | |
| 8 | | |
| 9 | Middle schools | |
| 10 | | |
| 11 | | |
| 12 | Secondary schools | Lower secondary education |
| 13 | | |
| 14 | | |
| 15 | | |
| 16 | | |
| 17 | Sixth-form colleges / Further education colleges / Secondary schools with sixth forms | Upper secondary education |
| 18 | | |
| 19 | Universities and other higher education institutions and further education institutions | Higher education and further education |
| 20 | | |
| 21 | | |
| 21+ | | Adult education |

The secretary of state for education is responsible for education policy in England.[3] The secretary of state and the Department for Education and Skills (DfES)

---

[2] Broadly the same system exists within Scotland, Wales and Northern Ireland, with compulsory education up to the age of 16, but with variations and differences of terminology.

[3] In Scotland, Wales and Northern Ireland, responsibility has been devolved to the Scottish Executive Education Department, the Welsh Assembly Department of Training and Education and the Department of Education in Northern Ireland (since suspension of the Northern Ireland Assembly on October 14 2002), respectively.

strongly influence the way in which education is provided through legislation[4] which includes detailed provisions relating to the standards and characteristics that school premises should have.[5]

The provision of primary and secondary school education is largely the responsibility of local authorities. There are 150 authorities with education services responsibility across England,[6] with similar arrangements applying in Wales and Scotland. Northern Ireland provides education through statutory education and library boards. Local authorities are responsible for ensuring that sufficient spaces are available in their area for all students of compulsory education age.

'Further education' refers to any education for students post-age 16 which is aimed at qualifications which are sub-degree level. Therefore, while further education in the sense of A-level qualifications is the normal entry route to higher education, in many cases further education is vocational-based learning and does not lead to higher education, or is an alternative to higher education for older students and adults. Further education is generally overseen by the Learning and Skills Council through the provision of financial support for school sixth forms, sixth-form colleges, further education colleges and a number of other education providers.[7] The white paper entitled "Further Education – Raising Skills, Improving Life Chances" and published in March 2006 proposes major changes to the further education sector. To date, PPP projects in the further education sector (other than schools projects) have been limited.[8]

The distinction between higher education and further education can be difficult to draw but, broadly, 'higher education' means education to degree-level standard. This includes undergraduate and postgraduate study and some professional qualifications. Courses are available at universities, colleges, institutions of higher education (including teacher training) and institutions of further education. In England, universities are funded through the Higher Education Funding Council for England, their own revenue-raising activities and investments and student fees.[9]

---

| | |
|---|---|
| 4 | The key education acts are the School Standards and Framework Act 1998 and the Education Act 2002 (although there are numerous other pieces of primary and secondary legislation). In addition, there a number of initiatives and other pieces of legislation which affect children and young people, such as the Children Act 2004, the Every Child Matters Agenda and children's trusts; it is important to have regard to these to understand the wider context within which education sits. |
| 5 | The Education (School Premises) Regulations 1999 SI 1999/2. Note that there is also legislation relating to disposal of school playing fields and shortly to be implemented legislation imposing standards for school meal provision. |
| 6 | In Scotland, there are 32 local authorities; Wales has 22 local education authorities and Northern Ireland has five education and library boards. |
| 7 | In Scotland, the Scottish Further and Higher Education Funding Council (SFC) is the body that distributes funding for teaching and learning, research and other activities in Scotland's colleges (and universities). There are 43 colleges and 20 higher education institutions in Scotland funded by the SFC. In Northern Ireland, the Department of Employment and Learning oversees and funds the statutory further education sector. The 16 further education colleges are free-standing incorporated bodies and are due to merge into six larger colleges. |
| 8 | Approximately 20 projects with a capital value of around £190 million. |
| 9 | In Scotland, the SFC referred to above funds the Scottish higher education institutions. In Wales, the equivalent body is the Higher Education Funding Council for Wales. In Northern Ireland, the Department of Employment and Learning currently oversees and funds higher education institutions. |

Education

## 2.2 Duty to provide compulsory education

The compulsory education system is typically organised within two tiers – primary and secondary. Primary schools may also have 'early years' facilities such as nursery schools and it is a small step to joined-up facilities of a collaborative nature between the health and education sectors such as Sure Start facilities, which are aimed at providing the best possible start for young children in areas of deprivation.

In a few parts of the country there are three tiers of compulsory education service, with middle schools taking pupils from primary schools at year five up to pre-General Certificate of Secondary Education at year 10. Many local authorities in recent years (eg, Bradford) have systematically removed their middle schools, but a number of local authorities still maintain that the benefits of this system outweigh disadvantages such as potential staff recruitment difficulties and, arguably, increased operating costs for their education services.

Local authorities are required to make particular provision for children with special educational needs and will usually seek to do so through special schools established for that purpose.[10]

An important point to appreciate in the collaborative nature of the UK education system are the roles played by faith-based schools and also the provision of independent but state-maintained foundation schools – both of which have been allowed to continue in conjunction with local authority overall management of the education system. With the exception of schools developed under the government's academies initiative (explained in more detail below), all state schools are 'maintained' by the local authority. This involves the provision of an annual budget for expenditure covering salaries, consumables, energy, rates and other charges, as well as the costs of maintaining the school facilities.

## 2.3 Financing the education system

DfES[11] is responsible for ensuring that the education system is properly financed. The stream of funding that comes through that department will cover both revenue expenditure and capital expenditure (in the form of grants and support for borrowing by the local authority) and, of course, support for the costs of a PFI project.

The manner in which a local authority then spends money on schools – in particular, the extent to which it makes money available for schools to utilise through their delegated budget – has been a matter of some controversy in recent years, with the government threatening periodically to remove the funding role of the local authority, with DfES then stepping in to provide funding directly to schools.

Local authorities are responsible for capital expenditure spent on maintained schools, with the exception of those that have voluntary aided status. Local authorities are assisted in making that investment through grants and support for local authority borrowing provided by DfES. Voluntary aided schools are dealt with

---

10  Increasingly, however, special needs pupils are integrated within mainstream education – particularly through co-location of facilities.
11  In Scotland, Wales and Northern Ireland, the principles of central government funding to local authorities with delegation to individual schools are also present. However, the arrangements differ in each case and significant differences exist.

separately – typically receiving 90% of relevant capital expenditure directly from DfES with a 10% contribution (this can be waived or contributed to by the local authority) from diocesan or other sponsoring bodies. Where a chapel or other 'non-educational' facility exists on a voluntary aided school site, the responsibility for the upkeep of this separate facility lies entirely with the diocesan body and the school governing body.

This allocation of responsibility (designed to ensure that the diocesan and other 'foundation' bodies continue to make a financial commitment to voluntary aided schools) has been effectively put to one side in the BSF programme, with DfES providing 100% support for capital costs.

### 2.4 Categories of school

There are a number of categories within which schools are classified.[12] A given category of school will have varying characteristics in the following areas:

- the constitution of the governing body – ability to appoint governors to the governing body can vary from category to category;
- whether staff are employed directly by the school or the governing body;
- how admissions criteria for the school are set and how they operate. Schools are expected to admit pupils into the school up to a pre-determined maximum number – if applications exceed that number, the admissions criteria will determine who is admitted. There are rights of appeal against decisions of the body that is designated as the admissions body for the schools concerned;
- ownership of the school and any playing fields, and the possibility of trustees having an interest – the position concerning foundation and voluntary aided schools is notable as schools in these categories typically have trustee interests in respect of the school site; and
- sources of capital for developing the school – for all but voluntary aided schools, capital is funded through the local authority.

Following consultation, the school organisation committee[13] has responsibility for provisions regarding continuance of the school, its expansion or even closure, changes in numbers of pupils and relocation or merger with another school.

Distinctions that exist between these categories are summarised in the table overleaf.

Current legislation (particularly as a consequence of the Local Government (Contracts) Act 1997) makes it possible for local authorities to participate in education PFI transactions. Such arrangements can extend to all categories of maintained school described above, enabling foundation and voluntary aided schools to participate. In all cases, however, the local authority will require the agreement of the governing body to the arrangements as explained below.

---

12  See Part 2 of the School Standards and Framework Act 1998, which established the new framework for school organisation.
13  Under the current Education and Inspections Bill it is intended that school organisation committees will be abolished.

Education

| Type of school[14] | Outline description |
|---|---|
| Community | Schools owned and operated by the local authority. |
| Foundation | Local authority funded, but in other respects independent of the local authority. Foundation schools receive capital investment through the relevant local authority. |
| Voluntary aided | Schools promoted by typically faith organisations such as Anglican, Roman Catholic and Jewish religions. |
| Voluntary controlled | Previously voluntary aided but brought into local authority control. |
| City technology college | The 2002 Education Act provided for these secondary schools. By agreement with the sponsor, these have typically become academies. |
| Academy | Independent (usually) secondary schools supported by DfES. Pupils are admitted without charge. Any outgoings are met through DfES funding and sponsor contributions. They are not accordingly regarded as local authority 'maintained' schools. |
| Trust[15] | Not a new category but instead a designation for schools that transfer to foundation status. |
| Special education needs[16] | These schools are to provide for pupils with special educational needs. There is a move to integrate these pupils into mainstream education, which has led to the closure of some such schools. |

2.5 **Composition and role of school governing bodies[17]**

Governing bodies of all maintained schools are corporate bodies created under education legislation. The governing bodies for community schools (including special and maintained nursery schools) fall into this category. Schools that have a foundation or are voluntary controlled or voluntary aided are corporate bodies with exempt charitable status (technically they will be regarded as excepted charities when the new charities legislation comes into effect).

---

[14] While schools in Wales broadly follow the same categories as England, significant differences exist in Scotland and Northern Ireland. In Scotland, the curriculum is not set by law, which gives greater freedom to local authorities and schools. There are mainstream comprehensive schools as well as denominational schools (mostly Roman Catholic) and some Gaelic medium schools. In Northern Ireland, secondary education is largely selective, with pupils going to grammar schools or secondary schools according to academic ability. There is a large voluntary school sector and Catholic maintained schools. There is a current initiative to create more integrated education.

[15] As proposed in the Education and Inspections Bill.

[16] One example of a special education needs school is a pupil referral unit which provides for children not otherwise in mainstream education, for example as a result of being excluded from school.

[17] Scotland, Wales and Northern Ireland all have broadly similar bodies, although in Scotland the reference is to school boards. Later references to powers of the governing body under the Education Act 2002 will apply only to England and in some cases Wales.

The precise membership of a school governing body varies with each type of school. Membership can comprise all or some of the following categories of individual:
- parents of pupils at the school;
- local authority-appointed governors;
- school staff;
- nominees of the school's foundation (where relevant); and
- community governors (appointed to represent community interests).

Governing bodies have been incorporated since the Education Act 1996. Prior to that time, individual governors acted as such and made their decisions collectively, but with a significant degree of personal responsibility for the decision concerned. With incorporation, the liability of an individual governor is now significantly reduced. Where a governing body exceeds its powers at law, no specific liability is imposed upon individual governors, although in acting as a governor every governor must be clear that he should avoid conflicts of interest and must act reasonably in participating within decisions taken.

A governing body is entitled to delegate functions unless delegation is prohibited by law.

For many years now, governing bodies have been given considerable flexibility in the use of financial resources available to the school for its maintenance. Subject to certain exceptions (eg, when a school is in special measures), a budget for the school will be established as required by law and funded through the local authority, but with considerable discretion for the governing body to determine its application across a range of expenditure for which that school is responsible.

Thus, it follows that individual schools can make decisions to apply funding in different directions. For example, choices will exist regarding the extent to which staffing is funded as opposed to additional maintenance of the school (eg, redecorating and planned maintenance).

An important issue in the context of PFI transactions is that since the governing body is funded to make its own decisions as to the extent to which it requires facilities management services including maintenance services associated with its accommodation, these arrangements do not sit well with a PFI transaction under which a unitary charge is payable for serviced accommodation. How can the local authority ensure an affordable transaction where by law it is obliged to give the governing bodies discretion in the use of their budget?

The answer lies in the entering into of a contractual arrangement between the governing body and a local authority, the terms of which provide for the governing body to agree to pay back to the local authority a proportion of its delegated budget based on a formula agreed and set out within the contract (typically known as the governing body agreement).

A key element of the government's education reforms has been to allow governing bodies greater flexibility and freedom in the conduct of the school. This has led to initiatives such as the development of extended schools, the development of innovative arrangements including federation of schools and greater cooperation between schools, both formal and informal.

## 2.6 Extended schools[18]

A key policy within DfES at the present time is to secure, over the next few years, a position under which all secondary schools (and, where appropriate, primary schools) play a more substantial role within the communities that they serve, utilising the school facilities out of normal hours. This extended school agenda is the subject of various policy documents (available through the DfES website), and is supported by changes in education law that have brought about a significant extension in the potential role played by a school governing body.

Under Section 27 of the Education Act 2002, a school governing body now has a specific discretionary power to arrange for the use of its facilities for purposes of a charitable nature. This is an important restriction on how the governing body should operate – the power has been conferred in conjunction with the extended school agenda and therefore the power does not extend to utilising the premises on a commercial basis. Governing bodies will be entitled to cover their costs of operation, but should not seek to make a commercial profit from the utilisation of the school out of hours, other than to fund the financial requirements of the school.

Where a PFI contractor wishes to take control of the school out of usual hours (eg, where it has guaranteed a minimum amount of commercial revenue within the PFI arrangements), care will have to be taken to ensure that, through the governing body agreement, the local authority places itself in a position to confer the exclusive rights to utilise facilities that the PFI contractor will require.

## 2.7 Federation and other innovative arrangements

Following the Education Act 2002, schools have the opportunity to work together more formally than ever before.

The concept of schools cooperating together is not new and existing arrangements (frequently called 'soft federation') continue. Essentially, soft federation is an informal arrangement under which schools provide resources to or share resources with each other.

The Education Act 2002 creates a new concept of hard federation – enabling several schools to be combined into a single constitutional entity under one governing body. Up to five schools can agree, without further approvals, to cooperate in arrangements of this kind – larger federations require the approval of the secretary of state, which will be given under a power for the schools concerned to apply for innovative practices.[19] Arrangements of this kind are increasingly being adopted across England, particularly in the context of campus developments comprising feeder primary, secondary and related special schools.

---

18  Scotland has a similar extended school programme. Wales has a less formal programme, but with similar principles. Northern Ireland has recently announced an extended schools programme with £10 million of funding.

19  A little-known power within the Education Act 2002 permits the secretary of state to approve arrangements under which school governing bodies enter into innovative arrangements that are calculated to enhance the position of the school. Successful schools have been encouraged to consider and, if appropriate, take advantage of this particular power. Essentially, the power allows governing bodies to work outside the confines of legislation that would otherwise limit the powers of the governing body to enter into, for example, commercial transactions.

## 3. Education PFI and PPP in other jurisdictions

### 3.1 Introduction

As is noted later in this chapter, a key driver for the ambitious school building programme on which the UK government has embarked is the urgent need to secure educational transformation with a view to attaining ever-higher quality of educational outcomes.

That transformation extends well beyond the buildings that students are taught in, going to the heart of the way students learn and the challenge and opportunity presented by technologies – both information and telecommunications.

In other words, the education system needs to catch up with and reflect, to the advantage of students and those involved in the teaching process, technologies now available to enhance the quality of the educational experience.

The need and desire for educational transformation are not unique to the United Kingdom – they present a challenge to all nations.

The parlous position that many education systems are in is ably summed up as follows:

*The state of the buildings in which teachers and students are required to work is nothing short of deplorable in many communities. There are literally hundreds of schools in Victoria with buildings designed 40 years ago with an expected life of 20 years, but they are still in use. The dreaded portable or demountable classroom is a common feature of schools in high growth corridors. Some schools and long-standing sturdy buildings are utterly dysfunctional as far as modern pedagogy is concerned because they were built on factory lines for standard class sizes and little flexibility as possible without costly renovation.*[20]

It follows that countries which have noted the progress made in the United Kingdom in the creation of various forms of PFI and PPP arrangement, and which have embraced this way of transforming public service infrastructure, inevitably look towards the model to see whether it can contribute to the modernisation of education facilities that is manifestly required.

The potential of the PFI and PPP model, and more generally, the potential for involvement of the private sector in education services, is even more profound if consideration is given to one of the key objectives found within the millennium development goals of the United Nations.

Goal Two is the achievement by 2015 of universal primary education so that children everywhere will be able to complete a full course of primary schooling. The achievement of this goal will in turn create significant demand within developing states for even higher levels of education, which will make even further demands on the infrastructure delivery arrangements within the country concerned.

---

20   "A new vision for public schools in Australia", Brian J Caldwell, Managing Director, Education Transformation PTY Limited.

## 3.2 PFI and PPP education projects in Europe

Many European countries have embraced the PFI model in an effort to drive up school building investment. For example, in the Netherlands, although projects of this kind were slow to develop initially, achievements are now being realised, with the first schools project having been concluded. Similar initiatives in Portugal, Italy and Greece also accommodate plans for education building programmes utilising PFI. Other EU member states are actively taking forward public sector investment plans that include provision of privately financed schools.

Particularly notable is Ireland, a nation that was among the earliest to identify the potential advantages of privately financed solutions, taking forward potential projects from the late 1990s onwards. UK bidders keen to see their businesses develop and achieve critical mass through investment overseas were eager to capture the opportunity presented and a number of schemes have now gone forward, including school rebuilding programmes.

The position in mainland Europe is not quite so straightforward. One interesting feature has been the inability of central government in many European states to develop coordinated initiatives across the entire country.

The legal and administrative arrangements under which communities are governed within many European countries differ very significantly from the position in the United Kingdom. Local autonomy frequently means that decisions as to whether to take forward proposals for new schools and for the rebuilding of schools with privately financed solutions are very much dictated by local political considerations and the willingness to promote enabling legislation.

A further factor to be taken into account is the basis on which a legal relationship is established between the public and private sectors. Early experience in the Netherlands involved the adoption of contractual principles effectively borrowed from the United Kingdom. For various reasons, this approach proved not to be the most effective, with recourse subsequently being had to the Dutch Civil Code. Now a PPP expertise unit is seeking to develop more customised standard documentation to assist in the efficiency of the procurement process.

However, the existence of the European Investment Bank has helped to encourage many decision makers to consider seriously privately financed solutions. The European Investment Bank (owned by the EU member states) now has an active programme of lending to schemes that lead to improvement and modernisation of education systems. With its ability to lend to private sector entities (including private finance concessionaires), the European Investment Bank has become a significant player within privately financed transactions. This is a significant advantage to the encouragement of such schemes, particularly to their affordability to the public sector.

## 3.3 Private finance in Australia

Australia is also recognised as a territory in which private finance has made considerable strides.

The Australian government was quick to identify the advantages of private finance as a contributor to public service and infrastructure development, and has taken forward schemes across various sectors, including education. One of the first projects to be completed involved a group of schools within the Sydney metropolitan area.

The model as adopted in Australia has considerable similarities to that within the United Kingdom. The government of New South Wales has actively promoted schemes involving two large (nine and 10-school) groups of projects known as the New South Wales Private Finance Project.

### 3.4 United States

The education system in the United States is in many respects very different from that in other areas in which private finance has been adopted to provide education facilities. Given the federal nature of the United States, individual states have their own autonomy in the delivery of education services. This involves many different models of school ownership and funding, but a noteworthy technique adopted across many states is to secure capital investment in the education system through the issue of public bonds which are sanctioned by a democratic vote within the communities to benefit from the bond issue, with the proceeds being utilised towards school investment activities.

The bonds are promoted by the relevant school board and achieve credit status through the ring fencing of local taxes that are raised to service the financial requirements of the bond.

While this model leads to achievement of capital investments, it necessarily requires considerable political support within the communities concerned because of the direct impact on taxation.

It is perhaps unsurprising that, given the increasing demand for modernisation of schools, many states are looking at the PFI model. Indeed, approximately 50% of all states have passed enabling legislation designed to accommodate new methods of delivering schools to include, where this is considered appropriate, a privately financed solution.

## 4. Education PPPs

### 4.1 Introduction

Education PFI/PPPs have covered a wide variety of different types of project. We have seen projects involving nurseries, primary schools, secondary schools, further education and higher education institutions. Generally, these projects have focused on providing accommodation and building related services rather than any core or even support teaching functions. However, we have also seen a number of projects which do go further. We have seen a number of education joint ventures which, while not providing teaching functions, do provide a number of services that support teachers and schools well beyond the bricks and mortar – the VT 4S joint venture with Surrey County Council, for example. In addition, beyond the schools sector there have been a number of training and outsourcing projects that could properly fall within the ambit of education PPPs.

We first look at the primary and secondary school building and maintenance programme under PFI in the United Kingdom, which is the most significant

Education

education PPP sector, and then move on to consider the impact of the BSF programme. Finally, we consider some other types of education PPP.[21]

## 4.2 Schools PFI

*(a)* *In general*

Schools PFIs began with the Sir John Colfox School in Dorset, which opened in September 1999. They continue today as a separate method of procurement in Scotland and Wales. However, in England,[22, 23] schools PFIs have now been subsumed within the BSF programme. While schools PFIs in England will still exist and form part of BSF, they are unlikely to be procured other than through the BSF programme.

Schools PFI projects in the United Kingdom[24] have been some of the largest and most successful. Since 1996 there have been approximately 140 schools PFI projects, with hundreds of schools built and maintained with a capital value in excess of £5 billion.[25] While England has seen the vast majority of the schemes, there have been significant numbers of projects in Scotland and, to a lesser extent, Wales and Northern Ireland.[26]

As in most most other sectors, the driver for schools PFI was the desire to introduce investment into public buildings in a manner that provided value for money and incentives to keep the buildings maintained to a high standard over the long term. Schools in the United Kingdom had suffered from underinvestment and it was recognised that school buildings were costly to maintain, unsuitable for modern teaching methods and a barrier to improving educational attainment.

There has been a wide variety of schemes in terms of the numbers of schools involved, the types of school and the level of new build compared to refurbishment works. As the sector has developed, projects involving multiple schools have increasingly become the norm (grouped school projects), as they provide better value for money.

The sector has been highly competitive, with over 30 different consortia involved and an active secondary equity market. The sector has survived a number of setbacks, including the failures of Ballast Wiltshire and Jarvis (probably the biggest schools PFI contractor at the time), but in terms of attracting new investment and delivering new buildings it must be seen as a success.

In many ways the schools sector is very similar to other PFI accommodation projects and many of the same procedures and standard form documents apply. The

---

21  International education PPPs were considered earlier in the chapter.
22  And to a certain extent Northern Ireland.
23  The last schools PFIs outside of BSF are currently in procurement, with Doncaster the last due to reach financial close.
24  As discussed already, schools in Scotland, Northern Ireland and Wales have devolved authority for PFI. Schools in England are now dealt with under BSF, although there may still be PFI projects within BSF.
25  Figures from the Partnerships UK projects database.
26  Scotland has approximately 20 projects, with a capital value of £1.4 billion. Wales has five projects, with a capital value of £113.9 million. Northern Ireland has three projects, with a capital value of £35 million (although Northern Ireland has a significant programme of investment planned). All figures from Partnerships UK Projects Database.

intention here is not to set out a summary of all the key PFI contract clauses or risks, but rather to focus on areas where the schools PFI project agreement differs from other accommodation projects or where there are areas giving rise to particular concerns. We also do not consider the procurement process for education PPPs.[27]

By way of background, the latest schools standard form of PFI project agreement is the 4Ps[28] version dated May 2005. In addition, the BSF standard-form schools PFI project agreement is also available and has a number of differences from the 4Ps document.[29]

While we are not attempting to describe in detail all the elements of a PFI project, in order to see the schools sector in context, it is helpful to summarise briefly a 'standard' PFI accommodation project.[30]

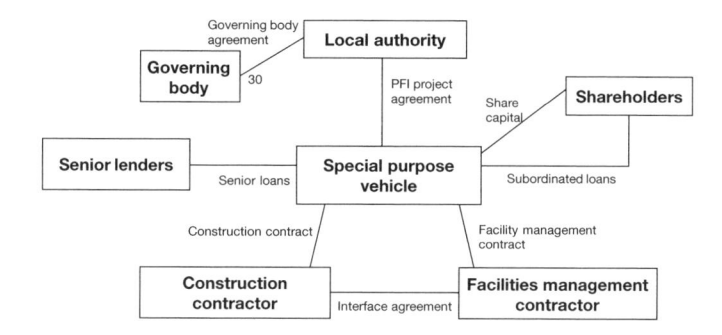

As with most accommodation PFIs, a consortium bids for the PFI project and then delivers the construction or refurbishment of school buildings through the establishment of a special purpose vehicle (SPV) and a subcontract with a construction company. On completion of the works, the special purpose vehicle maintains, through a facilities management subcontract, the buildings throughout the term of the project. In addition, the special purpose vehicle, through the facilities management subcontract, provides associated services such as cleaning, catering and grounds maintenance (some of these 'soft services' may be provided by the public sector).

A key feature of accommodation PFI is that the public sector pays the special purpose vehicle only from completion of the works and spreads the capital costs over the term of the project. This means that the special purpose vehicle secures funding

---

27   The procurement process will depend on the nature of the procuring authority. For local authorities, the process is in principle no different from other PFI schemes.
28   4Ps is a public sector advisory service that provides support to local authorities that are undertaking PFI/PPP transactions.
29   The latest BSF PFI agreement is on the Partnerships for Schools website and is the version issued in March 2006. It is likely in due course that the 4Ps version will adopt the changes. In any event, given that PFI in England will be procured only through BSF, the 4Ps version is largely redundant. Both the 4Ps and BSF PFI agreements have been endorsed by Partnerships UK as being consistent with Her Majesty's Treasury's Standardisation of PFI Contracts Version 3 (SoPC3) guidance.
30   The roles of the governing body and the governing body agreement were set out earlier in this chapter.

from equity investors[31] (usually 10% of the required funding) and from senior lenders such as banks or the capital markets (usually 90% of the required funding), and repays them over the life of the project from monies received from the public sector. As with most other accommodation PFI projects, another key feature is that the public sector pays only to the extent the school is available and services are correctly provided. Considerable time is spent defining the meaning of when areas of the schools are 'available' and the key performance indicators for measuring how services are performed. If these are not achieved, a payment mechanism translates the failures into a monetary amount which is deducted from the payment made to the SPV.

As a rule, under schools PFI it has not been practical on a value for money basis to transfer demand risk. By 'demand risk', we mean the risk that the public sector or end users do not want to use the building. So in the context of a school, even if classrooms are empty because there are insufficient pupils, then provided the SPV is meeting its contractual obligations to maintain the building and provide services, the public sector will be required to make payment in full.

However, in certain education sectors – notably student accommodation – there have been PPP arrangements which transfer some or all of the demand risk to the private sector.

There are also a number of key differences between the education and other PFI sectors.

*(b)* *Comparison with other accommodation PPPs*

*(i)* *Stakeholders*

Unlike some other forms of PFI where there is a single procuring authority and limited involvement from other parties, schools have a multitude of interested parties.

There are a huge number of interested parties, from central government (DfES) through to the local authorities and the governing bodies of schools to the head teachers, other members of teaching staff, unions, parents, pupils, the local community and cleaners and caretakers.

In addition, schools are particularly sensitive, being a front-line service. They interface with the public and do so in an area, alongside health, which has suffered from underinvestment and is very important to the public.

On top of this, as discussed earlier, there are many different types of school, each with different constitutional arrangements and structures, and governments regularly seek to introduce new structures[32] to help deliver better education.

*(ii)* *Purchaser/user split*

One of the effects of the school organisation in the United Kingdom is that, unlike most other PFIs, there is a split between the people procuring and contracting and paying for the PFI (the local authority) and those people using the school on a day-to-day basis (teachers and pupils).

---

31  The equity investors will require a return on their investment. In this regard, note the Argyll and Bute Schools PFI project, which is the first to include a not-for-profit structure.
32  For example, academies and trust schools.

While this is generally understood and well managed, it can give rise to certain problems. For example, schools and teachers are not always aware of the detail of contract negotiations and agreed specifications. This can lead to misunderstandings between the school and the SPV and its subcontractors.

*(iii)*    *Vandalism*

One risk of particular concern in schools projects is vandalism. Broadly, the public sector is responsible during the school day (subject to the benefit of insurances), but the private sector is responsible out of school hours – the issue being one of control. However, the drafting remains complex, and the private sector must comply with detailed notification requirements and demonstrate that it did not cause the loss and is subject to onerous rules as to proportionality.

Given that insurance is in place, the real issue is who bears the costs of the insurance deductible.

Issues also arise regarding damage caused by excluded pupils and visitors to the school.

*(iv)*    *Insurance*

"Arson attacks on schools are serious and frequent. 20 schools a week suffer an arson attack. A third of these happen during normal school hours. Around 90,000 children are affected by school arson each year."[33] Statistics of this sort have meant that insurance issues, such as unavailability and cost increases, are particularly acute in the schools sector. Until recently, Zurich Municipal was the only insurer in the UK schools PFI market.

Insurers are increasingly getting involved in design and often require safety features such as automatic sprinklers or no flat roofs in order to provide insurance or reduce premiums. Zurich has produced a design guide which helps to minimise the costs of insurance.

*(v)*    *Multi-site projects*

Another feature of many schools PFI projects is that they involve multiple numbers of schools and sites (grouped schools projects). Northampton schools PFI, for example, comprises 41 different schools.

While this is not necessarily an insurmountable challenge, and the private sector generally prefers bigger schemes, it does cause logistical issues in terms of additional resources, phasing of works and additional stakeholder involvement. Even though there may be a single procuring authority, there is a need to deal with each individual school and head teacher.

*(vi)*    *Soft services*

Along with other PFIs, there is a current debate as to whether asking the private sector to carry out soft services delivers value for money. Within schools in England there are particular issues in the standard of school meals. PFI contractors have found

---

33    Arson Prevention Bureau.

themselves subject to criticism for their catering.[34] Sometimes this criticism may be justified, but it is important to acknowledge that they are working to limited budgets set by the local authority, and that persuading children to eat more healthily requires input and determination from a number of people – not just school meal providers.

(vii) *Information and communications technology provision*

Information and communications technology is a key part of providing education, but other than provision of cabling it has not been a key part of schools PFI. However, BSF will seek to change this with a more integrated approach to IT and the provision of school buildings.

(viii) *Out-of-hours use*

Another feature of schools PFI is that the buildings and facilities are commonly used beyond the normal school day. This is encouraged because of the political desire to place schools at the heart of communities and the extended schools agenda. There is also the desire to generate third-party income from the use of school facilities, to help the affordability of the project.

This gives rise to a number of issues which must be carefully set out in the contract. Examples include:
- the costs of additional services needed to keep the schools open for longer;
- additional cleaning;
- what happens if damage is caused by third parties; and
- what happens if third-party income cannot be achieved (particularly as third-party income projections have often been optimistic).

Confirming which party will bear the risk in scenarios such as these is important to establishing a successful partnership.

(ix) *Term times and holidays*

Another feature of schools PFI is the impact of holidays on the programme of construction works and maintenance of the buildings.

As a rule, schools and other education establishments require handover of buildings some time in late summer to enable them to be ready for the start of the academic year in early September. This can cause problems if delays in closing the project cause the construction programme to move. This can lead to pressure on the contractors to reduce their build period, start on site early or delay the programme for a whole year, or for the local authority and schools to accept a handover at a different time – usually at the Christmas or Easter holidays.

In the context of maintenance, most programmes are based on the ability to have six weeks during the summer holidays to carry out maintenance works. From time to time, there is mention of amending the term times for schools and this could have an impact on the cost of maintenance and services required as well as the ability to carry them out.

---

34   The 'Jamie Oliver effect', after the well-known television chef.

*(x)    Other school-specific issues*
There are a number of other school-specific issues that sometimes cause problems:
- Working near children is clearly a sensitive issue and provisions dealing with police checks into employees' backgrounds and local authorities' rights to exclude individuals are particularly relevant.
- Sales of surplus land to generate income to assist with affordability issues are sensitive. In the case of sale of playing fields, this requires consent from the secretary of state.
- There are the usual concerns about the impact of construction works on the use of existing buildings. While this is in principle no different from other sectors, this can give rise to particular concerns given the proximity of children to the works, disruption of teaching and, in particular, disruption around exam time.
- Finally, although not just an issue for PFI procured schools, the impact of design on the functionality and performance of schools is critical. Teaching and learning methods are currently undergoing significant changes, and the ability of the design of the buildings and the integration of information and communications technology to support and improve educational outcomes is increasingly important.

## 4.3   Building Schools for the Future

*(a)    Background*

As mentioned previously, the schools PFI programme in England has been radically overhauled and now forms part of a more ambitious education programme called BSF.

Introduced in 2003, BSF is the government's programme for delivering a step-change in the standard of secondary school buildings.[35] BSF is a key part of the government's plans to improve educational attainment and social welfare for young people. The programme will be delivered through a partnership between the public and private sector. Its aims are impressive and ambitious. It will be the biggest investment in education for 50 years, and over the 10 to 15-year life of the programme all secondary schools in England will be renewed or rebuilt.

The scale of BSF allows the opportunity to move from an attitude of repair and make-do to one of rebuild and renewal, with a more strategic approach to funding, design and procurement of buildings.

BSF applies to all areas of England. Scotland and Wales are not included within its remit, although Northern Ireland has its own version of the programme. BSF is delivered in waves of approximately 10 local authorities each year, with funding and entry into a particular wave allocated to those local authorities most in need of investment based on relative educational and social need.

To help deliver the BSF programme, the government with Partnerships UK has set up an advisory body, Partnerships for Schools (PfS). PfS will support the government and local authorities in selecting areas to receive investment,

---

35    Now also to include primary schools.

developing innovative and effective models to streamline procurement and creating long-term public private partnerships to deliver the programme. As part of this process, PfS has established a number of framework advisory panels to help local authorities efficiently choose advisers that have the relevant knowledge and skills.

*(b)* *Aims*

The aims of BSF are ambitious and are matched by significant funding commitments. For 2005 to 2006, the capital investment for new building works and information and communications technology is £2.2 billion; this investment is repeated year on year throughout the life of the BSF programme. Investment for the initial projects has been committed, although funding for future projects will be subject to final confirmation in later government spending reviews.

The programme is split into areas based on all secondary schools within an individual local authority boundary. This focus on the whole of a local authority area can lead to fairly large differences in:

- the number of schools within an area;
- the current standard of school accommodation and levels of attainment;
- the educational visions of the local authorities;
- the local authorities' views of private sector involvement; and
- the particular challenges facing individual local authorities.

Given the potential differences between local authorities, it is imperative that the private sector treats each authority accordingly and provides a specifically tailored product.

Local authorities are required to make a submission to DfES to receive BSF funding. Funding applications for BSF projects will be assessed according to rigorous school improvement criteria and funding will not be released until the criteria have been met. This will require local authorities to consider including academies and other options for new schools in their plans. Depending on the make-up of a local authority, it may not receive all its funding in a single tranche. Some of its schools may be allocated funding in an early wave while others may not get funding until some years later.

For individual local authorities the size of the investment is significant, providing a once-in-a-lifetime opportunity to modernise their secondary school estates. For example, most of the initial local authorities have projects worth around £100 million of new works, which rises to several hundred million by the end of the BSF programme.

*(c)* *Differences from PFI*

Although each local authority has its own approach to BSF, the message from central government is clear. BSF is not PFI with a few minor tweaks; BSF is designed with educational transformation in mind and the provision of new buildings without a significant improvement in educational standards will be viewed as failure.

Although BSF involves massive construction projects, at its core is the desire to improve educational attainment. In the first wave of projects it has been acknowledged in some quarters that the projects brought to the market and the private sector responses have been too construction dominated. There is a central government desire to make sure future waves, while securing the delivery of the construction works, give a stronger focus to information and communications technology and educational provision. Those bidders that understand this and reflect it while listening to the needs of the individual local authorities will be the most successful in the long run. As a result, it is likely that the private sector will reconsider the make-up of its bidding consortia and look to place information and communications technology and education at the heart of their offering.

*(d)* *The strategic partnership*

BSF has introduced a new method of procurement through a strategic partnership. Through a tender process, a private sector partner will be selected by a local authority to form a local education partnership (LEP) with the local authority and PfS. The LEP will be responsible for assisting the local authority in developing its education vision and for procuring that necessary capital projects are carried out. The LEP will procure the required projects through a variety of means, such as PFI, design and build construction and long-term maintenance contracts. The exact mix of work will depend on the requirements of the individual local authority, although it is anticipated that about 50% of the work by value will be carried out through PFI. The LEP will be a dynamic organisation which will procure projects as and when the local authority is allocated funding, and which will be incentivised to seek out opportunities for new projects and innovative ways for the local authority to fund projects.

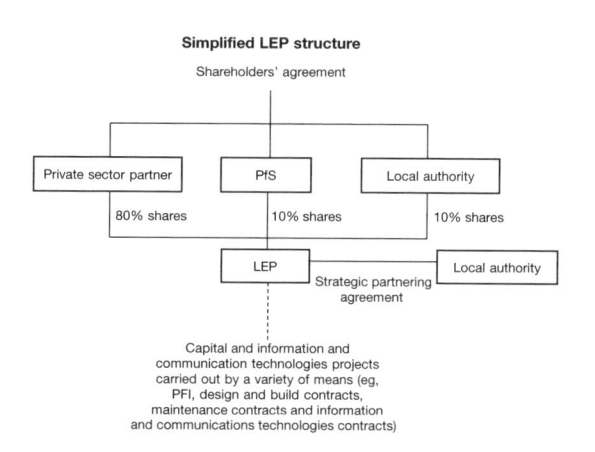

**Simplified LEP structure**

Shareholders' agreement

| Private sector partner | PfS | Local authority |
| --- | --- | --- |
| 80% shares | 10% shares | 10% shares |

LEP —— Local authority
Strategic partnering agreement

Capital and information and communication technologies projects carried out by a variety of means (eg, PFI, design and build contracts, maintenance contracts and information and communications technologies contracts)

There are standard form documents dealing with the setting up of the LEP and its relationship and obligations to the local authority. These are mainly set out in a strategic partnering agreement between the LEP and the local authority. A separate shareholders' agreement linked to an agreed business plan provides the working arrangements for the LEP. At the heart of the strategic partnering agreement, and what the private sector is fundamentally bidding for, is a 10-year exclusivity for the private sector partner to provide educational support services, design, construction, facility management and information and communications technology services in respect of major capital projects involving the secondary school estate within that local authority. The local authority, having committed to that exclusivity, receives through the strategic partnering agreement a number of protections for the local authority to ensure it receives value for money.

*(e)*   *A programme of investment*
For those familiar with the National Health Service (NHS) local improvement finance trust (LIFT) model there are a number of similarities within the LEP model. However, it is also true to say there are a significant number of differences. NHS LIFT and the LEP are illustrative of a general change in PPP procurement in the United Kingdom to programmes of investment which seek to achieve:
- a reduction in the procurement burden on the public sector;
- faster and cheaper procurement for future projects;
- greater value for money and efficiencies through a partnership between the public and private sector; and
- a vehicle that has the flexibility to bring together different funding streams and to integrate different projects while having a single point for making clear and consistent decisions as well as benefiting from economies of scale.

It is worth considering the benefits of an investment programme in more detail.

A programme of investment is generally structured so that it allows a more integrated and coordinated approach than a one-off procurement by a single authority. This coordinated approach applies across geographical areas, different public services and over a period of time. This enables a joined-up approach to strategic investment decisions so that different public sector bodies can coordinate their capital investments in the most efficient manner. In the context of BSF, a school co-located with health and social service provision would be a good example of an integrated approach.

Additionally, a programme of investment allows a number of projects to be 'batched' or brought together, particularly as the investment can be phased over a period of time. This has savings in procurement costs and makes the overall opportunity for the private sector more attractive. In many cases, particularly in NHS LIFT, the individual size of the projects would not justify a partnership arrangement, but when aggregated together they provide a cost-effective investment opportunity. In the case of BSF, while the individual projects are larger the batching approach creates a total investment opportunity in many cases well in excess of £100 million. In BSF, the LEP is a focus for the various investment opportunities. Over time, the LEP will enter into different projects: mostly secondary school PFIs and construction projects, but also information and communications technology projects and, potentially, health and regeneration schemes. In principle, there could be dozens of schemes over the 10-year life of the LEP. The number of schemes, in part, will be a measure of the success of the partnership between the public and private sector.

One of the key features of programmes of investment is that they have a 'national' and 'local' dimension. Nationally a body is needed – in the case of BSF, it is PfS – to manage the programme as a whole and enforce standardisation to ensure a common approach and procurement savings. Locally, the relevant public bodies – in BSF, the local authorities – apply the programme to their own area but reflecting the national approach.

While a programme of investment has many benefits, there are potential downsides:

- Complexity – with an integrated approach it is likely to it take longer to get public sector bodies to agree among themselves on the best way forward and this can lead to delays and additional costs.
- Local versus national approach – to procure efficiently, the programme needs to be rolled out in a consistent manner. However, local procuring authorities need to buy into this and national/local issues can cause tension. In BSF we have seen a number of variations on the 'standard' LEP model, even within the first few projects.
- Flexibility/uncertainty – while having a £200 million programme of investment is attractive to a private sector bidder, if in reality only, say, £70 million will be committed on day one, what is the level of efficiency savings that can be achieved? The private sector will be reluctant to take risks on public sector future investment decisions and so will be nervous about discounting its initial cost on the hope of getting future work. To the extent it does so, it may build in an additional cost to reflect the risk of not getting this work. In addition, the set-up and running costs of the programme can be significant, and if new projects do not come through as expected, this can cause financial problems. Given the complexity of individual projects, there may also be question marks about the procurement savings that can be achieved, particularly if the partnership is not working as well as had been hoped.

(f) *Scope of BSF*

A key feature of BSF, and one that cannot be underestimated, is the scope of BSF and the corresponding amount of integration that is required. This integration occurs at a number of levels, but critically it exists between the various services which the public sector requires to be provided; and it further exists within the supply chains of the private sector in how it delivers those services.

In respect of the services required by the public sector, BSF cannot be viewed in isolation: it sits within and alongside a number of wider government initiatives, such as the Every Child Matters strategy and the 14 to 19 initiative. As well as the more general government strategies, there are a number of issues within the existing education framework that impact on BSF. Two of the key issues are the integration into BSF of voluntary aided schools and academies. The Education and Inspections Bill introduced into Parliament in February 2006 provides for trust schools; these will be another layer that will need to be recognised within BSF. Different legal frameworks means that different approaches are needed to make these fit within BSF.

Another feature of the LEP is the ability for it to bring together funding streams and to deliver joined-up services with schools at the heart of a community. The BSF programme seeks to find ways of joining up funding with health and social services, to encourage the creation of facilities for the whole community.

In respect of the integration of the supply chain, the LEP will be the delivery mechanism for the local authority to help ensure that where projects are separately procured by the LEP they are able to function as a coherent whole, and that schools and the public sector are not overburdened by having to deal with multitudes of contractors. Particularly in the case of information and communications technology interfaces with construction and refurbishment works, this represents a significant challenge, and bidders and strong supply chain management and offerings which protect the public sector from interface issues will be well placed.

(g) *Current progress*

Significant progress has been made. The BSF programme is now firmly established: there are around 15 projects in the market, six at preferred bidder stage, and the first financial close has recently occurred.[36] There is also considerable private sector interest, with over 30 bidders and around 20 different shortlisted consortia.

However, there remain challenges ahead. Despite improvements, procurement still remains slow, especially when contrasted with the previous PFI schools programme. Bidding costs have been much higher than for grouped schools PFIs, and there is concern that there may be a lack of competition for future waves of BSF as bidders look for less expensive opportunities and smaller players are forced out of the market.

The government and PfS have recognised these concerns and are looking to address them. Where possible, they are looking to speed up procurement by bringing forward local authorities in later waves where they have a project that is ready for the market. They understand the issues around bid costs and are seeking to reduce these; they are also looking to make standardisation effective while ensuring local authorities understand the structure and are comfortable with it.

The next 12 months will be a critical time for the BSF programme. Wave 1 and pathfinder projects need to close to timetable and start delivering bricks in the ground and other benefits; Wave 2 and other programmes need to come to market to create some liquidity and also need to progress quickly and cost effectively through the procurement stage.

## 4.4 Other forms of education PPP

(a) *Private sector engagement in education service delivery – generally*

As noted earlier, education PFI and education PPP projects are largely about the buildings in which education services are provided. The delivery of the education service is left to the public sector to continue to provide.

In other words, the education sector has not (at least not yet) taken in a significant way the bold steps adopted within the NHS to involve the private sector in the actual delivery of services to the public.

---

36  Bristol BSF.

There are exceptions to this rule in certain parts of the education sector, as explained below. In addition, within this section we deal with the challenge presented where a certain element of the payment for the accommodation or other facilities is linked to tangible improvements in educational attainment or even demand for the service itself.

*(b)* *Payment by results*
In the early days of PFI there was considerable debate about whether the benefits to public service should be an element of the payment mechanism under which the private sector was paid. Without this element there is purely and simply infrastructure provision, with the public sector then left to provide the public services from within that infrastructure for better or worse. The argument ran that the private sector would be better incentivised to provide high-quality accommodation on a continuing basis if payment were in some way linked to the outcome of the use of the accommodation.

Attempts to link payment to anything other than the pure performance of the building have proved fraught with difficulty through the life of PFI/PPP. The prison service gave up seeking to link demand for places to the actual payment to be made at a relatively early stage.

As PFI moved into the IT sector the question needed to be looked at again in terms of the importance that an effective information and communications technology infrastructure could make to the learning experience of pupils and students. Would it be possible to secure a managed service arrangement for information technology that could be, at least partly, based upon a performance-related payment linked in turn to positive outcomes in the education system?

Education is potentially an interesting candidate for this particular approach in view of the amount of data that is, as a matter of course, collected within the UK state education system. Information readily available within any local authority area will include:
- the performance of pupils within a given school relative to other schools – based on the Scholastic Assessment Test assessment of the national curriculum;
- the existence of truancy and absenteeism figures; and
- claims records in relation to school vandalism.

The first of these forms of measurement was of particular interest to the education service in its promotion of PFI procurements. Probably the first local authority to seek bids for a full PFI supported information and communications technology service was Dudley in the West Midlands, which entered into a procurement exercise resulting in a contract being placed with RM Plc in January 1999.

RM provides a managed service to all schools and certain other education establishments within Dudley, based largely on a payment associated with the delivery of the managed service. A certain element of the payment is based on improving standards within a local authority that, prior to the award of this contract, had been recognised through Office for Standards in Education inspections of individual schools and the local authority itself as needing substantial improvement to its education service.

The willingness of bidders to take an approach that includes a results-based payment represents a leap of faith on their part, given the lack of direct influence the service provider has over outcomes within the education system concerned. However, further contracts have been awarded on a basis that includes results-based payments including:
- the Army Foundation College, Harrogate, operated by Jarvis in partnership with Nord Anglia as education service provider for the Ministry of Defence; and
- a sixth-form college for the Ministry of Defence.

In addition, further information and communications technology contracts have been awarded with result-based payments (eg, the London Borough of Newham) and a key element of the bidding requirements of BSF is performance-based payments within the information and communications technology service charge.

The common interest that then arises between the education authority and its private sector partner in terms of outcomes is to be regarded as an important success of PFI/PPP.

*(c)* **School administration**
As well as projects to build and maintain school buildings, there have also been arrangements where local authority responsibilities for school administration have been outsourced to the private sector. These can arise through intervention or voluntarily. Intervention occurs where DfES deems a local authority to be failing in respect of its education functions and requires it to outsource these to, usually, a private sector education provider. There have also been a number of voluntary arrangements, such as Surrey County Council's joint venture with VT Education and Islington's recently renewed intervention arrangements with Cambridge Education Associates. However, the local authority still retains strategic decision-making powers and the statutory duty to provide education services.

The nature of the outsourced services depends on local circumstances, but examples of such services include inspections services, careers guidance, special educational needs, pupil welfare, school development services, performance monitoring and developmental planning, and national literacy and numeracy strategies.

The outsourcings can give rise to transfer of employee issues and views on whether they lead to improvements are mixed.

*(d)* **Student accommodation**
A number of higher education institutions in the United Kingdom have entered into PPP arrangements for the provision of student accommodation. This sector is not as heavily regulated as the schools sector and, therefore, there is not the same standardised approach seen in the schools PFI market.

A number of different structures have been used, but a significant number are based on project finance solutions using an SPV that repays the senior loans from the rental income from students. Different risk allocations are present, but often we see the private sector taking demand occupancy risk so that it takes the risk of insufficient numbers of students wanting to occupy the property. There is a cost associated with transferring the demand risk in terms of higher borrowing costs, but for many higher education institutions this is seen as a price worth paying.

(e) *Training projects*

Considering education PFI/PPPs in their widest sense, a large number of projects outside the schools sector involve elements of education or training. While some of these are simply the provision of accommodation where the procuring authority undertakes some training which is ancillary to the more general use, for example a large hospital with a teaching capability, other projects relate to bespoke training facilities, including where the private sector is responsible for the actual teaching or instruction.

Within the United Kingdom, these 'training' projects have generally been focused within the defence sector and the police and fire sectors.

(i) *Defence training projects*

In the United Kingdom, the Ministry of Defence has undertaken a number of projects involving PPPs for the provision of training and training facilities.

There have been more than six PPPs for the provision of flight simulation equipment and training. Currently, the multibillion-pound UK Military Flying Training System is in procurement. This a major tri-service programme (involving the Royal Air Force, the Royal Navy and the Army Air Corps) to provide a comprehensive flying training system for a number of types of aircraft and crew members. The private sector together with the Ministry of Defence will deliver the flying training, including some instruction and procurement of equipment and facilities.

In addition, there have also been PPPs for the training of naval fire-fighting units, a £300 million project for training in respect of Astute submarines and a £600 million outsourcing of the army training estate accommodation.

The Defence Training Review is also currently in procurement. This is a major programme to improve and modernise the delivery of six areas of specialist Phase 2 and 3 training.[37] The training will be provided on a tri-service basis and will involve rationalising existing facilities into national centres of excellence. The areas of training include engineering, logistics, police, personnel administration and security, languages, intelligence and photography. Indicative costs are in excess of £10 billion. The contract length is likely to be 25 years and the Ministry of Defence is keen to include some element of payment by results. Preferred bidders for the two Defence Training Review packages are due to be announced during the course of 2006.

(ii) *Police and fire training projects*

Although not as numerous or as large as in the defence sector, there have been a number of bespoke training facilities in the police and fire sectors.

---

[37] Phase 1 training is basic training to join a service. Phase 2 is professional/trade training and Phase 3 is continued professional development.

These include the development of a new £40 million firearms and public order training facility at Gravesend, London, for the Metropolitan Police. This is operated by Equion and provides state-of-the-art training accommodation. While instruction is not outsourced, the accommodation provided is a bespoke training establishment. Similar facilities exist at the Cleveland and Durham Tactical Training Centre.

There have also been two fire and rescue training centres which provide state-of-the-art training facilities and instruction. These have been developed as PPPs between VT plc and the Somerset, Avon and Gloucestershire Fire Authority and the South Wales Fire and Rescue Services, respectively.

# Defence

Dan Hood
David Nelligan
Simmons & Simmons

## 1. Introduction

### 1.1 PFI/PPP in the UK defence sector

The procurement requirements of various defence departments are often some of the largest and most complex requirements in the market. Procurement is required not just of services (including training services), but also of accommodation (office, training, mess and residential) and military equipment (from smaller vehicles to key military aircraft and ships). Accordingly, there is significant interest in defence circles as to the best (and most cost-effective) procurement routes. It is understandable that in the United Kingdom the Ministry of Defence (MoD) looked to utilising private finance models in its procurement strategy as this procurement model was initiated in the 1990s.

The MoD entered into its first contract pursuant to the Private Finance Initiative (PFI) in 1996 – the German White Fleet contract for the supply of support vehicles. Since then the MoD has signed a total of 53 PFI contracts with a private sector capital investment value of over £4 billion, which represents approximately 9% (by value) and 4% (by number) of all completed UK government PFI projects. The MoD has a further 12 PFI projects in procurement with a total capital value of approximately £4 billion.[1]

The use of PFI has gained momentum following the MoD's Strategic Defence Review of 1998, which recommended using cost-effective purchasing processes to provide for the ministry's requirements on a value-for-money basis.

Public-private partnership (PPP) models other than PFI, such as contractorisation or strategic partnering, have been used where the long-term potential demands of the project mean that the MoD must ensure the contractual structure retains sufficient flexibility to meet requirements which may change substantially during the term of the contract.

Further, novel structures have been developed (and there is some debate as to whether some of these fall under the umbrella of the term PPP), such as alliancing (as proposed for use in relation to the ongoing aircraft carrier project) or project delivery model (to be used in the Military Flying System project), also known as an 'integrator' model to reflect the role that the prime contractor fulfils. Broadly, where

---

[1] Figures as at December 2005 - Ministry of Defence PFU report, "Review of MoD PFI Projects in Construction and Operation".

the complexity and size of a project warrant using a contracting structure other than the PFI and this approach is determined to be both appropriate and value for money, the MoD has demonstrated a willingness to consider such alternatives. However, for the majority of MoD projects where some form of PPP is appropriate, the use of PFI is most likely.

However, the use of PFI in the defence sector has had its critics. The procurement of projects using PFI has in some cases taken a long time and is expensive for bidders. The MoD has recognised these concerns and in 2005 established the Private Finance Unit (PFU), which is intended to ensure that privately financed projects have effective support in respect of commercial, procurement, legal and financial issues associated with such projects. The PFU supports projects in procurement and those in actual operation. Although it is not limited to looking at PFI projects, its particular focus to date has been on such projects.

The experience in the United Kingdom with different procurement routes (both good and bad) will provide valuable lessons for other jurisdictions.

Whichever procurement route is selected, the project stakeholders must always bear in mind that although defence projects share many similar features to other PPP projects, they will have unique features which require special consideration such as the importance of security issues, the use of specialist equipment, interaction with the authority and the overriding need for operational continuity.

## 1.2 The success of MoD PFI procurement to date

In December 2005 the MoD PFU published its report entitled "Review of MoD PFI Projects in Construction and Operation". This review and report was initiated by the director of the MoD PFU in order to take stock of how the PFI had performed in practice as at September 30 2005 (excluding IT and small capital value projects).

The report stressed that it did not seek to compare PFI to other procurement methods employed by the MoD and that all the projects were in either the construction phase or the early years of operations. It therefore acknowledged that there is a continual need to monitor performance over the lifetime of the contract. The key findings of the report were as follows:

- MoD PFI projects substantially deliver projects on time and within budget;
- MoD PFI projects are performing well and are delivering the services required; and
- Long-term PFI contracts are flexible enough to accommodate future change and to deliver on a sustained basis.

The report made further positive observations and recommendations in relation to best practice. It also identified a number of areas where the MoD could secure additional benefits from PFI procurement such as having effective and simplified performance regimes and ensuring that management teams have sufficient resources and support.

Overall, however, the report concluded that the good performance of MoD PFI projects provides a solid case for continuing with the use of PFI to deliver capability where it is appropriate and cost effective to do so.

## 1.3 The future of procurement using PFI models

Her Majesty's Treasury has issued two reports in recent years which have considered procurement using PFI models. The most recent report, "PFI: strengthening long-term partnerships", examined the progress made in PFI since the first report, and set out the intentions of Her Majesty's Treasury for the future development of PFI. Much of this remains to be put into practice through further detailed policy guidance. There are some interesting new proposals which will, if implemented, have significant implications for all PFI projects, including those in the defence sector:

- Development of new procurement vehicles - other contractual structures, such as project delivery models (along the lines of that proposed for the UK Military Flying Training System project), should continue to be developed where these new structures both capture the benefits of PFI and develop additional benefits.
- Duration of contracts - sector-specific caps on the length of PFI projects are to be introduced to reflect the optimal period over which the contracting authority wishes services to be provided and so as not to restrict unduly long-term flexibility.
- Types of service suitable for PFI - 'soft' services (eg, catering, cleaning and portering) should be included in a PFI project only where their inclusion can be clearly substantiated.
- Commercial terms - all commercial issues should be resolved before a preferred bidder is appointed in order to maintain competitive tension and prevent significant changes being agreed after that appointment.
- Improving the design process - projects should be properly defined and scoped before being released to the market. Her Majesty's Treasury intends to consult with the private and public sectors on this, commencing later in 2006.
- Funding competitions - funding competitions should take place for projects of a value in excess of £50 million once a preferred bidder has been appointed.
- Improving partnership - a non-binding partnership agreement or shared vision document is to be developed that will sit outside the actual PFI contract but is intended to define how the parties will work together.

How those issues will be dealt with and Her Majesty's Treasury's plans will be put into practice remains to be seen. In particular, a number of the proposals will be subject to consultation with the public and private sectors before their precise detail is determined. These issues are relevant to all jurisdictions and debates, and implementation of these issues should be closely followed by stakeholders interested in PFI models.

## 1.4 Standardisation of MoD PFI contracts

Most stakeholders in the UK PFI industry have acknowledged that standardised wording for the key contract between the contracting authority and the contractor should be adopted. It is agreed that this has generally assisted in reducing the cost and timing of procurement using the PFI model, and ensures that stakeholders can have some certainty of the commercial positions adopted by the contracting authority.

In the context of defence projects there are a number of issues which are particular to the defence sector such as security, the need for continued operations, specialist equipment and interface with the MoD and its other contractors. Some of these issues lend themselves to standardised contract drafting; others, however, will be relevant only to particular projects or types of project and therefore are not appropriately addressed by standardised contract drafting.

In defence PFI projects in the United Kingdom, two forms of standardised wording are relevant. First is the Standardisation of PFI Contracts Version 3 (SoPC3) issued by Her Majesty's Treasury in April 2004 (and amended in December 2005). SoPC3 sets out detailed guidance and standardised wording for use in PFI contracts.

The second is the soon to be released template PFI contract issued by the MoD PFU ('MoD Guidance PA'). The MoD Guidance PA has been developed by the PFU specifically for use on MoD PFI projects. It has been issued to industry stakeholders in a consultation process and is expected to be issued in the second half of 2006. Although MoD Guidance PA is specific to defence projects and includes standardised drafting for issues that are relevant only to defence sector projects, it is based on SoPC3 and standardised contracts from other sectors (in particular, the schools guidance contract).

These standardised contracts are an excellent basis for identifying key issues on defence PFI/PPP projects regardless of the jurisdiction.

## 2. Procurement law issues[2]

### 2.1 Article 296 of the EC Treaty

Most contracts which are let by the MoD under PFI will exceed the thresholds above which the public procurement rules should apply. Article 296 of the EC Treaty, however, provides an exemption from both the provisions of the EC Treaty and the public procurement rules for matters relating to national security and defence.

It is therefore possible for member states to invoke Article 296 and, as a result, not apply the public procurement rules in respect of awarding a defence PFI contract.

Despite this ability, the MoD has historically applied a narrow interpretation of when Article 296 will apply. In addition, even when Article 296 will apply, the MoD will normally follow a procurement process similar in nature to the negotiated procedure set out in the public procurement rules. Adopting such an approach both increases transparency and, where more than one bidder is taken through the process, should create pressure to keep pricing and terms competitive.

However, there is a general perception that there is widespread use of Article 296 by other member states to derogate from the public procurement rules.

---

[2] Acknowledgement for the detail of this section: Ammar Al Tabbaa, EU and competition law department, Simmons & Simmons.

## 2.2 European Commission Green Paper

In September 2004 the European Commission issued a green paper on defence procurement and invited views on three key proposals:

- the development of a non-binding code of conduct for defence procurement;
- the adoption by the commission of an interpretative communication clarifying the scope of Article 296; and
- a new directive setting out a procurement regime specific to the defence sector.

In response to the green paper, the European Parliament has suggested that more pressure should be brought to bear on national defence procurement agencies to alter their practice of near-automatic recourse to Article 296, and that measures should be taken to ensure that defence procurement is covered to a larger extent by EU legislation.

The European Parliament also urged the commission to take a tougher stance against unjustified use of Article 296.

There has already been some indication that the commission is willing to take action against members that rely on security derogations. For example, the commission found that Italy had infringed the security derogation rules when applying exemptions for the procurement of helicopters for use by the police, fire service and other emergency services.[3]

## 2.3 European Defence Agency code of conduct

The European Defence Agency announced in November 2005 that its participating member states had agreed a voluntary code of conduct for defence procurement. The code is intended to apply to contracts falling within the scope of Article 296. As of July 1 2006, subscribers to the code will, on a reciprocal basis, undertake to open up to suppliers based in each other's territories all defence procurement opportunities of €1 million or more where the conditions for the application of Article 296 are met. However, there are a number of exceptions, covering certain sensitive areas such as the procurement of research and technology, nuclear weapons, chemical and/or biological goods and services and cryptographic equipment. There is also a potentially broader exception for follow-on goods and services, but in any of these cases an explanation must be provided to the agency.

Other main features of the code include the following:

- The participating member states are free to join or to cancel their participation at any time. There are no sanctions for non-observance of the code.
- In the interests of greater transparency, participants agree to provide information relevant to new defence procurement opportunities to the agency for posting on a single internet portal.
- All providers will be evaluated on the basis of transparent and objective standards.
- Contract award criteria will be made clear from the outset and selection made according to the fundamental principle of the most economically

---

[3] European Community press release IP/05/1598 of December 14 2005.

advantageous solution, taking account of particular security-related issues, such as security of supply.
- All unsuccessful bidders that so request will be given feedback after the contract is awarded.
- Member states may proceed in exceptional circumstances without competitive procurement for reasons of pressing operational urgency or for extraordinary and compelling reasons of national security.

It is intended that the agency will act as a central monitoring body, to promote transparency and accountability. In addition to informing the agency where they find it necessary to award a contract without a competition, subscribing member states will also inform the agency when they disapply the state aid rules or the EU merger control regime on the basis of Article 296.

It is recognised that the success of this regime very much depends on reciprocal support and cooperation, at both an industry and governmental level, in particular to ensure continuity of supply. The agency also hopes to agree with industry a code of best practice in the supply chain, to extend the benefits of competition down the supply chain. Clearly matters will evolve over time and these arrangements will be kept under review.

## 2.4 The European Commission's next steps

Having considered the European Parliament's report on the green paper, the submissions of the other respondents to the green paper and the steps taken by the agency, the European Commission outlined its proposed next steps in December 2005. It made clear that, in the course of 2006, it intends to adopt an interpretative communication clarifying the scope of Article 296 and providing guidance on the scope for member states to derogate legitimately from the public procurement rules when awarding defence-related contracts. In parallel, the commission intends to begin preliminary work on a potential new directive setting out bespoke procurement rules for the defence sector and addressing cases where derogation under Article 296 is not appropriate. The commission also welcomed the work undertaken by the agency, which it believes to be complementary to its own initiatives.

In effect, therefore, the commission appears to be pursuing or endorsing all three of the proposed initiatives contained in the green paper, as per the recommendation of the European Parliament. There is a sense, however, that the commission recognises that there are considerable political hurdles to overcome before a new directive is adopted. The Interpretative Communication will be a non-legislative measure that reduces the risk of member states getting the law wrong, which should ensure better application of existing law. It will set out the principles governing the use of the derogation in the light of European Court of Justice (ECJ) case law, and will clarify what member states are required to show in order to demonstrate that the conditions for the application of the derogation are met. However, the commission considers that this communication is unlikely to be sufficient to resolve the inadequacy of the existing public procurement rules with regard to the specific features of defence procurement, such as complexity, security of supply and confidentiality. Hence, the commission is not yet prepared to abandon the possibility of a new directive in this area.

3. **Special or golden shares**

Occasionally, governments seek to retain control of certain decisions which a contracting entity may make on the basis that such control is necessary to achieve certain policy objectives. Such control is not usually sought in PFI-style projects; it is occasionally used in PPP projects such as strategic partnering or on a privatisation.

This control can be achieved in a number of ways. First, the contracting authority can take or retain an equity stake in the contracting entity (which is often a special project vehicle). The MoD has done this in relation to the strategic partnering arrangements in QinetiQ (formed out of part of the business of the former Defence Evaluation and Research Agency, which was a trading fund within the MoD).

Alternatively, the contracting authority can take a 'special' or 'golden' share in the contracting entity. Special or golden shares are shares in a company with special rights attached to them. These rights entitle the holder (usually the government) to retain control over certain decisions of the company.

The European Commission generally views the retention of such special rights as a potential restriction to the free movement of capital.[4]

The use of special shares in relation to defence PPP has not been tested in the ECJ. However, the commission anticipates in its latest report that the use of special rights in privatised companies is being phased out, particularly in industry sectors where there is effective regulation. How this relates to the defence sector, however, remains to be seen and is likely to be determined on a case-by-case basis as the commission acknowledges that it is possible to justify the use of special shares, provided this is in line with the EC Treaty and ECJ rulings.[5]

4. **Issues of particular relevance to MoD PFI contracts**

As mentioned above, PFI projects in the defence sector have unique characteristics which differentiate them from other projects. In fact, many defence projects will have characteristics unique not only to defence projects generally, but also to that project or type of project (eg, there will be different issues with equipment procurement projects and provision of training projects and accommodation projects).

The characteristics result from the particular requirements of the authority (in the United Kingdom, this is the MoD), and how these requirements are addressed is key to achieving a successful project. It is important for all stakeholders to understand that the needs of the authority will need to be balanced with the reasonable requirements of the private sector, including the funders. Stakeholders will have to assess what they really require (in the case of the authority) and what they can really deliver (in the case of the contractor), as many of the requirements

---

4   European Commission, Commission Staff Working Document "Special rights in privatised companies in the enlarged Union - a decade full of developments", July 22 2005.
5   *Ibid*, page 9.

of the authority can be accommodated but at a cost in terms of flexibility, timing of delivery or price. This is, in fact, one benefit of PFI procurement: it forces parties to assess the real need for particular requirements and the real limitations on the ability to deliver.

Although the issues that arise in defence PFI projects will differ depending on the nature of the project, it is useful to highlight some of the key issues common to all defence PFI projects. We have not identified below issues that issues that are common between PFI contracts in defence and other industry sectors with which the reader might already be familiar.

### 4.1 Security

A key distinguishing feature of defence PFI contracts is the importance of security issues. Security concerns affect a number of areas within a PFI contract, including those outlined below.

#### (a) Secret matters

The disclosure to the contractor of secret matters due to the nature of the services/equipment being provided by the contractor and the need for the contractor (and its employees and subcontractors) to keep such information secret will be of paramount importance to the authority. Any breach of this obligation will obviously have security and political implications and is very sensitive for the authority. The authority unsurprisingly will want to reserve the right to terminate the contract (and the employment of any employee or subcontractor). Under the proposed MoD Guidance PA, the contractor will be paid on such termination the outstanding senior debt and not the usual amount payable on termination for contractor default. This is on the basis that the lenders cannot effectively control the breach of the security provisions and they should not be disadvantaged as a result of the breach.

This approach assumes that the contractor can dispute the termination for breach of security, although this may not be possible in all circumstances where the nature of the security breach cannot be disclosed. In these circumstances, the contractor might think it appropriate that it be compensated in some way on termination for security breach (on the basis that the termination right for security breach may be used by the authority when it is not justified/proportionate).

In certain circumstances, the authority may be prepared to accept termination of the subcontractor/employee that caused the breach of the security provision rather than termination of the contract as an acceptable remedy. While this may be the case, the authority will usually want to reserve its rights to terminate the contract in any event.

#### (b) Ownership/control

The identity of the owners of the contractor and the subcontractors is also of significant importance to the authority for security reasons. The authority will be concerned to know whom it is ultimately dealing with and ensure that they all satisfy the necessary security requirements and have included in the contracts (in the case of subcontractors) the necessary security obligations.

*(c)* **Security clearance of staff**
The contractor will need to ensure that its employees/subcontractors are security cleared to enter onto the sites and/or perform the services. Failure to obtain such clearance can affect the delivery of services (and payments under the payment mechanisms), and accordingly the risk must be allocated between the parties. The MoD generally takes the view that this is a risk which can (and usually is) borne by the private sector.

4.2 **Need for operational continuity**
The primary function of the authority is to be able to provide a fully deployable military force at all times. The provision of services, equipment and accommodation under a PFI contract must not compromise the ability of the authority to perform this function. Careful consideration must therefore be given in the contract to issues that on other PFI projects will not be of such importance, as the following examples bear out:

- Specific remedies for delay in provision of services/equipment may need to be considered. The delay in delivery of key equipment (ie, ships or aircraft) or services (ie, training) may have an impact on the operational capability of the authority. In other sectors, the remedy for delay in providing the services by the required start date is generally the non-payment of the unitary charge. In defence projects, this might not be acceptable as the authority will need to continue with the existing arrangements (which might be more expensive) or put in place alternative arrangements for a short period (ie, short-term leases of equipment).

- The contractor may be required to operate close to the front line (ie, the equipment provided under the PFI contract may be used in front-line operations and will be at risk). In these instances issues of control of contractor personnel and liability for damage to equipment (and availability of insurance) will be particularly important.

- The authority will require rights to step in or direct the contractor to take specified actions in certain 'crisis' situations. In these instances, the authority will require action to be taken quickly and may want the right to take such action itself. This may result in damage to the assets of the contractor and impact on the contractor's ability to perform its obligations once the crisis is over (ie, if the authority requires demolition of facilities or new facilities to be built which interfere with the contractor's operations). In return for this flexibility, the contractor (and its financiers) will require the contractor to be entitled to receive payment as if it were performing its obligations under the contract. The contractor will also seek to recover losses under third-party contracts which arise as a result of such action, although this could result in large payments to the contractor where third-party revenue is a significant component of the project financing structure. The authority will need to consider carefully what obligations it will have to compensate the contractor for in such circumstances.

- The authority may require rights to step in to mitigate the consequences of relief events (events which are the fault of neither the contractor nor the authority, such as fires, earthquakes, riots, actions by utilities, national fuel shortages, strikes and floods). Relief events are generally the risk of the contractor (the contractor will suffer deductions to the extent that it is unable to perform due to the relief event, but will not be subject to termination because of the relief event), which can (and has the incentive to) manage them. However, this might result in the authority not having the required operational capability. In such circumstances, the authority might consider it can take action which the contractor is unable to take to overcome the effects of the relief event and will want to reserve the right to take such action. In addition, the authority may want to have the ultimate right to terminate the contact if the relief event continues for an extended period, the contractor is prevented from performing its obligations and the authority would need to incur significant capital expenditure to overcome the effects of the relief event. In such circumstances, the MoD Guidance PA provides that compensation will be equal to that payable on termination for *force majeure* on the basis that the relief event is also a no-fault event. The authority will be interested to include this right of termination to ensure that it has the flexibility to consider alternative procurement routes which will not be affected by the relief event and therefore ensure it is able to meet its operational requirements.

### 4.3 Military personnel

Many of the PFI projects entered into by the authority will include a significant role for existing military personnel. In some cases in the United Kingdom, these personnel are transferred to the contractor under the statutory obligations and are transferred to the private sector. In other instances, the contractor requires the skills of the military personnel and obtains these skills by seconding them into their organisations.

In addition, the UK MoD has the concept of contractors on deployed operations (CONDO) and sponsored reserves. These two concepts are similar, but different. However, both provide a useful potential force multiplier, as the contractor provides personnel to provide support functions, allowing the full-time military personnel to focus on their core competencies and tasks.

The MoD's policy on CONDO[6] applies to all contractor personnel working with the armed forces on deployed operations. Sponsored reserves are contractor personnel who are also reservists, who may be called out to serve as part of the armed forces as required. Unless and until sponsored reserves are called up, while working on deployed operations, they are subject to CONDO policy. Once called out, they are treated as military personnel and therefore are no longer subject to CONDO policy.

(a) CONDO

CONDO covers any contractor personnel deployed into a joint operations area or theatre of operation to provide commercial services to deployed operations and

---

6   Contained in JSP567 2nd Edition, May 2005.

exercises (and could therefore cover a range of contractor personnel, such as providing logistics services or technicians providing technical support on the deployment of unmanned aerial vehicles).

In addition to CONDO policy, the MoD has developed a new DEFCON 697 (published in January 2006 following consultation), notes for guidance and an associated interim DEFSTAN 05-129 (yet to be formally agreed by all authorities concerned with its use), each relating to the use of contractor personnel. However, the MoD recognises that, due to the potentially varied nature of the circumstances in which different contractors will be required to operate, these provisions and guidance will not be appropriate in all cases.

CONDO policy emphasises that use of contractor personnel must provide an assured service, which must be attractive for the contractor while providing value for money for the MoD and ensuring that the operational circumstances are as safe and secure as possible for the workforce.

CONDO policy details further provisions relating to, among other things:
- the status of contractor personnel;
- the requirement to carry identification cards (to ensure that they are entitled to treatment as prisoners of war under the Geneva Conventions if captured; and
- guidance as to the bearing of arms and wearing of uniforms (not permitted, as this would compromise their status as civilians under the Geneva Conventions).

*(b)    Sponsored reserves*

The services provided may be extremely important to the MoD and the MoD may wish to receive those services even where the environment is not entirely benign. However, it is recognised that civilians should not be required to operate at the front line. To counter these concerns and the concern that civilian contractors could legitimately refuse to operate in such environments (and thereby deny the MoD the required service), the concept of sponsored reserves was developed.

The Reserve Forces Act 1996 created sponsored reserves as a new category of reservists. They are trained in basic military skills and may be called out for military service.

Sponsored reserves will normally be employees of the contractor and the contractor will be responsible for their actions, performance, control and discipline (but such personnel will also be subject to elements of the Service Discipline Acts). From the point at which they are called out, they become subject to MoD authority and discipline. Contractors therefore will seek to agree that the MoD accepts all responsibility for their actions and the performance under the contract for the period that the sponsored reserves are called out.

MoD policy makes it clear that sponsored reserves are not intended to be used as a substitute for front-line troops and capabilities. However, they do provide a useful bridge to cover situations where it would be inappropriate to use civilian personnel.

### 4.4   Flexibility

Another key requirement of the authority is to ensure sufficient flexibility in the PFI contract to enable the authority to achieve its changing requirements over the length of the contract, and to ensure that the services provided are kept as up to date as possible and incorporate any improvements in delivery that may arise.

The need to reflect the changing requirements over time is very important to the authority, given the uncertainties as to the authority's requirements over extended periods due to the nature of international security and the ever-changing technological developments in the defence sector. The contractor (and lenders) will seek to ensure maximum certainty to enable it to meet its debt service obligations and provide a sufficient return on the equity investments made by the contractor. The change procedures will need to address these concerns in a fair way, recognising the needs of all stakeholders.

The authority will also seek to ensure that the contractor is incentivised to keep the services up to date and identify ways to improve service delivery. This is essential to ensure that the authority can provide the best facilities for its personnel and enable it to maximise its operational capabilities. This can be achieved by structuring periodic reviews to identify ways to improve service delivery and attaching rewards/deductions for effecting such reviews.

There is also the scope for the contracts to reflect the changing requirements over time as defence forces will potentially contract. The ability of the contractor to accept a reduction in demand over time will depend on the ability of the contractor to manage that reduced demand. This is an example of where the authority will need to consider the realistic needs of the contractor if it wishes the contractor to take this risk. The authority cannot in such circumstances impose significant restrictions on the ability of the contractor to generate third-party revenues, for example.

## 4.5   Specialist equipment

PFI involves the supply of a service (or capability) in return for which the authority pays a unitary charge. How that service is provided is generally left to the contractor - provided it meets the performance standards required in the relevant contract, the contracting authority will generally be happy. The authority should recognise this and, in particular, that ownership of the assets used to deliver the service need not always rest with the authority.

That said, careful consideration needs to be given to what will happen to the assets on termination or expiry of the contract - particularly where the PFI contract has replaced assets which would otherwise have been procured on a conventional basis. In addition, in defence contracts, the nature of the assets involved may dictate that the authority, rather than the contractor, on the basis of national security or the public interest, should own them. This is particularly relevant in the event of termination triggered by the contractor's insolvency, where the authority may wish to obtain the assets from a liquidator or administrator. Striking an appropriate balance between the interests of the authority and the contractor in relation to assets and covering all likely scenarios is therefore extremely important.

## 4.6   Interface

Defence projects will almost certainly never operate in a vacuum and will need to integrate with the authority and its other contractors (be they PFI contractors or other contractors). For example, all contractors will need to interface with the communications systems of the authority. These interfaces will have a significant impact on the risk transfers that are achievable under a PFI contract.

On certain projects there is the chance to ensure that the risks associated with obtaining services from multiple suppliers is mitigated by use of a central 'integrator' which will provide services itself and manage the outputs from other suppliers.

4.7 **Depth/experience of the contracting community**

Many of the services procured by the authority are supplied by a limited range of suppliers. Stakeholders will need to consider carefully the impact that this will have on the usual PFI contracting terms. For example, there will be issues with intellectual property, particularly on termination (see below), and also potentially in respect of the compensation payable on termination. In the United Kingdom, the compensation on termination regime applicable for contractor default which has been adopted in SoPC3 might be inappropriate in such circumstances. This is because there might not be a liquid market which will enable a market price to be determined for the purposes of the compensation on termination regime (ie, there may be only one supplier of a particular piece of equipment and no other market player will be willing to tender for the contract on termination as it will be unable to perform a contract tailored for the original supplier); and the alternative (the re-tendering procedure which determines the amount of compensation payable by considering future payments of the unitary charge and the costs to the authority which will be incurred following termination (including remediation costs and the costs of a replacement service)) might not deliver an acceptable outcome to the parties. The stakeholders in such a situation will need to consider carefully how the compensation regime will work so as not to advantage unfairly one party.

In addition, it is important that PFI does not lead to unsuccessful bidders leaving the sector, resulting in a limited market when the authority seeks to obtain other services now or in the future. Accordingly, the authority needs to ensure that the contractor uses competitive tenders when subcontracting its obligations in respect of a project. Although the contractors and lenders view the subcontracting strategy as their risk (ie, the unitary charge from the authority will not change as a result of the prices in the subcontracts changing over time), they will ultimately have an interest in there being as competitive a market as possible for the purposes of calculating compensation on contractor default, as mentioned above.

4.8 **Intellectual property**

The extent to which the authority will wish to own intellectual property and rights to use intellectual property (including by third-party subcontractors) will vary on a project-by-project basis. The issues may be straightforward or highly complex, particularly where multiple parties and sublicensees are involved.

At its most basic level, the authority will be concerned to ensure that it has all rights necessary to obtain the required services during the contract term and, following expiry or termination, retains the ability to continue receiving the service (whether provided in-house by the authority or by a new service provider). In relation to software, this will include ensuring that the authority has sufficient access to source code and to grant access to such source code to its third-party contractors. Particularly in respect of defence equipment, this can be an extremely difficult negotiation with contractors.

4.9   **Insurance**

Insurance is critically important to all stakeholders in all PFI/PPP projects. The nature of defence projects, however, has certain implications for the standard risk allocation adopted on PFI projects in relation to insurance.

In particular, given the nature of the services to be provided, the possible locations where service may be required and the underlying assets required to deliver such services, insurance cover may not always be available (or not generally available on commercial terms). The standardised contracts contain provisions to address unavailability of insurance; however, given the nature of the projects and the likelihood of unavailability, a more careful review of these provisions may be warranted.

4.10   **Risks which are different on defence projects**

Certain risks which are relevant for other projects may also need to be reconsidered in the light of the nature of the defence project. For example:

- the nature of defence PFI projects mean that the usual provisions relating to *force majeure* may need to be modified if services are to be provided in theatre and/or during hostilities (ie, the contract may need to provide detail of what services are to be provided in these circumstances);
- the use of facilities/assets by military personnel may lead to damage of the facilities/assets by such personnel. The risk can generally be managed by insurance, but in some instances it cannot be, or the damage is less than the deductible. In these circumstances the authority and contractor must agree who is best placed to manage this risk (or at least take responsibility for it); and
- damage to authority equipment located on the contractor's site may not be covered by insurance and the contractor may not have the financial resources to meet any claim for damage to such equipment, even if it is caused by the contractor. These interfaces are complicated because of the nature (and cost) of the authority equipment. For example, the services provided may be of small value but may involve working around expensive assets such as aircraft or tanks. The contractor will not be in a position to accept liability for damage to an aircraft or tank unless it significantly increases its unitary charge to cover for such risk. It is unlikely that this will be a cost-effective way to address this issue.

## 5.   Future of PFI/PPP in the UK defence sector

5.1   **Defence industrial strategy**

In December 2005 the MoD published its Defence Industrial Strategy white paper, which followed on from the wider 2002 Defence Industrial Policy.

It demonstrates a willingness to engage with industry to discuss the government's wishes and defence capability requirements, to identify any gaps between the government's aspirations and the views of industry, and how best to address them. In particular, the strategy identifies which industrial capabilities the government wishes to retain in the United Kingdom for defence reasons.

The white paper identifies long-term partnering arrangements as an opportunity to incentivise industry to drive down costs, but to allow increased profits where these are earned through improved performance. This suggests that PFI, and particularly PPP models, are increasingly likely to be used, where appropriate.

The white paper identifies that competition is often a useful mechanism for driving long-term value for money into a project, but is not always appropriate. Coupled with the recognition that contractors should be entitled to earn improved profit margins based on good performance, it will be interesting to see how this approach will be translated into PFI and PPP contractual drafting.

In particular, the white paper identified that a key focus for the near future will be on sub-systems and support, rather than replacing platforms (and those platforms either in the process of procurement or to be procured must be upgradable such that they can incorporate future developed sub-systems). How this will affect the appetite for, and shape of, PFI and PPP projects remains to be seen.

## 6. Conclusion

PFI is developing into a tried and tested means of delivering projects. The use of alternative PPP approaches remains sufficiently infrequent to warrant careful consideration of the appropriateness of such approach on a particular project. It should also be borne in mind, however, that PFI projects are still relatively young and there remains plenty of time to learn further lessons as to how they may best be put together and operated. The lessons from the experience in the United Kingdom are equally relevant to, and should be carefully studied by, all stakeholders in other jurisdictions.

As PFI and PPP projects mature further, no doubt other, different models will also develop, drawing on the experiences of the MoD and its advisers obtained through the negotiation, construction and operation of the structures used or in train today. For example:

- if the alliancing model proposed for the ongoing aircraft carrier project is successful, this may also be found to be appropriate for future large-scale projects of this nature; and
- the Defence Industrial Strategy white paper suggests that it may be appropriate to use an integrator model for the delivery of the Future Rapid Effects System fleet capability. Other, highly complex large-scale projects (eg, the UK Military Flying System project) already underway will adopt such an integrator model, and there will no doubt be other future projects for which this structure will also be appropriate.

# EU procurement

Matthew Hall
Ashurst

## 1. Introduction

The EU public procurement regime seeks to ensure that public bodies and specified private bodies awarding contracts above certain minimum values do so in a manner that permits open and non-discriminatory competition for the contracts in question. The idea is to open up the public procurement market and to ensure the free movement of goods and services within the European Union.

The basic structure of the regime is that relevant purchasing bodies must advertise in a specified format their contracts for the purchase of works, supplies or services which are above the relevant value and then follow a specific procedure leading to the award and then signature of the contract. Aggrieved third parties are provided with rights to challenge award procedures and decisions which they consider not to have been run in accordance with the obligations of the regime.

## 2. Operation of the rules

### 2.1 Structure

The first EU public procurement directive dates from 1971. The European Commission[1] (through its Internal Market Directorate General) started a major review of the various directives then in force in May 2000, with the publication of its original proposals for modifying the regime. After what became a very long gestation period, in April 2004 two new EU public procurement directives came into force.

The directives can be found at http://europa.eu.int/comm/internal_market/publicprocurement/legislation_en.htm#package. However, in relation to purchases in any particular EU member state, it is necessary first to consider the implementing national legislation, which transposes the requirements of the directives into national law.

The new regime consists of the following:
- the Public Sector Directive (2004/18/EC), which applies to service, supply or works contracts entered into by public bodies other than utilities in relation to a utility activity (see below); and

---

[1] The European Commission is one of the institutions of the European Union. Its four main roles are to propose legislation to the European Parliament and the European Council, to administer and implement EU policies, to enforce EU law (jointly with the European Court of Justice) and to negotiate international agreements.

- the Utilities Directive (2004/17/EC), which applies to service, supply or works contracts entered into by utilities (ie, public and certain private bodies operating in the water, energy, transport and postal services sectors) relating to a utility activity.

The directives apply to the 25 EU member states. Except in relation to the application of the Utilities Directive to the provision of postal services (where an additional 35 months were permitted), in all states the directives were required to be implemented by January 31 2006. As further states join the European Union, the directives will apply to them.[2]

Two existing EU directives dealing with third parties' rights to remedies - the Compliance Directive and the Utilities Remedies Directive - remain in force. However, the European Commission is considering whether revisions should be made to those directives.

It should be appreciated that the various directives do not provide a complete public procurement law and certainly do not amount to a code covering all elements of procurement. A very large number of elements of the law, as are described below, are open to interpretation and to 'taking a view'.

## 2.2 Contract coverage

The directives essentially apply to contracts "for pecuniary interest concluded in writing" between a provider and a purchaser which provide for the provision of works, services or supplies. The term 'public-private partnership' (PPP) is not defined for the purposes of EU public procurement law and therefore, in principle, PPP contracts are treated under the directives in the same way as any other type of contract (and, in practice, the directives will govern the award of the majority of publicly procured infrastructure and other PPP projects).

However, the European Commission has, for the purposes of analysis, distinguished between:

- purely contractual PPPs, in which the relationship between the public and private sectors is based solely on contractual links; and
- institutional PPPs, which involve cooperation between the public and private sectors through the medium of a distinct legal entity. In this context, a contract for the purchase of goods, works or services may or may not be included.

Although this is a useful distinction to keep in mind, for the purposes of public procurement law it is still necessary in any particular case to consider the contractual framework from first principles. This framework requires first a consideration of whether the contract should be classified as one for works, supplies or services. 'Works contracts' are contracts for general building and civil engineering works

---

[2] Bulgaria and Romania are expected to join in 2007. Croatia and Turkey started negotiations to join on October 3 2005. In December 2005, the European Council decided to grant candidate country status to the former Yugoslav Republic of Macedonia, with which accession negotiations have not yet started.

(including demolition, installation and building completion work). 'Supply contracts' are contracts for the purchase or hire and for the siting and installation of goods. 'Service contracts' are contracts for services.

A sequential approach to contract classification is taken, with it being necessary to consider, first, whether the contract is a works contract because its 'predominant purpose' (which does not necessarily mean the highest-value element) is works. Then, if the contract is not a works contract, it is classified as a supply or service contract, according to which of the supply and services elements has the greater value. Service contracts then have to be classified as 'Part A' or 'Part B' contracts, with the rules applying in full only to the former type. (Part B includes services such as hotel and restaurant services, rail and water transport services and legal services; in particular, these are not subject to an advertising requirement under the rules – the only obligations relate to the use of technical specifications and the provision of post-award information.) A contract which provides for the supply of equipment and an operator is considered to be a service contract. Contracts for the purchase of software are considered to be supply contracts unless they have been tailored to the purchaser's specification, when they are considered to be for services. A final complication is introduced by the separate treatment of concession contracts (see below).

In practice, PPP contracts are usually for services. For example, a hospital or prison PPP (to construct and then manage and operate the facility for a period of time) is typically for services. The London Underground PPP, an upgrade and renewal project relating to London's underground train network, was categorised as a services contract although it involved the supply of services, works and goods (because the value of the services element was greater than the value of the works or supply elements). However, some PPP arrangements are works contracts – in particular, contracts for the construction and operation of motorways and other types of road are usually for works.

2.3   **Entity coverage**
A contract falls subject to the EU public procurement rules only if it is to be awarded by a body subject to the rules. The Public Sector Directive applies to the state, regional or local authorities, "bodies governed by public law" and "associations formed by one or several of such authorities or ... bodies". These bodies are known as 'contracting authorities'.

A body governed by public law is a body established "for the specific purpose of meeting needs in the general interest, not having a commercial or industrial character". Further, it must be financed for the most part by the state or by other public law bodies or have a board appointed by the state or by other public law bodies. There have been many recent European Court of Justice (ECJ) cases on the scope of this definition and, where the provision may apply, its applicability needs to be considered with great care.

The Public Sector Directive does not apply to contracting authorities which are utilities awarding contracts in relation to one of their utility activities. In such cases the Utilities Directive is relevant. In addition, the Utilities Directive applies to public undertakings (ie, undertakings over which the state exercises a dominant influence) and to private entities which operate on the basis of special or exclusive rights granted by a competent authority (in all cases, provided that the undertaking or entity is operating in a utility sector (ie, is for this purpose a 'utility') and is awarding a contract in relation to its utility activity).

In the context of PPP arrangements, it is important to note the latter type of utility. The inclusion of such private entities means that many entities which operate under a PPP arrangement can themselves be utilities subject to the rules. An example is a private company licensed to provide a light rail transport service. In addition, although not likely to be set up under a PPP structure, a privatised water company or a licensed private electricity supplier would *prima facie* qualify as a utility and accordingly be governed by the Utilities Directive in relation to contracts awarded relating to its utility activity.

The definition of 'special or exclusive rights' is therefore an important one in relation to the utilities regime generally and in relation to PPP arrangements specifically. A body is caught only if the rights limit the exercise of a utility activity to one or more entities and substantially affect the ability of other entities to carry out such activity on the same territory under substantially equivalent conditions. It is necessary to analyse on a case-by-case basis whether the entity in question possesses rights which have this effect on other entities.

The range of bodies caught by the two directives is therefore vast. Although coverage needs to be checked in any individual case, in principle they cover, among others, ministers, ministries/government departments, government agencies, local and regional authorities, police authorities, legislative bodies, court services and health authorities, as well as public or private utilities such as railway infrastructure providers, underground railway operators, water companies, electricity distributors and generators, and airport operators.

## 2.4 Thresholds

A contract is caught by the directives only where its estimated value (net of value added tax) is above the relevant threshold value. These are complicated (and change every two years) but, at the time of writing, are broadly as follows:
- services and supplies (public sector purchasers) – €137,000 for central government bodies (mostly government departments) and €211,000 for other public bodies (including local authorities) (€211,000 for all Part B service contracts);
- works (public sector purchasers) – €5,278,000;
- services and supplies (utilities) – €422,000; and
- works (utilities) – €5,278,000.

There are particular rules concerning aggregation, which are intended to prevent avoidance by the use of a series of contracts which individually fall below the threshold values.

As can be seen, in most cases a PPP arrangement will exceed this value and therefore the issue of thresholds is of little relevance in this context.

2.5 **Exclusions**

The Public Sector Directive and the Utilities Directive both contain a number of exemptions (referred to as 'exclusions'). In general, these are not of particular relevance in the PPP field. However, it is worth noting that they include exclusions relating to national defence/security-related contracts. Some military-type PPP projects will fall within this exemption. However, this is a complex area and the European Commission is in any event conducting a review of the application of the rules to defence procurement. There is also an exclusion where the contract is for the acquisition of land or an interest in it (including buildings). However, despite this exclusion, it is important to note that some purchases of buildings (if built to the purchaser's requirements) still fall subject to the rules as a works contract.

2.6 **Award procedures**

The fundamental principle underlying the EU public procurement rules is that a qualifying contract must be opened up to EU-wide competitive tender. As a result, in most circumstances, at the start of a tender process a notice (the 'contract notice' or 'OJEU notice' (*Official Journal of the European Union*)) must be submitted in the standard form to the EU Publications Office in Luxembourg for publishing in Tenders Electronic Daily, an online database provided by the European Commission at http://ted.publications.eu.int/official/. The time allowed for responses or tenders must then be no less than a set period (and it is necessary in any event to consider in any particular case what is a reasonable period). There are also other rules on publication, including obligations to publish notices giving advance warning of potential contracts ('PIN notices'), again on standard forms.

In awarding contracts, an authority is then obliged to follow one of four types of tender procedure (which will be identified in the notice):
- the negotiated procedure;
- the open procedure;
- the restricted procedure; or
- (under the Public Sector Directive only) the competitive dialogue procedure.

Under the open procedure, the authority invites potential providers to bid directly for the contract in response to the contract notice. Under the restricted procedure the authority invites potential providers to participate in a two-stage process:
- pre-qualification on a shortlist; and
- final participation in the submission of a formal tender.

Under the negotiated procedure, the authority negotiates the terms of the contract with one or more potential providers. There are many variations but, typically, the procedure is split into:
- pre-qualification on a shortlist;
- tendering to be invited to negotiate;
- selection of one or more parties for negotiation;

- negotiation; and
- appointment of a preferred bidder.

The competitive dialogue, which is available only under the Public Sector Directive, is new; it is directly relevant to PPP contracts and is therefore considered separately below.

A body subject to the Utilities Directive may choose which procedure it wishes to use. By contrast, bodies subject to the Public Sector Directive must in general choose between the open and restricted procedures, and are permitted to use the negotiated procedure (or competitive dialogue procedure) only in limited situations. This reflects the position under the old directive (except that the competitive dialogue procedure was not available). In the past, this has given rise to problems in relation to some PPP projects as it presupposes that providers will be able to submit tenders corresponding to precise descriptions of an authority's requirements (eg, precise output specifications relating to the provision of a particular service). Accordingly, the view had commonly been taken that the negotiated procedure could be used when PPP-type contracts were awarded by bodies outside the utilities sector. This was based on the exemptions for cases in which prior overall pricing was not possible or where specifications could not be drawn up with sufficient precision. These exemptions remain available (the former for works, supplies or services; the latter for services only), but it is to be expected (see below) that PPP-type contracts will now generally be awarded under the competitive dialogue procedure.

The highest-profile element of the selection process generally required by the Public Sector or Utilities Directives is the contract notice advertising the proposed contract. However, much of the directives deal with the rules concerning the conduct of the process following this advertisement, which are designed to avoid discrimination on grounds of origin and to ensure that all potential providers are treated on equal terms. These are in many ways the very core of the directives. The principal areas covered are as follows:

- Use of technical specifications in the contract documents (specification stage) - technical specifications identify the characteristics of the works, services or supplies which are required under the contract which is being procured. The new directives made very important changes to the existing rules concerning the use of technical specifications. The default position is no longer that 'European specifications' must be used wherever possible. Purchasers may now, if they wish, instead refer to performance or functional requirements. Further, where technical specifications are referred to, purchasers must accept equivalent products or services (although it is up to the provider to demonstrate the equivalence).
- Rejection of providers (part of the selection stage) - there are specific rules concerning the situations in which a purchaser may or shall not consider a potential provider for the contract in question. This includes the mandatory exclusion (in normal cases) of candidates (natural or legal entities) which have been convicted of the following offences: participation in a criminal organisation; corruption; certain types of fraud; and money laundering.

- Suitable economic and financial standing and technical or professional ability (part of the selection stage) - there are specific rules setting out the basis on which purchasers may identify the potential providers from which the selection of the winner will be made.
- Award criteria (the award stage) - contracts must be awarded on grounds which are specified at the outset. Purchasers are able to choose between awarding the contract on the basis of the 'most economically advantageous' offer or on the basis of the 'lowest price' offer. Only criteria which are linked to the subject matter of the contract (eg, quality, price and technical merit, but also including environmental characteristics as relevant) are permitted to be used to determine which offer is the most economically advantageous.

It is worth commenting specifically on one area which generated much debate during the period up to adoption of the directives: the relevance of social and environmental criteria in the award process. The basic position is quite simple: social, environmental and similar issues may be taken into account where they are relevant to the subject of the contract and consistent with the criteria allowed at each stage of the procurement process. Contract performance conditions are also expressly allowed (and may concern social and environmental issues), provided that they are not discriminatory, directly or indirectly. In reality, despite the intense (politicised) discussion on these issues, the position in this regard has not changed from that which applied (based on ECJ case law) before the new directives were adopted. This is considered further below.

## 2.7 Remedies/challenges/*Alcatel* provisions

Often of most relevance to potential providers experiencing a breach of public procurement law will be the remedies available. After all, it is only through enforcement of the remedies that an infringement of public procurement law has any practical impact. The threat is not only to the process itself. Challenges can also give rise to potentially significant costs and losses for purchasers, particularly if an award procedure is halted or suspended. In addition, purchasers face the potential of (political) embarrassment and a loss of credibility as procurers of projects.

The principal practical remedies available to aggrieved potential providers are:
- to make a complaint to the European Commission; and
- to bring proceedings before a national court for infringement of national implementing legislation.

In addition, it may be possible to complain to the relevant government body (eg, in the United Kingdom, this is the Office of Government Commerce). In practice, at least if a central government body is the purchasing entity, this can result in significant pressure being brought to bear on the entity in question.

A complaint to the European Commission is the cheapest and most straightforward option for an aggrieved potential provider. This path may ultimately lead to the commission taking action before the ECJ in Luxembourg under Article

226 of the EC Treaty against a member state for infringement of the relevant directive. However, any ultimate judgment is merely declaratory and the case is brought not against the purchaser, but against the member state in question. The court may grant an injunction to suspend execution of a contract pending judgment on the merits of the case (even after it has been awarded), but in practice this is unlikely unless the infringement is blatant and the matter comes before the court quickly.

Due to its various limitations, this process is often of little practical assistance in the public procurement field, where the principal concern of a third party is to win the tender (or to ensure a fair competition) and where the time periods are often very short. It is this issue with which the Compliance Directive and the Utilities Remedies Directive seek to deal. These two directives provide certain minimum remedies before national courts for breaches of the public procurement rules, although member states have discretion in relation to some aspects.

Broadly, under these directives breaches must be actionable by a third party "having or having had an interest in obtaining a particular [contract] and who has been or risks being harmed by an alleged infringement" (ie, a third party which would or could lose out as a result of the breach). Member states are permitted to require the third party to inform the purchaser of the breach and of the intention to bring proceedings. Member states are required to ensure that the remedies which are available include, in effect, an injunction to stop the award process, set aside and damages. The exact implementation of this differs procedurally and substantively from country to country. In addition, of particular note is that the directives permit member states to restrict the available remedies to damages once a contract has been concluded (ie, signed). This option has been taken up by, for example, the United Kingdom.

An issue which has given rise to much discussion and concern as to its impact on purchasing procedures, particularly for complex projects in which funding is being provided such as PPP contracts, is the requirement to implement the ECJ judgment in the *Alcatel Case*.[3] This case held that national courts in member states must, in all cases, be able to review and set aside award decisions on procurement contracts subject to the procurement rules. A subsequent ECJ ruling[4] clarified that there should be a period of time between the contract award decision and the start of the contract (signature) to ensure that complainants are able, in duly justified cases, to bring actions in the national court for these remedies. The commission held discussions with individual countries as to the form in which these requirements would be implemented into national law. In the United Kingdom, for example, the new implementing rules incorporate these requirements by providing for a 10-day mandatory standstill period between the notification of the award decision and the date of contract conclusion for all procurements subject to the full scope of the procurement rules. Participants must be informed of the start of the standstill and

---

3   C-81/98, *Alcatel Austria v Bundesministerium für Wissenschaft und Verkehr*.
4   C-212/02, *Commission v Austria*.

given certain information concerning the award procedure. They may request further information during the standstill.

In the context of PPP projects, uncertainty can arise as to the point at which the contract award takes place (and therefore when, under the *Alcatel* rules, a standstill period must or can start). In the United Kingdom, Office of Government Commerce guidance[5] states that the announcement of the appointment of a preferred bidder effectively brings to an end the competitive stage of the award process and is the earliest point in the process at which the award decision may be communicated.

Despite the elaborate remedy mechanisms that exist, it must be recognised that, in practice, it is often the case that a purchasing entity will be uncertain as to whether a particular course of action may or does give rise to an infringement of public procurement law but nevertheless, based on an assessment of the risks, decides to proceed down that course. The risks are, as noted, essentially third-party action through national courts or European Commission action (which ultimately means action through the ECJ). However, if a purchaser can satisfy itself that a third party is unlikely to complain to the commission (and that the commission is unlikely to find out about the infringement independently) or to take direct action in the courts (perhaps because it does not wish to 'bite the hand that feeds') or, even if it does, to have standing (because it has not been damaged), then it may well consider that any risk of a possible infringement of the public procurement rules is outweighed by the advantages to be gained (in terms of timing or the ability to choose its own provider without a tender process). This principle will no doubt commonly be applied in the context of the new competitive dialogue procedure, considered further below.

## 2.8 Relationship to international rules

There is a wider international dimension to EU procurement law due to the European Union's various relationships and treaties. The directives apply in Bulgaria and Romania (ie, to purchases by authorities in those states) under the Europe Agreements, and in Iceland, Liechtenstein and Norway under the European Economic Area (EEA) Agreement. Further, the European Union is a signatory to the World Trade Organisation (formerly the General Agreement on Tariffs and Trade) Government Procurement Agreement (with Aruba, Canada, Hong Kong China, Iceland, Israel, Japan, the Republic of Korea, Liechtenstein, Norway, Singapore, Switzerland and the United States). These arrangements provide (subject to certain limitations) access for suppliers from those countries to EU procurement markets and vice versa. The directives require member states to implement these General Procurement Agreement obligations in their national law. In the United Kingdom, for example, this has been done by including, as relevant, providers from relevant countries in the list of those gaining rights under the implementing rules.

---

5   March 2006; "OGC guidance note on the 10-day mandatory standstill period for public sector contracts".

## 3. Procurement process and state aid

The EC Treaty includes specific provisions (contained in Articles 87 to 89) restricting the ability of member states to grant aid (of whatever form) which "distorts or threatens to distort competition by favouring certain undertakings or the production of certain goods ... in so far as it affects trade between member states". Broadly, the provisions are intended to stop member states from unfairly supporting their own companies to the detriment of competing companies from other member states.

Aid can take a variety of forms including:
- state grants;
- interest relief;
- tax relief;
- state guarantees or holdings; and
- the provision or purchase by the state of goods and services on preferential terms.

The EC Treaty, however, allows exceptions to the ban on state aid where the proposed aid schemes may have a beneficial impact overall. Thus, for example, the following forms of aid are permitted:
- aid having a social character, granted to individual consumers;
- aid to make good the damage caused by natural disasters or exceptional occurrences;
- aid designed to:
  - promote the economic development of underdeveloped areas (regarded as particularly backward in accordance with EU criteria);
  - promote the execution of an important project of common European interest or remedy a serious disturbance in the economy of a member state;
  - facilitate the development of certain activities or areas; or
  - promote culture and heritage conservation.

The EC Treaty prohibits only aid granted by a member state or through state resources. Case law has established that this means that the advantage must come directly or indirectly from the resources of a state and the measure providing for this must be imputable to the state. This could raise issues in some PPP-type purchases, but needs to be considered on a case-by-case basis.

The decision as to whether aid granted by member states is permitted rests with the European Commission. The commission's role is therefore to monitor proposed and existing state aid measures by member states to ensure that they are compatible with the EU state aid rules. The commission has the power to require that aid granted by member states without the commission's approval be repaid by recipients to the public authorities which granted it. The member state must recover the aid immediately in accordance with domestic procedures.

In the context of PPP arrangements, aid arises principally where the terms of a contract for works, services or supplies are not normal commercial terms, as to price or other matters, or where the contract does not reflect a genuine need. The basic test is whether the purchaser acted as a 'market purchaser' would have done. If it did, aid is not involved. If it did not, aid is involved, this being the difference between the actual value of the contract and the value of a contract that a market purchaser would have entered into (with the difference being repayable). These principles apply regardless of whether the public procurement rules apply to a particular contract and accordingly state aid rules can in theory be used to attack any state contract.

However, if the purchaser runs an open, transparent and non-discriminatory procurement procedure, as it would do to comply with the public procurement rules, and the contract price is the market price established through that procedure, there is generally accepted to be a presumption that state aid is not involved. This was recognised in the European Commission's *London Underground* state aid decision of October 2002,[6] where the European Commission stated:

> ... *the Commission considers that when these types of infrastructure arrangements are concluded after the observance of an open, transparent and non-discriminatory procedure, it is, in principle, presumed that the level of any public sector support can be regarded as representing the market price for the execution of a project. This conclusion should lead to the assumption that, in principle, no State aid is involved.*

The commission, it will be noted, did not refer to compliance with the public procurement rules in this passage. It is not necessary for the rules themselves to be followed in order for the presumption of compliance with the state aid rules to be raised – an alternative open, transparent and non-discriminatory process can be used. Equally, if the rules apply and are not followed (in whole or in part), or the rules do not apply and an open, transparent and non-discriminatory procedure is not used, it does not necessarily follow that state aid will be found and there is no presumption to this effect. In these cases it is necessary to consider in the normal way the terms of the arrangements in order to judge whether a market purchaser would have entered into them. One element of this analysis could be the terms which would have been obtained following an open, transparent and non-discriminatory procedure.

## 4. General EC Treaty principles

Despite their incredible detail, the directives provide only an outline of how purchasers should operate and there are innumerable issues which are not specifically covered. In some cases, the position has been clarified by case law. However, in many other cases purchasers and providers must reach a view as to what is likely to be 'legal'. A particular problem is the application of the general EC Treaty principles, in relation to which, despite ECJ guidance, there remains considerable uncertainty.

---

[6] State aid N 264/2002 - United Kingdom; London Underground Public Private Partnership.

The ECJ has confirmed that, notwithstanding that the technical rules do not apply to a particular contract in part or at all (eg, because it is below the value thresholds or because it is a Part B service contract), purchasers concluding them are bound to comply with the fundamental rules of the EC Treaty. This means, in particular, that the principle of non-discrimination on the grounds of nationality must be complied with, which in turn implies, "in particular, an obligation of transparency in order to enable the purchaser to satisfy itself that the principle has been complied with". The obligation of transparency itself "consists in ensuring, for the benefit of any potential tenderer, a degree of advertising sufficient to enable the...market to be opened up to competition and the impartiality of procurement procedures to be reviewed". Put more simply, this means some degree of advertising, appropriate to the scale of the contract. In addition, it is clear that the general principles of equal treatment, proportionality and mutual recognition must be complied with by purchasers subject to the EC Treaty.

However, according to the ECJ, some degree of flexibility does remain. The following was held in *Coname*:[7]

> [the] transparency requirements ... without necessarily implying an obligation to hold an invitation to tender, are, in particular, such as to enable an undertaking located in the territory of a Member State other than that of the [purchaser] in question to have access to appropriate information regarding that [contract], so that, if that undertaking had so wished, it would have been in a position to express its interest in obtaining that [contract].

The European Commission has in recent years been very active in pursuing these types of case. A somewhat remarkable example is a case in which the commission pursued Finland in the ECJ for failure to ensure an adequate degree of advertising in relation to a contract for the supply of kitchen equipment worth €176,000 (which was below the relevant thresholds for the application of the public procurement rules). There are many other examples.

The precise extent of the obligations imposed by the EC Treaty on purchasers has not been clearly defined by the ECJ (in terms, in particular, of what form of advertising is necessary and how far the transparency obligation extends (beyond mere advertising) in any particular case). This creates uncertainty for purchasers, but can be to the advantage of providers, which are able to use this uncertainty to pressure purchasers into operating open tender procedures where otherwise they may not have done so.

However, the commission recently produced an "Interpretative Communication on the Community law applicable to contract awards not or not fully subject to the provisions of the Public Procurement Directives". This covers only contracts which are not covered because they are below the value thresholds or are Part B service contracts. However, there appears to be no reason not to apply the principles more widely (and indeed the communication also makes reference to service concessions).

---

[7] Case C-231/03, *Coname*, judgment of July 21 2005.

The communication, setting out the commission's views, requires the following analysis and procedure:
- Is the contract potentially of interest to economic operators located in other member states?
- If so, it must be advertised sufficiently so as to allow an undertaking located in another member state to have access to enough information to express its interest in the contract should it wish.
- The method of advertising depends on the facts of the case, but the greater the potential interest the wider the coverage should be. 'Adequate and commonly used means of publication' include the Internet, national journals, local journals and Tenders Electronic Daily.
- The content of the advertisement can be limited to a short description of the essential details of the contract and the proposed award method.
- There are obligations concerning the contract award procedure. In particular:
  - there should be a non-discriminatory description of the subject matter of the contract;
  - there should not be conditions which cause direct or indirect discrimination;
  - the principle of mutual recognition of diplomas and the like should be respected;
  - suitable time limits should be used; and
  - there should be a "transparent and objective approach" which includes full knowledge of the rules of the procedure.

It will be appreciated that this list does not differ significantly from the obligations of the directives themselves (particularly if the negotiated procedure is used). It remains to be seen whether the ECJ will support this approach.

## 5. PPP-specific issues

### 5.1 European Commission green paper and follow-up

At the time of writing the European Commission is involved in a significant public consultation in relation to the treatment of PPP contracts and concessions under the EU public procurement rules. In April 2004 it published for consultation a green paper on PPPs and EU law on public contracts and concessions. This resulted in the publication in November 2005 of a document setting out policy options for PPPs ("Communication from the Commission to the European Parliament, the Council, the European Economic and Social Committee and the Committee of the Regions on Public-Private Partnerships and Community law on Public Procurement and Concessions"). The suggestions were an interpretative communication dealing with the establishment of 'institutionalised PPPs' (bodies owned jointly by the public and private sectors), and legislation dealing with the award of concessions. Consideration of these measures is ongoing, but they will be of great relevance to practice in this area.

## 5.2 Use of the negotiated procedure and competitive dialogue procedure

Probably the most intensively analysed change introduced by the new directives (specifically, the Public Sector Directive) is the new award procedure which applies in the public sector only: competitive dialogue. This was introduced in response to a belief by the European Commission that the old public sector directives did not offer sufficient flexibility with regard to certain projects due to the fact that the use of the negotiated procedure is strictly limited to certain cases. It was not needed in the utilities sector because, as described above, utilities are free to use the negotiated procedure.

Despite the detailed and prescriptive drafting (13 sub-paragraphs are used in the Public Sector Directive to describe the competitive dialogue procedure), the scope and operation of the new procedure are far from certain. The basic position is that it can be used where a purchaser wishes to award a 'particularly complex contract' (ie, a contract under which it is objectively unable to identify the technical means capable of satisfying its needs and/or is unable to specify the legal and/or financial make-up of a project), and considers that the use of the open or restricted procedure will not allow the award of the contract. Essentially, the idea is that it will be used where a purchaser can identify its needs, but not how to meet them. The Public Sector Directive lists (Recital 31) "important integrated transport infrastructure projects", "large computer networks" and "projects involving complex and structured financing the financial and legal make-up of which cannot be defined in advance" as types of contract likely to satisfy these criteria. It will be appreciated that classic PPP-type contracts will often fall within one or more of these examples.

Under the procedure, a purchaser, following advertisement of the contract, opens a 'dialogue' with a limited number of potential providers in order to identify the solution or solutions which are capable of meeting its needs. This dialogue may relate to technical, economic (including price) and legal aspects. Tenders are then submitted based on the solution or solutions identified (these usually being the solution(s) of each of the participants as opposed to a solution common to all). Following this, tenders may be "clarified, specified or fine-tuned". The commission has indicated in its guidance on the competitive dialogue[8] that it considers that the room for manoeuvre at this point is fairly limited. The selected tender (selection must be on the basis of the most economically advantageous tender (as opposed to lowest price)) may then finally be clarified and confirmed. The commission indicates in its guidance that this "does not entail any negotiations solely with this [provider]". However, some change is expected at this stage. For example, the UK Office of Government Commerce indicates in its guidance[9] that this can include fleshing out of designs, finalising the contract documents, due diligence for financial backers and final consultation with the workforce and its representatives.

The commission's overall view is that the competitive dialogue is distinguished from the restricted procedure by the fact that negotiations concerning every aspect of the contract are authorised and from the negotiated procedure essentially by the fact that negotiations are concentrated within a particular phase in the procedure

---

[8] europa.eu.int/comm/internal_market/publicprocurement/docs/explan-notes/classic-dir-dialogue_en.pdf.
[9] www.ogc.gov.uk/embedded_object.asp?docid=1004572.

(the dialogue phase) (as opposed to all the way up to contract award). It is clear that the commission intends that the procedure will be used, and that there will be less tolerance for the use of the negotiated procedure where the strict rules governing the use of it are not satisfied. The green paper states "in the context of a purely contractual PPP, the ... competitive dialogue procedure ... will provide interested parties with a procedure which is particularly well adapted to the award of contracts designated as public contracts". The UK Office of Government Commerce has indicated that it considers the competitive dialogue to be more widely available as a procurement route than the negotiated procedure, while at the same time indicating that "the negotiated procedure should only be used in very exceptional circumstances [such as the] London Underground PPP".

It appears that, in practice, the competitive dialogue is likely to amount simply to a codified form of the classic PPP process which has been employed for many years in, for example, the United Kingdom under the negotiated procedure. (In fact, the United Kingdom lobbied hard to ensure that the Public Sector Directive text on the competitive dialogue fitted as closely as possible with UK best practice on the award of PPP contracts; and the Office of Government Commerce guidance on the competitive dialogue procedure states that it "is similar in many ways to the existing practice of letting PFI contracts"). For example, in PPP parlance, it seems that the tenders received based on the solution(s) identified can be described as the 'best and final offers', while the tenderer identified as having submitted the most economically advantageous tender can be described as the 'preferred bidder'. If this is the case, the anxieties expressed during the passage of the Public Sector Directive as to its negative impact on PPP (eg, due to the reluctance of bidders to go to the expense of working up full-blown proposals at an early stage in the procedure) will have been overdone.

The competitive dialogue is now being used extensively. A range of projects have been advertised under it, including:
- a services contract to provide data warehouse services relating to schools;
- a supply contract for a fire and security software management system;
- a works contract relating to the appointment of a development partner for a property development site; and
- a services contract to design, build, finance and operate a community energy scheme.

A further high-profile example is a supply contract advertised by Transport for London in the United Kingdom for the supply and maintenance of a fleet of hydrogen-fuelled vehicles.

5.3   *Coverage of 'concessions'*
Concession contracts are treated in a special way under the directives. This is important in the PPP context, in which concession-type structures are common.[10]

---

10   The European Commission has issued important guidelines on the issue of concessions – Commission interpretative communication on concessions under Community law, OJ C 121/2, April 29 2000.

In general commercial parlance, 'concessions' refers to many types of contract. However, for the purposes of the public procurement rules, they are contracts of a specific type: those under which the consideration consists of or includes the right to operate and derive income from the works or services to be provided under the contract. The provider, usually providing the funding of at least part of the relevant project, must take on a significant degree of risk (usually the risk concerns the extent to which the public will choose to use the works or services in question). Clearly, such private capital involvement is one of the principal incentives for public authorities in entering into PPPs.

There is significant case law on the issue of the definition of a 'concession' and individual projects need to be analysed closely in order to determine whether in fact they give rise to concession contracts within the meaning of the public procurement rules.

Service concession contracts (a service contract structured as a concession) are excluded from the ambit of the Public Sector Directive. Works concession contracts (a works contract structured as a concession) are excluded from many of the rules, in particular the requirement for a competition. The directive instead contains specific rules concerning the award of works concession contracts and of works subcontracts by works concessionaires. In practice, as most PPP projects are service contracts, when structured as a concession they are outside the directive. However, large infrastructure projects such as toll bridges and roads are, as noted above, usually works projects and therefore when structured as a concession are within the directive, albeit subject to a specific (limited) regime.

The position is different under the Utilities Directive. This directive completely excludes both works and service concession contracts. Thus, for example, the award by a utility of a contract which relates to its utility activity (and therefore *prima facie* falls within the Utilities Directive) falls outside the directive if structured as a concession. Similarly, the award by a utility which is such by virtue of its own contract (concession or otherwise) of a (sub) concession falls outside the directive.

However, the position is complicated by the application of the EC Treaty principles to public bodies. As noted above, even if the strict public procurement rules contained in the directives do not apply, in all cases it remains necessary to consider the application of the general EC Treaty principles. Therefore, for example, a public sector body will be unable to award a service concession without engaging in the appropriate degree of advertising even though such contracts are specifically excluded from the Public Sector Directive.

## 5.4 Consultations prior to award procedures

Purchasers can find it useful to engage in consultation with third parties prior to the commencement of award procedures. This can be useful, for example, to identify the precise specifications of a project or the contractual structures that might be suitable. Consultations of this nature are permitted, including with potential participants in an actual award process, but must be carried out with care and in particular in accordance with the principle of equal treatment of tenderers which underlies the directives.

One aspect of equal treatment which applies in this context is that consultation cannot have the effect of precluding competition. This could occur if, for example, the consultation resulted in specifications being set which limited the number of potential providers to one (because only it can satisfy the identified technical features) or favoured the firms that had been consulted.

Further, the consultation should not result in material information being made available to the consultees which other participants in a subsequent actual award process do not have. In order to deal with this issue, it is sensible to record the information made available to consultees so that it can be made available in any later procurement process to all potential providers. There are various ways of doing this, including video recordings of meetings.

## 5.5 Contract terms

PPP arrangements are by their nature often complex and lengthy. This means that it is common for issues to arise as to the application of the public procurement rules following signature of the contract and during performance. Again, the underlying principles of equality of treatment and transparency need to be borne in mind in considering this issue.

The European Commission's green paper accepts that PPP contracts must be able to evolve over time, including through the use of price-indexing clauses or other clauses "on condition that these identify precisely the circumstances and conditions under which adjustments could be made to the contractual relationship". However, it otherwise takes a strict approach, stating that if not covered in the contract documents changes are acceptable only in "unforeseen circumstances" or if they are justified on grounds of public policy, public security or public health, with any material change to the subject matter of the contract giving rise to a new contract (which therefore might need to be the subject of a new process).

The reference to 'unforeseen circumstances' is strange in this context, because many changes (eg, a requirement for an additional lane on a motorway due to unexpected traffic growth) which fall within this description would definitely not be considered by the commission to justify an amendment without a further competition. Leaving this aside, the practical position as to contract changes - particularly if a pragmatic view is taken as to whether a third party would have the standing to challenge - is probably not as strict as the commission sets out.

In practice, a purchaser should consider the effects of the particular change (ie, whether it materially favours the provider; whether additional works, supplies or services are introduced; the significance of the changes in terms of altering the whole object/scope of the contract) and the circumstances (ie, the reasons for the change; whether the changes are common industry practice). It is also relevant whether the possibility of change was considered as part of the award process. Most PPP projects include a formal variations mechanism, while others have provisions which allow for the project specifications to alter radically over time (particularly in military-related projects). On balance, it may be possible to take a reasonable view that a change giving rise to a new contract (and therefore a *prima facie* need to re-advertise) has not arisen in any particular case. In any event, it is always necessary to consider whether any third party would have or be likely to have standing to challenge any particular change (even if it discovers it).

## 5.6 Subcontracting

PPPs often involve material subcontracting arrangements. Specific rules and principles apply to subcontracts, which can be summarised as follows:

- In general, a project company which is itself a body subject to the public procurement rules (because it is a private utility with special or exclusive rights) must comply with the rules in the normal way.
- However, this does not apply to the arrangements of a project company where those arrangements (be they subcontracts to consortium members or to others) were considered by the purchaser during the award process (to the project company). This is sometimes called the 'umbrella principle'.
- This also does not apply when the derogation in Article 23 of the Utilities Directive applies. Pursuant to this provision, a project company may award certain services, supplies or works contracts to its affiliates.
- A project company which is not subject to the Utilities Directive has no obligations as to subcontracting under that directive.
- The exception to this is where the project company is a works concessionaire under the Public Sector Directives (ie, the holder of a works concession), in relation to which certain publicity requirements apply to the award of works subcontracts exceeding the relevant threshold, with the exception of contracts concluded with businesses that have formed a group in order to win the concession or their affiliated companies.

## 5.7 Creation of 'in-house' arrangements

An institutional PPP can be established either by creating a separate entity held jointly by the public sector and the private sector or through the private sector taking control of an existing public undertaking (this latter being privatisation or quasi-privatisation, considered below).

Public procurement issues potentially arise in relation to the establishment of a public/private entity only if, as would be the case in PPP arrangements, this is accompanied by a contract under which works, supplies or services are procured. A particular issue in this context is the extent to which a contract award to such an entity can be treated as 'in-house' (to the purchaser) and therefore outside the rules. There have now been a number of ECJ judgments on this issue, which are probably the most significant in recent years in relation to PPPs and are therefore worth some comment.

The basic principle (set out in the *Teckal* judgment)[11] is that the public procurement rules do not apply where:

- the purchaser exercises over the entity a control which is similar to that which it exercises over its own (internal to the purchasing entity) departments (the control condition); and

---

11   Case C-107/98, *Teckal*, judgment of November 18 1999.

- the entity carries out the essential part of its activities with the controlling purchaser or other controlling public bodies (the essential activities condition).

A later judgment (*Halle*)[12] narrowed this so that any involvement of a purchaser in the equity share capital of the separate entity – regardless of the percentage, and even if it does not give rise to any control or influence or veto over the actions of that entity - means that it cannot be treated as in-house. Finally, the recent *Parking Brixen Case*[13] confirmed that the *Teckal/Halle* rules also apply in relation to contracts falling outside the public procurement rules but which are subject to the EC Treaty principles. *Parking Brixen* further ruled that even a wholly owned subsidiary of a public body may not fall within the *Teckal* test if there are factors indicating that the company in practice operates to a large extent independently of its parent.

## 5.8 'Privatisation'-type arrangements

EC law does not discriminate between public and private ownership and accordingly the transfer of a company from the public to the private sector (or similar arrangement) is an issue for member states. However, public procurement law can apply where the transaction also has the effect of entrusting to the purchaser of the business or its affiliates the supply of goods, works or services under a contract with a public sector purchaser itself subject to the procurement rules.

It is necessary to consider such arrangements in the round so as to ensure that the privatisation is not in fact (or does not include) a disguised procurement. This is illustrated by the recent *Mödling* judgment.[14] That case concerned a purchaser which decided to establish a public company to take care of a waste management scheme which had been performed up to then by its own departments. This public company obtained the contract without a competitive tendering procedure and a few months later a private entity purchased 49% of the shares of this public entity. The private entity therefore became responsible for waste management operations within the geographical area of the municipality.

The ECJ held that it was necessary to examine the award taking into account all of the stages and their purpose. The arrangement was on this basis an "artificial construction comprising several distinct stages" (or a "device") pursuant to which a public service contract was awarded to a semi-public company 49% of the shares of which were held by a private entity. The *Teckal/Halle* principles did not apply and the contract should have been tendered in accordance with the rules.

The ECJ in this judgment did not consider the position in a case in which there is no intention to avoid the directives. One example of this could be a case in which, after entering into the contract with the public entity, the purchaser decides to privatise this company. Presumably, if there is genuinely no link with the contract, this arrangement will fall outside the rules. This type of arrangement raises the issue of how far contracts can be included as part of a privatised business. The generally

---

12  Case C-26/03, *Halle*, judgment of January 11 2005.
13  Case C-458/03, *Parking Brixen*, judgment of October 13 2005.
14  Case C-29/04, *Mödling*, judgment of November 10 2005.

EU procurement

accepted principle (at least in the United Kingdom, where there have been a very large number of such sales) is that they can be included where:
- they cover only pre-existing areas of work for which the purchaser has a clear requirement at the time the contract is made;
- the terms of the contract reflect, insofar as possible, the provisions of the previous arrangement;
- the contract includes terms that are normal for a contract of the type in question; and
- the duration of the contract is as short as possible.

However, there is some conflict here (which is unresolved) with the developing *Teckal* case law (see above).

5.9   **Choosing and excluding tenderers on the basis of social and environmental factors**

Purchasers often wish to, or are pushed to, take account of objectives beyond the simple performance of the contract when choosing potential providers. For example, they may wish to consider issues such as the economic development of their locality or a particular group of people or environmental impacts. The new directives were drafted in the light of ECJ case law, which recognises in particular that environmental and social factors may be taken into account in procurement processes. However, there are limits to this.

An analysis of the scope for taking these considerations into account needs to be carried out by reference to the various stages of a procurement process under the directives. These are:
- identifying the need;
- setting the specification;
- exclusion/selection (of those to be invited to tender or negotiate);
- award; and
- contract performance.

At all stages the general EC Treaty principles of non-discrimination, equal treatment and transparency must be respected. As far as the individual stages are concerned, there is most scope available early on in the process to take account of social and environmental issues. For example, if the need is for a hospital, the purchaser's awareness of local issues might lead it to identify locations in deprived areas in order to assist with their regeneration. Specifications set out the details of the requirement and there is significant scope to decide how to draw them up within the public procurement rules, provided that the specification is non-discriminatory and relevant to the products, services or goods to be procured. In the selection stage, candidates can be excluded on certain grounds, which can relate to social/environmental grounds such as breach of disability discrimination or environmental laws, and can be selected on grounds which include social/environmental grounds provided that the criteria are directly relevant to the subject of the contract.

In relation to the award phase (when the most economically advantageous offer is used), the award criteria must similarly:
- be relevant to the subject of the contract;
- relate to the specification; and
- be distinct from the selection criteria.

For example, an award criterion based on the percentage of local people employed would be irrelevant to the subject of the contract and discriminatory, and would therefore infringe the rules. Finally, it is possible to use contract conditions to support social/environmental considerations. However, the conditions should not be disguised technical specifications, selection or award criteria. Further, they must be advised in advance to the candidates (in the tender documents) and relevant to the subject of the contract.

## 5.10 Changes to specifications and other terms during the award process

Particularly in complex projects negotiated over a long period, it is common for purchasers to wish to make changes to matters such as specifications and conditions or award and selection criteria. The issue which arises is the extent to which this can safely be done without it being necessary to restart the award process.

The answer to this depends to an extent on when in the procedure the changes are made and also on which procedure is being run. In the context of PPPs being run under the competitive dialogue or, now less commonly, the negotiated procedure, there is in general probably more scope to make changes than there is in relation to contracts being awarded under open or restricted procedures.

A strict reading of the rules would indicate that the scope for changes is fairly limited, even under the competitive dialogue or negotiated procedures. However, in practice, there is significant scope to 'take a view'. Essentially, the issue is whether the introduction of the new element would have altered the course of the procedure, in that, for example, other potential providers may have responded to the OJEU notice or have passed through the various stages of the procedure. Therefore, in relation to any particular change, a purchaser should consider whether in fact this, if introduced at the outset, would have changed the process; if so, it should, to be safe, revert to whatever earlier stage in the process is needed so as to ensure fairness. This is a pragmatic solution which relies on the principles underlying the public procurement rules: transparency, objectivity and non-discrimination.

The acceptability of this at all stages of the procedure is supported by the European Commission's *London Underground* decision, which considered the award of three service contracts under the utilities regime using the negotiated procedure. These were very complex contracts, the award process for which commenced in July 1998 (with the publication of a PIN notice), with preferred bidders not being selected until May and September 2001. In its analysis of whether certain modifications to the contract terms after the selection of the preferred bidders would have caused discrimination or unequal treatment, the commission considered (among other things) it to be relevant that the final results of the process (including the elements negotiated after selection of the preferred bidders) would not have changed the outcome of the tendering procedure. The commission referred approvingly to the methodology adopted by the purchaser, which involved adjusting the offers of the other bidders to reflect the refinement made since announcement of preferred bidders. In other words, the purchaser had gone back in the process to check for unfairness. By implication, if it had found unfairness, it would have had to revert to that stage.

Another pragmatic consideration in this context is the likelihood of challenge and the ability of potential providers to challenge. On the former issue, in practice, as noted above, there may be an unwillingness on the part of potential providers to challenge their customers (the purchasers). In addition, there may, in practice, for example, have been no other providers (with a reasonable chance of being awarded the contract) which would have responded to a revised OJEU notice (reflecting the changed terms of the contract) in any event. On the latter issue, potential providers are also at some point likely to become time-barred from challenging. For example, in the United Kingdom proceedings must be brought very quickly (weeks if not days) after the grounds (the alleged infringement of the rules) arise.

# Partnerships UK

**Edward Farquharson**
Partnerships UK

The efficient delivery of projects is the core aim of a well-developed public-private partnership (PPP) project delivery programme. Achieving this objective will depend on the ability of the public sector to take a strategic approach to its engagement with the private sector and to take the lead in the process while listening to the views of the private sector and special interests.

The public sector must have a clearly developed policy coupled with an understanding of not only its own limitations, but also those of the private sector. This will require the public sector to play a central role in helping to develop the market, managing the pipeline of projects being taken to market and encouraging the development of alternative sources of supply. This in turn leads to improved competition, a key driver to achieving value for money for the public sector.

A well-developed and consistent policy needs to be visibly supported from the top, especially in the early days of a programme's development. Without this, it is difficult to generate the required level of private sector interest to invest the necessary time and resources to engage in what will initially be seen as a new and often alien procurement approach. This implies articulation from the highest levels of government of the public sector's overall objectives and its firm determination to pursue a meaningful pipeline of projects.

How can this be achieved?

PPP programmes raise a number of key implementation issues for governments.

First, the implementation of a PPP programme can significantly challenge existing government institutional arrangements and processes. This challenge usually exists across a wide range of government institutions: not only the sponsoring ministry for a particular project, but also other institutions such as the ministry of finance, state auditing bodies, procurement, investment appraisal and regional and municipal bodies, to name a few. Any solution to developing PPP implementing capacity must be holistic and acknowledge the fact that the challenges can cut right across different levels of government. This can pose difficulties in developing the necessary expertise in these institutions.

Second, many of the issues faced in implementing PPP projects are generic across sectors and levels of government. It is therefore better, where possible, to solve the implementing capacity issue once rather than repeat it each time for new sectors. This will also prevent institutions missing out on important cross-cutting issues.

Third, public sector PPP skills and experience can be scarce and expensive. This suggests that it is important to have a mechanism that can spread these resources efficiently over the entire PPP programme.

These three key issues - the challenge for a wide range of public sector institutions, the generic nature of many PPP issues and the need for efficient deployment of PPP skills - all suggest that some form of centralised response to implementation is required, especially if a coherent programme is to be developed across central, regional and local levels of government.

To be effective, such a central PPP unit will need:

- sufficient resources to attract and retain high-quality PPP expertise from the public and private sectors;
- clear senior government-level support; and
- effective channels to operate through government.

This suggests that any PPP technical unit should be located in, or under the wing of, a ministry that looks across line ministries: typically a ministry of finance, economy or planning, or in occasional instances, a prime minister's office. Clearly, this will depend on the structure of government and how the lines of command work in practice, but the key point is that such a unit can engage across the board without inter-sectoral issues getting in the way, and that its activities are associated with, and therefore treated as coming from, the highest levels of policy making and implementation.

At the same time, the issue often arises as to how to attract and retain high-quality staff. Associated with this is the challenge that PPPs require a wide range of disciplines, ranging from issues of public policy and procurement through to highly technical understanding of legal, financial and sectoral issues. While much of the detailed technical work for each project is usually best outsourced to specialist advisers, it is still important that the public sector has a firm grasp of the issues and is a smart client: after all, it is the public sector, as a client, that is purchasing services on behalf of the taxpayer, not the advisers. In any case, good advisers usually prefer to work for a client that understands what it wants. The implication, therefore, is that such a unit has the authority and resources to remunerate its people on a basis that is competitive with the private (and public) sector in each of the relevant disciplines. Retention of staff is vital to add to the effectiveness of such a unit, as it provides the public sector with memory of past deals, experience and lessons learnt. Similarly, secondments from the private sector can provide a quick boost in skills but, while a useful supplement, are not a complete or long-term solution to the problem.

By way of example, the United Kingdom's PPP Programme developed strongly following establishment of a central PPP taskforce in Her Majesty's Treasury (the UK government's ministry of finance and economy). This taskforce of personnel comprised a combination of public and private sector resources, mostly mid to late career, with backgrounds in project delivery, procurement, commercial contracts, economics, finance and law - with sector-specific and policy knowledge. Its skills were made available, free at the point of use, across the UK public sector, providing a specialist source of in-house PPP support in the earlier days of the UK Private

Finance Initiative (PFI) programme. The taskforce comprised 20 individuals (12 in respect of PPP project evaluation, procurement, contracts and implementation, and eight in respect of PPP policy). This support did not, of course, replace the need for individual procuring authorities to engage specialist private sector consultants on specific projects - in fact, one of the early jobs of the taskforce was to help authorities choose the right consultants and appoint them on the right terms, and guidance was developed to this effect. The taskforce worked closely with other specialist public sector bodies, such as the 4Ps Team, which implements the PPP programme in local authorities.

As the PPP programme developed in the United Kingdom, so the implementation capacity of the taskforce later evolved into Partnerships UK. Seeking to create a long-term career platform capable of resourcing equally from the public and private sectors, Partnerships UK was established by the Treasury as a joint venture with the private sector, with 51% of Partnerships UK collectively owned by the private sector. Partnerships UK's private sector shareholders saw that supporting the creation of such an entity would enhance delivery to market of well-structured programmes and projects as a key reason to invest - in fact, Partnerships UK is non-dividend distributing, although it does pay a fixed 6% return to all its shareholders on that part of their investment which is made by way of unsecured loanstock. Nevertheless, Partnerships UK firmly retains its public sector mission: its largest shareholder by far, at 44.6%, is Her Majesty's Treasury (the Scottish ministers own a further 4.4%). It has additional governance layers that would never be seen in a commercial entity, such as a wholly public sector staffed advisory council that ensures Partnerships UK is true to its public sector mission. Although Partnerships UK is not technically part of a government department, it continues to work closely with a team of around 15 officials in Her Majesty's Treasury who are supported by Partnerships UK, now staffed by nearly 50 professional staff organised sectorally and with cross-sectoral disciplines such as law and finance.

Given the extent of the UK programme, a number of sponsoring ministries have also developed their own PPP technical units (referred to as 'private finance units'). The extent of interaction between Partnerships UK and the ministry private finance units was intense in the early days of the PPP programme. Over time, as some private finance units have developed strong sector capability of their own, so the level of interaction has varied, as would be expected. In some cases, Partnerships UK has even seconded its own personnel into the private finance units to help individual ministries build up their own long-term PPP capability in developing their sectors.

In certain cases, where the sector programme is of a scale and homogeneity to justify the effort, Partnerships UK has formed programme-specific delivery vehicles in partnership with the sponsoring sector ministry. Two examples to date are in the primary healthcare (Partnerships for Health (PfH)) and secondary school (Partnerships for Schools (PfS)) sectors. Both PfH and PfS are forms of joint venture between Partnerships UK and the respective ministry, highly focused on delivering strategic investment programmes in their specific sectors over a number of years using a variety of procurement approaches. Each has a degree of autonomy and focus on its programme, while at the same time Partnerships UK's involvement helps to ensure that there is exchange of information and available best practice across government. In the United Kingdom, these programme-based units were established only after the government had built up a number of years' experience of PPP procurement and were justified by the extent of the programme taking place in the specific sector. In this way, the public sector can treat with the private sector on an equal footing of highly sector-specific skills and experience.

The need to establish some form of central capability appears to be increasingly recognised in other PPP markets – examples include:
- Partnerships Victoria in Australia;
- Partnerships British Columbia in Canada;
- the Treasury PPP unit in South Africa;
- the PPP Centrum in the Czech Republic;
- the investment unit in Mexico's Finance Ministry;
- the PPP unit of the Ministry of Finance in the state of North Rhine Westphalia in Germany; and
- Brazil's PPP units in the federal ministry of planning and at state levels.

As can be seen, a number of these units are based at state rather than central government level. This reflects the devolved or federal nature of the governments involved, rather than decentralisation of this capability for its own sake. Given that the private sector market is usually not equally segmented, there are often benefits in state-level units in similar markets coordinating their activities and sharing best practice where and if possible. Indeed, it is expected that a platform to enhance sharing of public sector know-how across the EU region will shortly be established by the European Investment Bank; this should be of particular help to governments that have more recently decided to develop their PPP programmes.

Looking more closely at the roles of these units, there are some subtle differences. In some cases, the units are more particularly focused on information gathering and dissemination; in others, on policy development and implementation, and even project support.

In the case of Partnerships UK, its activities broadly divide into policy implementation activities and project support. Of particular note on the policy work has been Partnerships UK's involvement with the development and enforcement of standardised PPP contracts. This activity has had a significant impact on reducing transaction times and costs and, equally importantly, in ensuring the quality of long-term PFI contacts entered into by the public sector. Partnerships UK also has a role, on behalf of Her Majesty's Treasury, to evaluate local government PFI projects that benefit from central support before they are launched on the market. Again, the emphasis is on quality control and consistency of approach to issues such as value for money and affordability, helping to ensure that wherever possible, projects that go to market are likely to be bankable, affordable and deliverable.

Equally, Partnerships UK, on behalf of the Treasury, runs a help desk that is available across the UK PPP spectrum for short-term enquiries. At the same time, Partnerships UK is frequently asked to assist a procuring authority in preparing a project for market, especially in new or more challenging sectors. This sort of engagement can last months or even years. Partnerships UK has also been asked by a number of overseas governments to assist in establishing their own PPP programmes, and this usually involves targeted interventions on strategic and best practice issues over the initial few years, sharing experience from the United Kingdom's relatively mature programme.

A very recent development for Partnerships UK has been the establishment of a support unit for operational PFI projects, ensuring that contract managers responsible for the day-to-day management of PFI contracts (over 500 such contracts are now operational across the United Kingdom) can benefit from technical support and sharing of best practice across the public sector.

Partnerships UK's role is not solely confined to PFI - it is equally active in developing other forms of partnership between the public and private sectors. This includes the commercialisation of IP assets developed by the public sector or in the application of IT PPPs. Moreover, as the boundaries between PPP and conventional public sector procurement become less distinct, so Partnerships UK has become increasingly able to apply some of the value-for-money enhancing principles and practices of PPP across general public sector procurement.

Fundamentally, as governments seek to develop more comprehensive approaches to risk appraisal and allocation in the delivery of public services, so the need for high-quality, dedicated and market aware capabilities will need to be fulfilled. Hitherto, one of the key issues to be addressed has been a lack of symmetry in capacity and market knowledge when it comes to engaging with the private sector, especially where long-term partnerships involving significant commitment of public sector expenditure are concerned. It is not too hard to see that governments will increasingly come to realise the need to develop the appropriate levels of expertise within the public sector as increasingly sophisticated forms of engagement with the private sector evolve in the quest for ever more efficient ways of procuring public services.

# Financing public-private partnerships: the changing market

Chris Brown
Norton Rose

The last few years have seen a slow but accelerating change from simple debt financing to more sophisticated finance structures. This is in part due to the procurement process, which deters innovation because sponsors try to minimise bid costs and funders thinly spread their resources across a wide range of projects to minimise their costs and increase the number of chances of winning. More recently, equity investors and financial institutions have been playing a greater role, particularly on the larger projects where there are fewer real bidders. Consequently, more sophisticated funding structures are being devised.

## 1. Impact of the term

Public-private partnership (PPP) contracts have terms that vary from 20 to 35 years. This was particularly challenging in the early years for the commercial bank market, which was not used to lending for such long terms. This led to some projects using more traditional forms of finance, such as leasing. For example, Ashford International rail passenger station was financed with a long-term lease because this was one of the few financial instruments available with a term in excess of 25 years. These tax-efficient instruments were deterred by Her Majesty's Treasury, which viewed them as merely reallocating tax, not adding value. As a consequence, there have been very few leasing structures. Longer-term PPP contracts have invariably been financed using bond finance. Indeed, in a few cases the term of the PPP contract has been extended as bond finance has allowed authorities to pay lower annual payments. As commercial banks have not been keen to finance for long terms, the margins have often been structured to encourage refinancing later through either new commercial debt or bonds. In fact, many commercial banks really participate in the market for the arranging fees, looking to sell down all, or nearly all, of their participation as soon as they can, so maximising the return on their capital. Hence, the long-term nature of PPP contracts has created an interesting dynamic which has encouraged bond finance and the monoline insurers, so vital to the use of bond finance, to enter the market. Over the last five years the original two to three monolines have expanded to six to seven recognised monolines.

## 2. Monolines

Monolines are large specialist insurance institutions whose primary business is the provision of financial guarantee insurance for financial obligations.

Monolines are normally licensed under New York state insurance law. The largest and best-known monolines include Ambac Assurance, MBIA, Financial Guarantee Insurance Company, Financial Security Assurance and XL Capital Assurance.

Monolines were a novelty in PPP in the mid-1990s but have now become more commonplace in the sterling bonds market. The European sector that has seen the most regular primary participation by financial guaranty insurers is the UK Private Finance Initiative (PFI) market. As this market began to evolve from one dominated by traditional bank lenders to a capital market where bond financing plays an important role, the opportunities for financial guaranty insurers have flourished. Wrapped bonds have been used in the United Kingdom to finance hospitals, roads, schools, rail projects, tunnels and public buildings, and gradually other European countries are opening up their public financing to the capital markets, with financial guaranty insurers involved in road financings in Italy, Spain, Portugal and France, together with airports, utility companies and healthcare in various European jurisdictions.

However, monolines have only very recently been used to wrap bank debt (see the Golden Ears bridge project below). The PPP market provides monolines with some strong fundamentals: a government revenue stream, the provision of essential assets and simple operating risks. Monoline insurers aim to minimise the risk inherent in issuing financial guarantees by taking only investment-grade risk (meaning that it is highly likely that the borrower will make full and timely payment of interest and principal when due).

Since the first wrapped debt transactions were completed in the market, the number of active players and funders keen to win transactions, and central government agencies pushing risks into the private sector's lap, has resulted in a deterioration of risk profiles. Although projects typically are now better structured, with all parties having a greater understanding of the risks inherent in these transactions, the credit protections which typically support PFI structures – cover ratios, reserve accounts, tails, liability caps and surety bonds – have been reduced. In this environment, rating agencies have sought to increase the level of protection on individual deals in order to continue to secure an investment-grade rating. This in turn has led to the current era in the PPP market of reduced numbers of bidders per project and fewer funders in the market, thereby reducing liquidity for large deals. However, while the number of bidders and banks has reduced in the market, the number of monolines has actually increased.

Set out below are some of the factors to be considered when assessing the merits of monoline involvement in financing projects. We have focused primarily on wrapped bank debt, this being the emerging concept in the PPP market at the time of writing.

## 2.1 Benefits of monoline involvement

- Marketability – monoline guarantees are used to enhance the marketability of debt, wrapping the debt such that the likelihood of full payment of interest and principal is enhanced and therefore the debt can achieve a higher investment rating from the rating agencies.
- Pricing – as the pricing of the debt is based on the rating of the monoline, rather than the underlying project, margins will be reduced to reflect the lower risk, thereby reducing the overall cost of the funding. This is also connected to the revised capital adequacy regime which will be brought in with Basel II, which applies to most financial institutions operating any sort of financial business within the European Union. Among other things, the new regime will allow banks to differentiate their capital treatment for particular assets and introduce credit assessments based on external rating factors. The current regime requires banks to set aside capital amounting to 8% of the principal amount of any loan to private corporate borrowers (ie, the special purpose companies set up to carry out a PPP project). The new regime appears to provide that the capital adequacy requirement for any AAA-rated debt to corporate borrowers is significantly less than now and for other debt. All other things being equal, this means the banks can obtain a greater return on the loan, which in turn enables the banks to reduce the margin. (Basel II should come into force in 2007.)

    However, the amount of the premium charged by the monoline to raise the underlying project rating to investment-grade category raises the effective margin.
- Tenor – the tenor of any loan will be limited by the term of the underlying project agreement. However, in circumstances where there is a lengthy concession term, the lender will be able to offer longer tenors due to the reduced exposure to the underlying project risks.
- Administration and management – monoline providers will require that they exercise all the decision-making powers that the lenders would otherwise have been able to exercise. This can simplify the administration and management of the loan, as in most cases it will need only to contact the monolines agency(ies) for a decision instead of talking to the agent for and/or the entire lending syndicate.
- Reduced hedge pricing through use of hedge intermediation – some monolines are able to offer hedging intermediation. The borrower enters an interest swap with the monoline, which then enters into a back-to-back swap with the banks. As the banks are hedging with an AAA-rated counterparty, the credit spread on the swap is reduced, thereby lowering the overall cost of the swap. The hedge intermediation structure is set out in the following diagram:

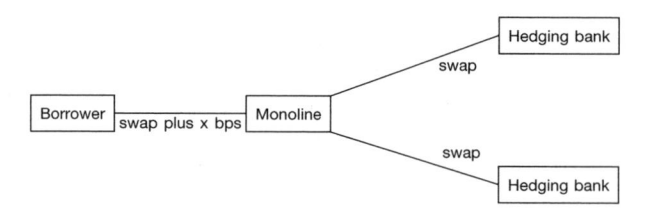

```
                                              Hedging bank
                                         swap
                                     ┌─────────┐
                   Borrower          │ Monoline│
                   ─swap plus x bps──┤         │
                                     └─────────┘
                                         swap
                                              Hedging bank
```

## 2.2 Limitations

- Guarantee is only for 'scheduled principal and interest' – the monoline policy will provide cover only for 'scheduled principal and interest'. Monolines tend to regard this as the fundamental basis for their cover and cannot generally be persuaded to cover other amounts that might become payable under the bond/loan agreement. The monoline policy will therefore often not cover:
  - tax gross-up;
  - default interest;
  - increased costs; or
  - commitment and other fees.
- Credit rating – monolines will require a 'shadow rating' from the credit agencies (normally at least two) in respect of the project. The shadow rating is the rating that would have been assigned to the wrapped debt if the monoline policy did not exist. The shadow rating will affect the pricing that the monoline will require in respect of its policy. As mentioned above, a monoline is unlikely to wrap a transaction unless the shadow rating is at least investment grade.
- Monoline default and voting events – the intercreditor documentation will need to make provision for both 'monoline defaults' and 'voting events'. A monoline default will arise if the monoline becomes insolvent, fails to make a payment or suffers a rating downgrade to less than BBB-/Baa3. The consequences of a monoline default are subject to negotiation. Particular regard should be had to:
  - the monoline's voting rights;
  - potential increase of margin;
  - cancellation and replacement of the monoline policy; and
  - suspension of premiums until the monoline is replaced or no longer suffers from downgrade in rating.
- Over-drawing – monolines may require the wrapped debt to be drawn down in a particular profile. If any wrapped debt is drawn down ahead of schedule (ie over-drawing), then they may not be guaranteed until the expected profile is achieved again. This is because the premiums will be sized and payable on the basis of certain assumptions as to the borrower's exposure at particular points in time

## 2.3 Case study

A recent illustration of a monoline wrapped bank debt transaction was the 2006 Golden Ears Bridge PPP project (GEB) in British Columbia. GEB involved the design, building and financing of a new bridge over the Fraser River with a concession period of 35.5 years. The structure diagram below illustrates the financing structure.

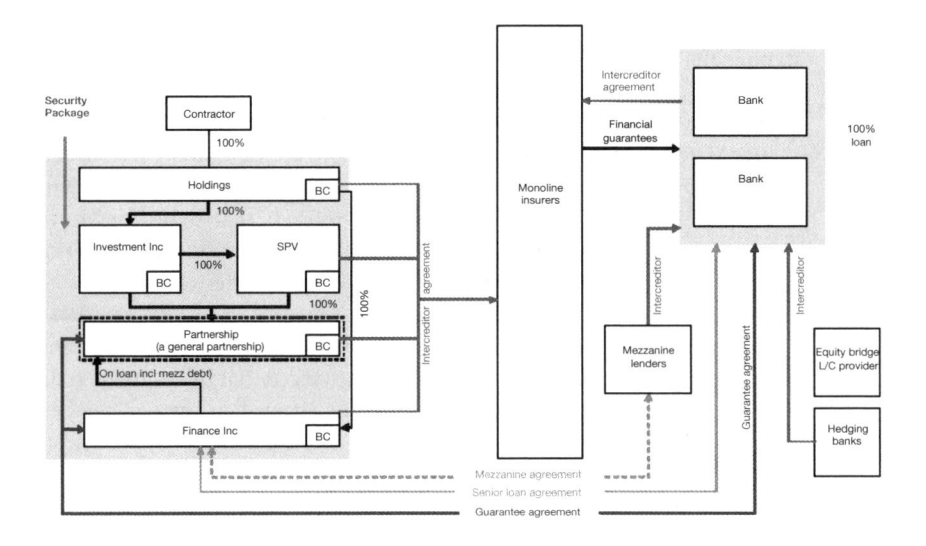

The senior debt (consisting of a term loan, a working capital loan and a standby loan) was provided equally by two banks. Both banks also provided a loan to cover the equity portion (this in turn was wholly secured by an equity letter of credit provided by the sponsor's corporate lender). One of the senior lenders also provided debt in the form of mezzanine debt. The senior debt was wrapped jointly by two monoline insurers on a 50-50 basis. The debt facilities also included a CPI swap. The CPI swap allows the project company to match its inflation-linked revenue streams into an inflation-linked repayment obligation, together with two hedging strategies, backed by the monolines.

The wrapped bank loan solution offered the sponsor a more competitive all-round cost of debt than was available with traditional bank financing, but without having to sacrifice any of the flexibility in structuring. Rather than being drawn down in one tranche, wrapped debt can be drawn down better to match the construction programme. For commercial lenders the monoline wrap means they can offer lower margins. Further, with the introduction of Basel II it is to be expected that this type of financing will increase as commercial lenders should not need to set aside so much capital.

3. **Refinancing in PPP**

Many banks see the PPP market as the obvious route for refinancing infrastructure once a project is commissioned. Typically, the financing cost for a PPP project is greater if the project includes a construction element. Lenders are notoriously wary of construction completion risk and price accordingly. Once construction is complete, the project is therefore partly 'de-risked' and, as a result, lower interest rates become available in the market. Sponsors will often then re-finance the project, triggering a cash windfall.

Financing public-private partnerships

The public sector, too, has indicated its desire to share the rewards of refinancing, inviting the possibility of some renegotiation of all contract terms to ensure the public purse obtains a benefit – indeed, in the United Kingdom, government guidelines were introduced in 2002 to ensure this would happen in the PFI market.

Her Majesty's Treasury negotiated with the private sector that, as from September 2002, the private sector would accept a voluntary code whereby PFI authorities would get 30% of any refinancing gains on projects that signed before this date (where the contract had not included arrangements to share the gains); PFI contracts signed after this date would provide for public authorities to receive 50% of any refinancing gains.

Arguably, the interests of both the public and private sectors in a refinancing are aligned. However, the public sector must be convinced that the gains are transparent and that any new risks assumed are worthwhile given their share in the benefit. In fact, there has been a considerable amount of misinformed hysteria from some political commentators. In practice, the public sector shares half the gain, which can be quite considerable, in exchange for increased compensation on *force majeure* termination (highly unlikely) or termination either voluntarily or by default by the public sector.

There are a great number of projects that could, in theory, be refinanced. However, many deals are too small to make refinancing worthwhile, due to break costs and incidental expenses. Further, most projects have no explicit profit-sharing provisions, and as a result a considerable amount of negotiation is required. Even when percentages are specified, contracts often have to be changed to make them suitable for refinancing with longer terms or with an alternative type of finance than originally envisaged.

Other developments in the PPP sector may impact on the feasibility and desirability of refinancing. As the secondary market evolves, further financial efficiencies are likely to be sought and the financial engineering needed to achieve these will become increasingly advanced.

There is likely to be an increasing number of PPP assets and their debt facilities being grouped together. This may encourage investors to refinance several projects in groups, using portfolios to enable the refinancing of less mature assets and develop further financial benefits.

## 3.1 Case study

An interesting example of a recent PPP refinancing was the refinancing of Tube Lines Limited (TLL) in 2004. TLL is responsible for the management, maintenance and upgrade of the assets and infrastructure of the Northern, Jubilee and Piccadilly lines of the London Underground following implementation of the London Underground PPP. TLL had initially sourced its funding from a group of senior and mezzanine lenders, entering into a number of agreements on December 31 2002 to fund the performance of TLL's obligations in relation to the PPP.

In 2004, TLL entered into arrangements for restructuring and tranching the existing funding in order to lower its aggregate cost of funds and release financing benefit to its shareholders. The diagram below illustrates the structure of the refinancing.

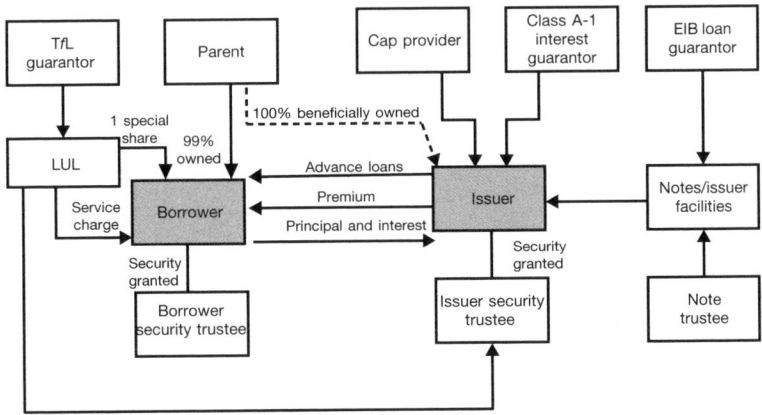

[Diagram: TLL refinancing structure showing relationships between TfL guarantor, Parent, Cap provider, Class A-1 interest guarantor, EIB loan guarantor, LUL, Borrower, Issuer, Notes/issuer facilities, Borrower security trustee, Issuer security trustee, and Note trustee. Flows include: 1 special share, 99% owned, 100% beneficially owned, Advance loans, Premium, Principal and interest, Service charge, Security granted, Payment under put option/mandatory sale.]

The capital structure for TLL's refinancing was arguably revolutionary in PFI bond structures. Instead of solely relying on the strength of the concession together with an external credit wrap, the tranched structure focused directly on the heart of the concession, Transport for London (TfL).

When the concessions were entered into in 2002, the government in the form of TfL (rated double-A by Standard & Poor's and Fitch) had committed to support TLL's payment obligations, agreeing that in a recovery scenario, it would guarantee at least 95% of TLL's debt, since the London Underground cannot be taken as security for any lending (termed the 'underpinned amount').

The refinancing was mostly by way of wrapped bonds issued by the issuer (a special purpose company established for the limited purpose of issuing the notes and entering into certain transactions and matters) and certain debt facilities. The issuer then on-lent any refinancing proceeds to TLL. The financial benefit was achieved primarily by a restructuring and tranching of TLL's funding so that a significant (and the most senior) tranche could rely completely for recovery on the support provided by TfL for the PPP, and thereby attract a lower coupon and charges. The debt was granted a double-A rating and 20% risk weighting.

The bonds were split into four tranches – A, B, C and D. The A and B notes (which made up the vast majority of the debt) were sold to a commercial bank and the European Investment Bank. The tranche A bonds are backed by the underpinned amount and guaranteed by a monoline insurer. This left only a small proportion of the debt (effectively the existing mezzanine debt portion) to be refinanced publicly, offering investors exposure to TLL's operational risk. This was achieved by issuing the C and D notes which were subordinated to the A and B notes.

The most important part of the refinancing was to reinforce the underpinning from TfL in order that the rating agencies and the banks would be satisfied that the notes provided a direct recourse to TfL. Mechanisms such as an issuer put option and a standstill agreement were reinforced to ensure timely payment in the event of an acceleration of the debt. In addition, in order to meet the refinancing bank's requirement for municipal risk, it was necessary to ensure that the deal would always be backed by a municipal body. In theory, it had been possible for the government to transfer responsibility for London Underground to some non-municipal body and, if backed by a letter of comfort, maintain the same rating. The government gave an undertaking that the deal would always be backed by a municipal letter of credit.

The participation of various creditors meant a big challenge was balancing their competing rights and powers. A tiered decision-making process was created, in order to give powers to make decisions to those creditors which will be most directly affected by them, while ensuring that decisions can be made effectively. Level 1 decisions, broadly concerning day-to-day, non-fundamental credit matters, are made by the monoline insurer. Level 2 decisions, which deal with more fundamental credit matters, are made by the B note holders. Upon the occurrence of certain events which are relevant to the look-through to TfL, decisions revert back to the monoline insurer and the A note holders.

The efficiency of the structure depended heavily on the A notes being sufficiently cheap to counter the higher costs of the unwrapped B, C and D notes. This was achieved with the introduction of a 'funding over time' mechanism for this tranche. Rather than being fully drawn at launch, with all the extra commitment costs that would entail, the A notes act like highly sophisticated variation bonds. At launch, the issuer sold the A notes and immediately repurchased them. It then entered into a swap agreement with the underwriter and the refinancing bank under which the two agreed to repurchase the notes according to a predetermined drawdown schedule over the course of the first review period (7.5 years).

Overall, the bond financing provided much more advantageous terms to TLL. The lower cost of funds achieved by the refinancing allowed TLL to release over £80 million in financial benefit to its stakeholders, of which 70% was made available to TfL.

## 4. Cheaper equity – secondary market

A key development in the PPP market in recent years has been the growing involvement of secondary funds. Initially, they focused on buying portfolios of equity in closed transactions, usually once the underlying PPP projects had reached practical completion. More recently, they have contracted to forward purchase the equity that contractors, operators and other investors have or are going to invest in projects. They have played a vital role in injecting liquidity into the market. In addition, there are further synergies to be realised, such as purchasing insurance in bulk and cutting the cost of back-office functions for completed projects. Because they are buying portfolios they can in effect lower the cost of equity by gearing-up.

## 5. Leveraged funds

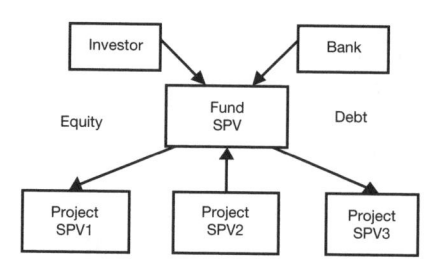

More recently, they have been teaming up with contractors and other sponsors to set up funds to invest in projects. Contractors can then enjoy greater liquidity, greater ease to exit the fund than SPVs and a more competitive equity product, through gearing. One cannot underestimate the importance the secondary market is having on the way that contractors and investors view the market.

6. **Credit guarantee finance**

Governments have watched for some time ever-increasing gearings, substantial refinancing gains and the wrapping or guaranteeing of debt. There has been a growing view that debt providers are taking too high a price for their product. There

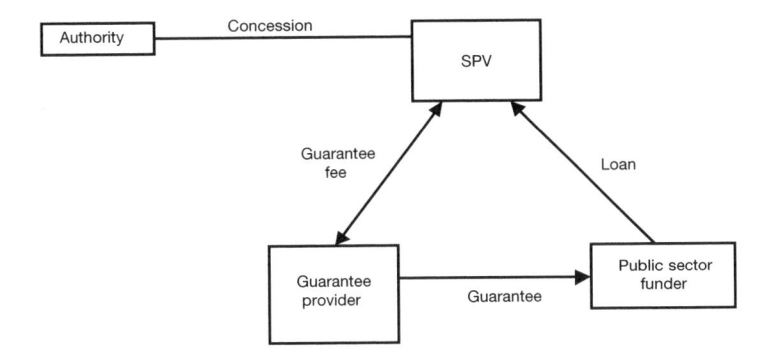

have been a number of projects financed by the government or relevant authority providing the debt with the private sector guaranteeing its repayment for a fee.

The public sector funder can access treasury funds at gilt rates; it lends at market rates (inclusive of effective guarantee fee margin). Overall, the public sector gets a much lower effective rate of finance. Yet as any good economist knows, the public sector gets cheaper funding in the market because there is an implicit guarantee from the nation's taxpayers. So far, governments appear not to have factored the cost of the guarantee into the benefit equation. It is time they did so. There seems to be an appetite in the public sector for this type of finance, so we should expect to see more.

7. **Trends**

So how will the market evolve in the near future? Basel II (currently scheduled to be introduced in 2007) is likely to lead to more wrapped debt or bond financing. Indeed, banks participating in a syndicated project loan may have differing capital requirements depending on their risk assessment models, which can change over the life of the loan. It remains to be seen how the market will manage this issue – perhaps through more wrapped debt?

As risk analysis becomes more sophisticated and the public sector becomes more astute as to how risks may be apportioned and supported, there is likely to be a greater role for a variety of debt in a deal. This has already started: the London

Underground refinancing, the E18 toll road in Norway and the Golden Ears Bridge are all examples. As well as bonds with different priorities, mezzanine debt is increasingly common.

The public sector, in driving down the cost of financing, is likely to play an increasing role in using its access to the capital markets to fund projects. In a strange way, we seem to have come back to where we started.

# About the authors

**Nicholas Avery**
Partner, Ashurst
nick.avery@ashurst.com

Nicholas Avery, LLB, is a partner in the London office of international law firm Ashurst. He holds a degree in English law and is a solicitor of the Supreme Court of England and Wales. He has 20 years' experience as a lawyer in London and New York, and has worked extensively in the finance of infrastructure assets under public-private finance programmes in the United Kingdom and in Europe, acting for financiers, project sponsors and public sector entities.

**Chris Brown**
Partner, Norton Rose
chris.brown@nortonrose.com

Chris Brown is a partner and heads up Norton Rose's infrastructure projects team. He has advised the public sector, contractors, investors and funders on some of the leading domestic and cross-border infrastructure transactions.

**Joss Dare**
Senior Solicitor, Ashurst
joss.dare@ashurst.com

Joss Dare is a senior solicitor in Ashurst's energy, transport and infrastructure department. Ashurst is one of the leading firms in the Private Finance Initiative (PFI)/public-private partnership (PPP) field, having advised on PFI/PPP projects in the United Kingdom alone with a total value in excess of £12 billion; it has a track record of delivering innovative, large-scale PFI and PPP transactions around the world. Mr Dare has 10 years' experience of project finance, advising public sector clients, sponsors, funders and subcontractors on PFI and PPP projects of all types across many jurisdictions. He has advised on many road projects, including real and shadow-tolled deals, as well as those involving availability payments – both in the United Kingdom and elsewhere in Europe. In addition, Mr Dare has advised on landmark PFI/PPP deals in the accommodation, custodial, health and defence sectors.

**Edward Farquharson**
Project Director, Partnerships UK
Edward.Farquharson@partnershipsuk.org.uk

Edward Farquharson coordinates Partnerships UK's international work and has over 20 years' experience in debt and private equity finance in infrastructure businesses in the United Kingdom, Asia, Latin America and Africa. This includes 10 years with CDC Capital Partners (both London based and, before that, Southern Africa), where he led the infrastructure team responsible for developing an equity and debt portfolio of road, rail, airport and port projects in Asia, Africa and Latin America.

Previously, Mr Farquharson was involved in developing limited recourse project financings at Morgan Grenfell, including the Dartford Crossing project, the Channel Tunnel and Woodside Petroleum North West Shelf gas project. He was also based for a period in Brazil where he established Morgan Grenfell's Sao Paulo-based business.

Mr Farquharson has an MBA from Manchester Business School and is an alumnus of London Business School and INSEAD. He has a degree in philosophy, politics and economics from Oxford University.

## Matthew Hall
Partner, Ashurst
matthew.hall@ashurst.com

Matthew Hall, MA (Cantab), has been since 2003 a partner in the Brussels office of Ashurst, a leading international law firm advising corporates and financial institutions, with core businesses in M&A, corporate and structured finance. He deals with all aspects of EU and UK competition law, including merger control, state aid and issues arising out of trading agreements and practices. He has extensive experience of dealing with the European Commission and national regulators in the United Kingdom and other jurisdictions. In addition, he has a specialist practice in the area of EU and UK public procurement law. He is qualified as a solicitor in England and Wales.

## Dan Hood
Senior Associate, Simmons & Simmons
Dan.Hood@simmons-simmons.com

Dan Hood is a senior associate in the Simmons & Simmons projects group. He has extensive experience of advising public and private sector clients, both in the United Kingdom and internationally, in the defence, transport, technology, media and telecommunications, and financial sectors in relation to PFI/PPP and outsourcing work. He was a member of the Simmons & Simmons team which worked on the PPP of the Defence Evaluation and Research Agency, which won *The Lawyer's* Projects/PFI Team of the Year 2003 award. Mr Hood represents Simmons & Simmons as a member of the Nuclear Industry Association and is a regular speaker on PFI/PPP issues. He also is the author of the England & Wales chapter in the forthcoming publication *A Practical Guide to PFI/PPP in Europe*.

## David Nelligan
Partner, Simmons & Simmons
David.Nelligan@simmons-simmons.com

David Nelligan is a partner in the Simmons & Simmons banking group, specialising in project finance. He has advised on some of the largest defence projects in the United Kingdom, including advising the sponsors on the Colchester Garrison project and the Ministry of Defence on the Defence Training Review project. He has also advised sponsors, funders and awarding authorities on other projects in a range of sectors in the United Kingdom, Europe, Africa and Australia.

## Cameron Smith
Partner, Ashurst
cameron.smith@ashurst.com

Cameron Smith, LLB, BCom, is a partner in the energy, transport and infrastructure department of Ashurst in London. He holds degrees in law and commerce and has specialised in PFI/PPP projects and other project-financed transactions for over 12 years, while based in London, Tokyo and Melbourne.

In particular, Mr Smith has led Ashurst teams on a number of leading PFI/PPP transactions in a variety of sectors, including 10 separate prison and custodial sector projects. In addition, he has been heavily involved in a number of design-build-finance-operate roads, light rail projects, hospital projects and other government accommodation projects in the United Kingdom and Europe.

Mr Smith led the legal teams on the three most recent prison PPP deals to reach financial close in the United Kingdom, and is also editor of one chapter of a leading PFI looseleaf text.

# About the authors

**Paul Smith**
Partner, CMS Cameron McKenna LLP
paul.smith@cms-cmck.com

Paul Smith is a partner in the infrastructure and project finance group of CMS Cameron McKenna, specialising in privately financed projects under the UK government's PFI/PPP. He originally qualified as a quantity surveyor with a major UK contractor before specialising in PFI, in particular the early PFI hospital projects. He re-qualified as a solicitor and trained with the firm, focusing on PFI, and is a member of the Law Society of England and Wales. During this period and since qualification, Mr Smith has been involved in a variety of PFI/PPP projects in a variety of sectors, including advising sponsors and lenders on a number of projects in the health, infrastructure, defence, education and courts/custodial sectors. Mr Smith became a partner in the firm in 2004.

**Frank Suttie**
Partner, Beachcroft LLP
fsuttie@beachcroft.co.uk

Frank Suttie is a partner within the Beachcroft projects practice. He has been an adviser to the private and public sector in relation to local government and health from the outset of the PFI, advising on a range of projects involving outsourcing, PFI and PPP. He is lead partner for the firm's engagement to the Partnerships for Schools (PfS) legal panel, advising local authorities and governing bodies parties in relation to Building Schools for the Future (BSF) procurements and advising PfS directly on the integration of voluntary aided schools and academies into the initiative. Current engagements include Knowsley BSF (first wave) and Liverpool (second wave). Mr Suttie is recognised in both the Legal 500 and Chambers Legal directories for his work on PFI and PPP projects.

**Giles Taylor**
Partner, Beachcroft LLP
gataylor@beachcroft.co.uk

Giles Taylor is a partner within the Beachcroft projects practice, based in London. Over the last 10 years he has advised on a wide variety of PFI and PPP schemes across the education, health, transport, energy, defence, accommodation and housing sectors, both in the United Kingdom and internationally. He has particular expertise in the education sector, including schools PFI, student accommodation and the BFI programme.

**Tom Winsor**
Partner, White & Case LLP
TWinsor@whitecase.com

In 2004 Tom Winsor joined White & Case's London office as a partner and as head of its international rail practice.

From 1999 to 2004 he was UK rail regulator and international rail regulator, at a time of considerable turbulence for the British railway industry. He was also the national competition authority for the British railway industry, and heard and disposed of cases alleging anti-competitive behaviour and abuse of dominant positions.

Mr Winsor was a member of the group of nine economic regulators of the United Kingdom and the senior member of the convention of European rail regulatory authorities.

Mr Winsor's practice at White & Case embraces railway and infrastructure projects in the United Kingdom, Europe and Asia (including railway concessions and financings), and also covers advice and assistance to clients in regulatory dynamics, competition cases, price reviews, investment protection measures and connected matters.